PRIVATE LIVES

PRIVATE BLUES

Lawrence M. Friedman

P|R|I|V|A|T|E LIVES

Families, Individuals, and the Law

HARVARD UNIVERSITY PRESS

Cambridge, Massachusetts

London, England

2004

Library of Congress Cataloging-in-Publication Data

Friedman, Lawrence Meir, 1930–
Private lives : families, individuals, and the law / Lawrence M. Friedman.
p.   cm.
Includes bibliographical references and index.
ISBN 0-674-01562-2 (alk. paper)
1. Domestic relations—United States—History. I. Title.

KF505.F75 2005
346.7301'5—dc22   2004047519

To Leah, Jane, Amy, Paul, Sarah, David, and Lucy

Contents

Acknowledgments

This book grew out of a series of lectures, originally delivered in August 2002 in Santiago, Chile, as the Fondación Fueyo Lectures at Diego Portalès University. I want to thank Dean Carlos Peña for his support and encouragement. The present version, however, is much revised and expanded. I want to thank Paul Lomio and the staff of the Stanford Law Library, including Erika Wayne and David Bridgman, for their tremendous help in chasing down obscure and not-so-obscure references for me. Thanks are due, too, to my assistant, Mary Tye, who was so helpful with the manuscript. I also want to thank two anonymous reviewers of the manuscript for their helpful comments. I have tried, successfully I hope, to take their suggestions into account. I also wish to express my appreciation to those students who helped me, particularly Catherine Crump and Julia Martinez. I profited, too, from the valuable comments of Joanna Grossman and the research on divorce in San Mateo County, California, done by Albert Lopez. And, as always, I want to thank my family for all the things they mean to me.

1

Family Law in Context
An Introduction

The basic theme of this book is the transformation of family law in the past hundred years or so. A key subtheme is the decline of the family (legally speaking) and the rise of the individual. Family, of course, is a collective concept. A single person can be a household, but it takes two or more people to make a family. Modern life, like life in all human societies and at all periods of time, is family life. But the family today is far different from the family of yesterday. It is essentially a coming together of *individuals;* it is an arrangement of individuals, for individuals; it is much more brittle, malleable, friable than in the past. And the family, as such, no longer has much legal status or meaning. Family law is still a vital, significant field of law; but it has become a law about *individuals*—individuals, to be sure, as they exist in relationship to other people, that is, to their "families." And because family law is a law about *individuals* it is also a law that stresses the primacy of *choice,* of free and voluntary actions.

In traditional societies, the legal and social situation was radically different. Traditional societies differed in many ways from each other, and it is easy to reduce them to cartoons. But generally speaking, in these societies, a person's rights and duties flowed from his or her status in society or within the family. Men and women, old and young, noble or commoner, son or daughter, mother or father: these were only some of the many relevant categories. The family, or clan, or extended family, was often the real locus of rights and duties, rather than the individual member. Very often, too, the father or the senior male in the family had overwhelming power over the other members; this was true in the older strata of Roman law, where the oldest male ancestor had total control over all of his descendants; nobody under his jurisdiction, male or female, could marry without his consent.[1] This was an extreme case; but in the law of many other peoples and societies, the father or male head of the family had awesome authority.

Modern society has traveled a long way in the other direction. What is the master trend in the history of family has also been, arguably, the master trend in the history of law in general, or even perhaps the history of society. That is, the family as a legal unit dissolves; and the individual members rise to power. In the middle of the nineteenth century, Sir Henry Maine, in his classic study *Ancient Law* (1861), described the movement of law in "progressive societies" as a movement "from Status to Contract."[2] Rights, in other words, no longer depended on gender, birth order, rank, or caste. They were now (according to Maine) matters of individual choice, of voluntary behavior. Individuals—men, women, and children—had rights; families or groups did not. Society was made up of atoms, not molecules. Each of these atoms was, in important ways, legally equal. Family law, law in general, and indeed society as a whole rested on this foundation of equality. And voluntary agreements (choices) rather than inborn status were at the core of social behavior.

Of course, this statement is something of an exaggeration, and was even more so when Maine wrote his book. Most of us find it hard to describe nineteenth-century England as a country made up of people with equal rights. England was a monarchy, and although the Queen was not particularly powerful, she was in some ways at the apex of society; in any event, the nobility, the landed gentry, and the great merchants owned the land and the wealth; they ran the country; they dominated public and private life. Women did not vote, did not hold office, and were shut out of most occupations. Legally and socially they were subordinate to men, and this was particularly true of married women—their property was under the control of the men they were married to. Generally speaking, they had no right to enter into contracts, to buy and sell property, to make wills and testaments. Until deep into the nineteenth century, religious minorities had no vote; indeed, the vote belonged chiefly to men of property. Property was king. In the United States, women were perhaps a bit better off than they were in England; but married women in most states had the same disabilities as those in England until the latter part of the century.[3] Black slavery was not abolished until the 1860s; and even after emancipation, most African-Americans were poor, illiterate, and little better than serfs. In the southern states, where most of them lived, they were virtually tied to the land; and by the end of the century, black people had effectively lost the right to vote or hold public office. Those who dared to speak out, or to offend against the code of the white south, put their very lives at risk.

The situation today is dramatically different in England, in the United States, and indeed in all of the developed countries. One of the most striking trends of the late twentieth century, in the United States and elsewhere, has been the rise of what I have called plural equality.[4] By this I mean the collapse of the notion of a single dominant ethos, a single dominant race, culture, code of morality. During most of American history (and for most of the history of *most* nations), a fairly clear structure of social dominance was in place. This was true even of the United States, despite its democratic nature, and even though America was extremely democratic in nineteenth-century terms, as De Tocqueville and others recognized. In the United States, too, there was freedom of religion, and there was no established church. Minority religions were tolerated; people could build churches, mosques, and synagogues as they liked. The Constitution, and public opinion, allowed people to exercise their religions freely.[5] But toleration is not the same thing as partnership. The public, official culture was drenched with the spirit and the substance of Protestant Christianity. The schools were so partisan, so Protestant, that Catholics felt obliged to set up their own school system.

Most Americans took it for granted that public life did and should reflect the values of the majority. Other people were, so to speak, guests in a house they did not own.

By the late twentieth century, the situation had changed considerably. True legitimacy, a true place in the sun, was now defined much less narrowly. Symbolic power was extended to other races, religions, and ways of life. Officially, at least, the United States has become multicultural. The President sends greetings to his Moslem, Jewish, and Buddhist countrymen on their sacred days. Public life includes many symbolic gestures of this kind; and Jewish, black, Chinese, and gay citizens hold office, even high public office. Remarkable changes have also taken place in the relationship between women and men. The old doctrines of subordination are gone. Women vote and sit on juries; women serve in the state legislatures, in Congress, and occasionally even in the governor's mansion. Women flock to the medical profession and are beginning to penetrate the upper echelons of finance and big business. A quarter of all lawyers are women. There are two women justices on the United States Supreme Court. Civil rights laws insist on equality of the sexes in the workplace, in education, in the law. According to law, men and women are totally equal.

Only somebody very stubborn or naïve, however, would argue that there is gender equality in society at large. This Utopia is still far off in the distance. And women have perhaps made the *least* progress toward equality inside their families. They still have to shoulder the main burden of housework and child care. Most women work, and millions of women have to drag themselves home to their second job: the family. For middle-class people, the husband's job or career usually takes priority over the wife's, though this is somewhat less so than it was in the past. Women still suffer from domestic violence, from sexual harassment and abuse. But if we look backward, to the past, we have to admit: the changes in gender relations are tremendous, far-reaching, and important. And they are changes, in the main, that go in the direction of plural equality.

My aim in this book is to describe and explain these changes as they relate to family law and personal privacy. It is a huge job—maybe impossible—to try to explain why these changes occurred. A few factors are obvious. A free market system, technological and scientific developments, the huge, well-off middle class in Western countries, leisure time, urbanization, the mass media, the rule of law—all of these have been important elements of change; and they are also linked in complex chains of causation. These factors have produced the kind of society that prevails in the developed countries of Europe and North America, and in such countries as Japan and Australia. Of course, no two of these countries are the same. Finland is not France, and France is not Japan. But there are similarities; and the similarities are probably more striking than the differences. Also with regard to legal culture: these countries all share a common legal culture, the culture of modernity.[6] One social and legal trait that they hold in common is the one I have described: the rise of the *individual* as the locus of duties and rights.

Everything in modern society conspires to buttress the primacy of the individual, and his or her wants, desires, aspirations, and habits. Nothing, for example, is more characteristic of modern society than advertising. Our days and nights are drenched with it. Advertising surrounds us every day, in our homes, on the streets, in our newspapers, and on television. It pops up on the Internet. It screams at us in public places. It even appears at times as writing in the sky. Advertising is a core feature of capitalism, of a market system. And advertising, whatever the product, whether cars, breakfast cereal, the services of lawyers, or a new kind of shoe polish, conveys a double message. One is a message about the product; the other is unspoken, but crucial and essential. It is the ideology—one might almost say the religion—of advertising, of markets in general. This ideology is based on consumption, on private wants and desires. The message is aimed at an audience of individuals, each watching in his or her own private space. Advertising is aimed at the individual *you*. It tells *you*, the watcher, the reader, the listener, what to buy and what to use: what products will make you stronger, more beautiful, sexier, what soap will make your clothes whiter, what toothpaste will brighten your teeth, what car will make you feel more alive, more daring, more attractive; and so on, endlessly.[7]

Advertising, loathsome as it is at times, annoying, intrusive, and shallow, may be essential to the modern economy and to a free society in general. Modern law, including family law, evolves along with society; and in the Western countries, the developed countries, it evolves along with that peculiarly modern brand of individualism I have mentioned. Such a statement, naturally, papers over both a great deal of complexity and a great deal of variation, from generation to generation and from country to country. As the saying goes, the devil is in the details.

The paths of change are nonetheless clear. Family law has indeed moved from status to contract—in the sense, as Milton Regan has put it, first, that the "law is more willing to enforce agreements that tailor family life to individual preference"; and second, that "the law is more solicitous in general of individual choices in family matters."[8] The modern laws of marriage—and divorce—are worlds apart from traditional marriage and traditional ways to end or get rid of a marriage. Marriage was once a matter for the kinfolk to decide, not the woman and the man. In many traditional societies, the family arranged the marriage, fixed the price, made all the preparations. Often the bride and groom never laid eyes on each other until their wedding day. This was true for a Japanese woman of the late nineteenth century who later happened to move to the United States and who wrote a fascinating book about her life. She had a happy marriage, to a man her brother found for her, and whom she never saw before her wedding day. Her sister, her mother, all the members of her family had marriages of this sort. She never questioned the right of her brother—the head of the family once her father died—to pick out her husband. This same brother, however, had rebelled against the system. He backed out of an arranged marriage at the last minute. This was considered a terrible disgrace to the family. His father banished him—never spoke to him or of him again, and treated him as if he had died. Ironically, after the father died, the brother became the head of the family; and proceeded to arrange a marriage for his sister— a form of marriage he himself had rejected.[9]

Japan of course was not the only country that was patriarchal, or the only country where families arranged marriages for their children.

Arranged marriages are still the norm in India, even among members of the middle class. Families were often involved in ending marriages as well as in beginning them. In some societies, marriages cannot be dissolved at all. In others—for example, in traditional Islamic societies—men (but not women) can end a marriage easily. In still other societies, any decision to end a marriage has to involve the families of husband and wife. (Matters of dowry or bride-price, for example, have to be worked out.)

Most young people in the developed world would find any system of arranged marriages both incredible and intolerable. Nothing could be more individual, more personal, than choosing a life partner;. Young people usually hope their parents would approve of their chosen partner; but if not, the marriage goes on anyway. After all, it is not the parents who are getting married. It is not their life, but their children's life, that is at issue. This seems completely self-evident to us; but the situation is different in societies where marriage joins two families, not two individuals.

Nowadays marriage is supposed to be, above all, a matter of partnership and love. Of course romantic love, and love marriages, are not modern inventions; they are not the result of the steam engine, the railroad, and the telephone. They have always been staples of literature. Novels, plays, poems, and songs all depend on love and love stories, perhaps more than any other themes. What could be a purer romance than Shakespeare's sixteenth-century tragedy *Romeo and Juliet*? The two "star-crossed" lovers meet, fall hopelessly in love, marry secretly, and are united in the end in death. Yet it is a feud between the lovers' two *families* that sets the tragedy in motion; Juliet's father had chosen a husband for her, never dreaming that she had already pledged herself to a man, and an enemy of the family at that. The story pivots on the tension between the customary way of arranging marriages and the reality of a passionate, overwhelming love.

Law follows custom and reflects social understandings: this much is obvious. The power of parents to choose mates for their children has vanished from modern Western society and, indeed, from legal norms as well. Parents do not have to approve of the mates their children choose, unless the children are underage. Under the French Civil Code of 1804, parental consent was necessary for daughters until age twenty-one, and for sons until age twenty-five, although the code did recognize the general principle of free choice.[10] In the United States, in general, the power of the parents even over young people has been shrinking. In Ohio today, if the bride and groom are minors, the parents must consent;[11] in Texas, young brides and grooms—fourteen to eighteen years old—need this consent (but a court order can substitute for parental consent in some cases); and in Washington state, eighteen-year-olds can marry, and the statute makes no mention of parents at all. For grown children, there is not a hint of parental control remaining in the law of the United States and, indeed, of Western countries generally.

This right to choose a life partner is only a piece of a larger right—the right to choose a basic style of life and to make major life choices freely, without society, or the state, interfering. In family law, this leads to what Milton Regan has called the "optional family"—that is, a menu of choices: staying single, cohabiting, or marrying; and, whether married or not, deciding whether or not to have children. He also speaks of the "negotiated family"—that is, the fact that "family relationships are less likely to be organized around common expectations of behavior"; each family, each couple, each person works out the principles, desires, and behaviors that will constitute their own family life.[12] What is "optional" is of course a matter of pure choice; what is "negotiated," however, implies other people—a partner, spouse, children. This term reminds us that one person's choice affects, and is affected by, others.

The primacy of choice, nonetheless, has to be emphasized. And some aspects of choice, in American law and in the law of certain other systems, are given the somewhat incongruous and misleading name of the right of privacy. This right is linked closely to choices about sex and marriage. For this reason, it is an essential part of the story I mean to tell. It is the subject of the last chapter of this book. "Privacy" is a complicated concept. In some ways, it is an odd concept. It may seem strange to talk about the decision to use a condom or the birth-control pill, or the right to be openly gay, as a matter of privacy. What is involved, of course, is the right to make *private* choices—free from the interference of the government. In the law, disputes over this kind of privacy relate, above all, to issues of sex, family, and reproduction.

Privacy and family are related, too, in an even more organic way. The home is the seat of the family; and the home is also the seat of private life. "A man's home is his castle" is one of the most famous slogans of the older common law. When this axiom was first enunciated, a man's home was a castle mostly for people who actually lived in castles (or at least in mansions). The poor had no privacy. The legal slogan actually has to do with searches and seizures, arrest warrants, and the like; but it does express an important idea: the home is the haven, the island of immunity, the place of private life. For the average person, this became so only in the nineteenth century. The nineteenth century was the century of the home, the family, the private sphere. In the bosom of the family, too, people learned (as they always had) the norms of society—how to live, how to govern their impulses; they learned what was right and wrong behavior. Private life was the foundation of public life.

In the twentieth century this situation changed radically. The family lost its monopoly on the power to train, mold, and socialize children. It lost this power not only to schools, but to also to radio, movies, and television, and to the peer group. The outside world came bursting into the home. A man's home was no longer a castle; it was open, porous—it was, above all, an entertainment center. The media blurred the boundaries between the public world and the private world. The family was transformed; so too was the very concept and meaning of privacy. The right of privacy means the right to be left alone, the right to a private life, the right to some kinds of secrecy and seclusion; but it also means the right to make personal choices—about marriage, sex, babies—choices that may be, and often are, anything but private. Perhaps what joins all these disparate ideas together is the concept of free choice, including the choice to "go public" or not.

The privacy issue is tied to the family in yet another way. The family (or rather, the traditional family) once had a kind of state monopoly.

Men and women could have sex legitimately only if they were married—that is, if they formed a family. Only "families" in the traditional sense could have babies. If you wanted sex, you were supposed to get married. If you wanted babies, you were supposed to get married. Sex and babies were otherwise (officially) off limits.

Of course, not everybody played by the rules. There was sex outside of marriage, and there were babies born outside of traditional families. But official society sharply condemned illicit sex and illicit children. The modern concept of the right of privacy (including choice of lifestyle, sex partners, and whether to have children) has helped to burst open the notion of family, remolding the family and destroying its monopoly on babies, sex, and intimate life. Sex and reproduction, after all, are at the very heart of marriage and divorce, and family law in general. But modern society and modern law have gone a long way to uncouple sex and reproduction from (formal, traditional) marriage. In a way, the "privacy" cases of the Supreme Court—cases on contraception, abortion, gay rights—are a new branch of family law, and an essential one at that.

I have described what I (and many others) consider the master trend in the growth and development of family law. It is a trend toward the enthronement of the individual, and individual choice. But at every step of the way there has been opposition and conflict; and this too is part of the story. Moreover, choices do not take place in a vacuum. What I choose for myself has an impact on other people. A married woman, for example, in most states today has the right to end the marriage. This is her free choice. But what if her husband would choose not to? Her choice trumps his choice. There are, in modern law and life, many instances of this sort of conflict. A divorcing husband and wife may both want custody of their child. An adopted child may want to find her birth mother; the birth mother may not want to be found. "Choice," then, does not mean a lack of conflict. Conflict is everywhere, in every society. Only the terms and conditions of conflicts change over time and space.

How can a society resolve these conflicts? There is no single answer. No single, simple answer is possible. As a result, many such conflicts make their way into the courts for resolution. One function of courts in this society is precisely to resolve conflicts for which there is no obvious, rational solution.

The story should not be read as an account of the decline and fall of the family. The family has not dissolved. It has changed and broadened. It has become more elastic. In some ways, it is a much weaker institution. But it still has a vast reservoir of strength. This can be seen even—or especially—in the demand for gay marriage. Many conservative people read this demand as a sign of moral decay. But it is testimony to the idea and ideal of the family. It is simply a demand for a more elastic definition of legitimate marriage. And, paradoxically, it is a demand for the right of two people to give up some of their rights of free choice: the right of two men, or two women, to put themselves under a legal and social yoke that they are now quite free of. After all, same-sex couples who choose civil commitment, where it is available, cannot simply walk out on each other; gay marriage implies gay divorce.

This book is about the evolution of family law, and the law of privacy, in the United States. But the United States is not an isolated country; it is part of the developed Western world. The story of American family law is in many ways very much like the story of family law in other advanced industrial countries. Of course, American law has its own peculiarities; so does the law of other nations. No two countries are alike. Each has its own quirks, its own zigs and zags along the common path. Although my main emphasis is on the United States, I will try to situate American law in a broader, comparative context.

A few simple premises underlie this book. These are premises that underlie the study of law and society in general. For one thing, I treat legal phenomena as dependent variables. Social forces shape the legal order. Law is not and never has been an autonomous kingdom. It does not live in a world of its own. The legal system is part of society; it tends to fit its society like the glove fits the hand. Feudal societies produce feudal law; market systems produce law adapted to free markets; a welfare-regulatory state produces its own sort of legal order.[13] (Actually, it is in a way misleading to say that a feudal society *produces* feudal law, and so on; a certain kind of legal order is what *makes* a feudal society feudal; a certain kind of legal order—rights of contract, sale, property—makes a capitalist society capitalist; and a welfare state is a state with laws about old-age pensions, health care, and so on.) What is true of law in general is true for the field of family law as well. It is a product of society, and it reflects, in its general contours, the social structure, social practice, and social debates within its society.[14] Here too it is impossible to disentangle family structure from legal structure. After all, the words "marriage," "divorce," "adoption," and "custody," though they are part of everyday language and everyday understanding, are also *legal* terms. The law defines what is and is not a marriage, and what is and is not a divorce.

Family law is a well-recognized field of legal practice. It is bread and butter for thousands of lawyers, in the United States and elsewhere.[15] It is a practical concern for all these lawyers, and their clients. Family law has, in addition, special theoretical interest for scholars interested in the study of law and society. In our time, laws are commonly borrowed, diffused, exported, and imported. We can make a rough distinction between two kinds of law. One kind is, in a way, technological. Technology travels easily, and although technology affects culture deeply, it is itself independent of culture. An automobile is an automobile is an automobile, whether it is in Tokyo or Moscow or Buenos Aires or New York. A cell phone is a cell phone; a computer is a computer. There is no such thing as a Chinese cultural cell phone, or a Brazilian style of computer. Some laws and legal institutions seem to be of this type. They move easily from country to country. Some highly technical matters of commercial law migrate with apparent facility. Perhaps—just perhaps—rules of corporate governance fall into this category, although this can be debated.[16]

Other branches of law seem to be less technological. They are deeply rooted in the culture; they change slowly and travel badly. Family law is usually cited as the chief example of this type of law. A computer may be a computer in Iran or Saudi Arabia; but a marriage in these countries is not at all like a marriage in France or in Finland. Gender relations, laws about sex—these seem to be deeply cultural, deeply specific. Of course, many countries have borrowed family law from somewhere else (usually as part of a wholesale adoption of legal codes). Japan and Turkey are famous instances. But some people are skeptical as to whether these translations "take."[17] Moreover, a country like Saudi Arabia, which may be only too eager to adopt certain legal rules and institutions from the West, would never dream of accepting Western family law. It is completely foreign (the Saudis say) to their culture.

No doubt it is true, up to a point, that family law does not travel or transfer easily. Nobody can impose a regime of family law on a society the way an income tax law can be imposed, or a law regulating stock exchanges. Any attempt to do so is likely to be futile. No: family law has to develop organically, within society. But this does not mean that it is therefore exceedingly tough and resistant to change. In fact, family law is much more malleable than many people believe. The changes come from inside society, not from outside, to be sure; but they are changes nevertheless. In point of fact, family law has been changing rapidly, almost in a revolutionary way, over the past century or so. It may have changed as much as corporation law or commercial law has changed, and possibly even more. This is so because the family itself has been changing with whirlwind speed. Victorian family relations and family law seem almost as quaint and outmoded (in some Western countries) as the Victorian horse and buggy.

For the most part, the changes in family structure are familiar and obvious. Families are smaller than they once were. The birthrate has declined in all Western countries; in some of them (Italy, for example), the birthrate is so low that the population is shrinking. The Catholic Church still officially bans contraception, but nobody pays much attention. The extended family is all but dead. In 2004, Chile, the last important holdout, passed a law providing for absolute divorce; everywhere else in the Western world divorce was already legal—and extremely common. The relations between men and women, between parents and children, have been redefined and recast; the family is much more democratic—or, if you will, anarchic. Patriarchy is in retreat. At one time, as mentioned, the father was the head of the family in almost every conceivable way. His word was law. The family, for example, was a "little commonwealth" in Puritan thought. Everyone in this commonwealth was subject to the will and the wishes of the father, just as people in the larger society were subjects of the King.[18]

In modern Western societies, the kings are gone (or are powerless ribbon-cutters) and the father is no longer king of the family. This is true both socially and legally. The family has changed in other ways too. For one thing, people live longer than they used to, thanks to sanitation, good food, and modern medicine. Few parents die young. Divorce has replaced death as a cause of family breakup. Long life has reduced the supply of orphans, and this has had an impact on the law and practice of adoption. People talk about the graying of society: more old people, and more old-old people. Instead of a bumper crop of babies, there is a bumper crop of old folks. This profoundly affects the politics and policies of the welfare state. Welfare policy, in turn, both reflects and influences norms about the duty of children toward their elderly parents. The state has essentially taken over a role that children used to have. Longevity has also affected the meaning and importance of inheritance. If your parents live into their nineties, you may well have to wait until you are sixty-five before you inherit their money. This means that lifetime transfers—money for college, for a down payment on your dream house—are more important in your life than inheritance.[19]

Basic changes in society, such as the increase in wealth and leisure and the development of more open and democratic structures, have freed individuals from many of the ropes and chains that bound them to tradition. The zone of human choice has expanded greatly. The Western middle class lives in what I have called the republic of choice.[20] The right to choose (a way of life, a partner, a style of eating, dressing, making love) is a fundamental idea in contemporary society. How fundamental varies somewhat from country to country. Each society has its own unique constellation of ideas and behaviors. But everywhere we find that the broad trends are quite similar in form, in direction, in substance. The zone of choice is everywhere expanding. Consider, for example, the position of women in every Western society compared to (say) two centuries ago: women's position is different in Japan or Korea than in Sweden or the United States, but the overall trend has been the same.

I want to make one point very clear. The *idea* of choice, I feel, is enormously important to people today, and the zone of choice has widened in modern society; but this zone is not infinite. It is, in fact, narrower than most people think. People in general are not conscious of the constraints and limitations that their culture imposes. The average Joe or Jane is not a trained anthropologist. Joe buys a shirt, Jane buys a blouse, and each thinks this was entirely their choice, their taste, their decision. Of course, in a way they are right. Nobody held a gun to their heads and said, "Buy this or else." But fashion limits—or even dictates—the range, the choice, the menu of blouses and shirts. People do not stop to ask themselves *why* a certain style seems so attractive. Only yesterday it may have seemed ugly or outmoded. Nor do they ask why men wear shirts and pants and never wear skirts, and women wear skirts and blouses and sometimes pants and shirts. Free choice is a reality, but always within limits, within boundaries. Society, social norms, fashions, habits—these fix the boundaries, in ways that often defy rational explanation. Most of us are not consciously aware of these boundaries. We simply accept them, automatically. We live inside compounds that have invisible walls.

A second point: I am trying in this book to describe and explain. Whether the changes I discuss are good or bad is a question I want to leave mostly to the reader. But of course I have my own notions of good and bad, and they will often be quite apparent. I am also aware that there is no such thing, really, as mere description; each description is also an interpretation. Moreover, the story I want to tell is extremely complex. At every point, there are counter-stories that could be told. Some segments of society cling to the good old ways, honor them, and work for them. They hope that the looseness, the permissiveness, the excessive choices of modernity are only a passing phase; they hope that the good old days can come back. On this last point, they are surely wrong—history never repeats itself. But who knows what the future may bring? Perhaps some variation on family life that we cannot even imagine today. A traditionalist vision of the future might be closer to what will actually happen than the vision of the hippie or the revolutionary.

Choice has its enemies, and they are not just the traditionalists. This is the age of the individual, an age in which privacy flourishes; and zones of choice in the developed countries are evident. But it is also the age of massive state power—the age of big government. And the age of big institutions, too: gigantic corporations, for example, whose tentacles cover the globe. Bigness is power; and both government and enterprises have power to control and shape individual lives. The twentieth century was a century of democracy and freedom, but it was also the century of genocide, and of the worst dictatorships of all time, murderous regimes of unprecedented virulence and strength. It was the century of Hitler, Stalin, and Pol Pot. And today, technology poses a severe threat to privacy and autonomy: threats from wiretapping, electronic surveillance, and dossiers that computers generate. The media are a double-edged sword. They are, in one very real sense, profoundly liberating. They spread messages of freedom and choice. Despite their crass commercialism, and their supine and timid posture in the face of controversy, television in the Western countries has an underlying ethos that is, despite itself, brash and antiauthoritarian. All dictators feel compelled to restrict and censor the media. But technology and the media can also be amazingly intrusive. The era of Big Brother is no longer science fiction. New devices and techniques threaten the principle of privacy. They are, or can be, powerful enemies of basic human dignity. I will return to this general theme at the end of this book.

2

Marriage and Divorce
in the Nineteenth Century

The history of family law in the United States, like that of any country, is a story of great complexity.[1] The nation was established by Europeans—mostly from Great Britain—and it inherited a tradition of Christian marriage and family life. Much of that tradition has survived over the centuries. Other bits and pieces have changed or disappeared.

In this chapter, I single out and discuss a few aspects of the history of family law. One of them is the doctrine of the so-called common law marriage.[2]

Common Law Marriage

A common law marriage was a marriage by agreement, a marriage that began when a man and woman simply made a contract with each other to be married. Although historically and in religious terms marriage was supposed to be a sacrament, in American law, marriage was, to use a phrase that appears over and over again, a "civil contract." Blackstone called it that; and so did American jurists and courts.[3] It was, of course, a most peculiar contract. If two people have a contract to buy and sell a horse, they can call the whole thing off by mutual agreement; but the two parties to the "civil contract" of marriage are stuck with their bargain, unless they go to the trouble of getting a divorce—no easy matter during much of America's history. Moreover, as one writer put it, parties to an ordinary contract "can fix its terms to suit themselves"; but in the marriage contract, once the parties enter into it, "the law fixes absolutely its terms."[4]

Marriage, then, was a status—entered into, to be sure, by agreement. The doctrine of the common law marriage carried the idea of the agreement to a kind of logical extreme. If a man and woman merely said the right words to each other, that was enough in law to make them validly married. No witnesses, no ceremony of any sort was needed. The two were bound to each other from that moment on. Their children were legitimate. They had the same property claims on each other that any husband and wife would have—no more and no less than two people who got married in a cathedral before a crowd of hundreds of witnesses and guests, dressed to the nines, and in a ceremony conducted by a bishop.

In England, too, secret and informal marriages were at one time a common practice, and this was also the case in other countries (for example, France).[5] After all, for the poor, ceremonial marriage was a serious expense. In England, the law seemed to accept these marriages, until the passage of Lord Hardwicke's Marriage Act in 1753. This important statute destroyed the legal basis of informal marriage. The very title of the law was "An Act for the Better Preventing of Clandestine Marriages." From then on, all "Banns of Matrimony" had to be "published in an audible Manner in the Parish Church, or in some Publick Chapel," for three Sundays in a row. A recognized clergyman (of the Church of England) had to perform all marriages, and marriages had to be "solemnized in the Presence of Two or more credible Witnesses" and entered in a registry. Moreover, anyone who tried to conduct a marriage in violation of the act was guilty of a felony and liable to be "transported to some of His Majesty's Plantations in America."[6]

What is now the United States was then a collection of British colonies; independence did not come for more than twenty years after the passage of Lord Hardwicke's act. But informal marriage had a very different fate in the United States. The act of 1753 did not apply to "any Marriages solemnized beyond the Seas;"[7] and indeed, Lord Hardwicke's path was not the American path. The doctrine that had been driven out of the mother country survived and thrived in the former colonies. After the Revolution, in a series of important cases, the independent states generally recognized the common law marriage as totally valid and legal.

Why was this so? Where did the idea of the common law marriage come from, and why did it persist? In some ways, this is an easy question to answer. In many societies, informal marriage is the norm. Informal marriage had deep roots in custom and practice. It was apparently quite common, during the colonial period, for people to "marry" informally. Their neighbors seemed to accept the idea that these marriages were morally, if not legally, sound. One minister in Maryland was said to feel that if such marriages were not valid, then nine-tenths of the people born in his area were bastards.[8] "Informal" marriages were not always totally informal. There were at times required customs and rituals—for example, breaking a coin. Whether the law recognized "breaking money" as a form of marriage or not, people in the community regarded it as a sign of commitment.[9] Texas had an institution called "bond marriage." A man and woman signed a written agreement containing the usual marriage vows. The document—which was witnessed—was really a form of engagement. It often had a forfeiture clause: if either party backed out, he or she would have to pay.[10] Whatever one can say about a bond marriage, it was hardly the sort of thing Lord Hardwicke had in mind.

In Texas and elsewhere in the United States, particularly in the West, there was a serious shortage of clergy. This was undoubtedly one reason to accept common law marriages and other informal types of union. An Anglican minister, Charles Woodmason, who traveled to the back country of South Carolina in 1766 in order to bring his religious message to this rather wild area, reported that "thro' want of Ministers to marry and thro' the licentiousness of the People, many hundreds live in Concubinage—swopping their Wives as Cattel, and living in a State of Nature, more irregularly and unchastely than the Indians."[11] Woodmason was probably exaggerating. Many of these couples likely did not think they were living in a "state of nature." But the shortage of ministers certainly encouraged informal ways of getting married.

The Texas-style bond marriage was a clearly defined custom, with a strong dash of formality; even breaking a coin was a ritual or ceremony. They were also, for the most part, public acts. Most states recognized marriages, however, that were totally informal—with no evidence to back them up and nobody to confirm that the couple had actually exchanged the right words or vows in private. But like all legal doctrines of any importance, the common law marriage was hardly a historical accident. We should ask, then: what use was it? What purpose did it serve? Reported cases make the answer fairly clear. Money, land, and inheritance: these were the points at issue. The common law marriage was a device for settling claims to property. It protected "wives" of informal unions and their children when the marriage ended with the death of one party, usually the "husband." That was its major function.[12]

The United States was, in a sense, the first middle-class country. No factor explains more of the twists and turns in American law, and the nature of American society in the nineteenth century in general. The United States was the first country in which ordinary people owned some capital: a farm, a plot of land, a house. Questions of title, inheritance, and mortgage do not enter the lives of people who have nothing and own nothing—serfs, tenant farmers, and the like. Once people have property, once they own something, they become consumers of the products of the legal system. Now family law becomes significant for them. A man is dead; he owned an eighty-acre farm. Is this woman his widow? Are these children legitimate heirs?

The doctrine of the common law marriage protected the rights of a woman who had lived with a man in a stable relationship. It protected the rights of their children as well. Since common law marriages were completely informal, there was almost never any actual proof of the marriage; judges simply assumed an agreement to marry. If a man and woman lived together, had children, and led respectable lives, if the community thought they were married, then practically speaking they *were* married. These facts raised the presumption of a common law marriage.

Who could prove otherwise? The doctrine also protected the reputation of the couple and their children at a time when sex outside marriage was a scandal. Indeed, in most states sex outside marriage was a crime in the nineteenth century. For these reasons, most American states accepted the doctrine of the common law marriage. A few grumbled and did not; but they were a distinct minority.

Some examples of the doctrine at work will illustrate its social utility. One important case, in the early nineteenth century, turned on a woman's right to a pension. The plaintiff claimed she was the widow of a man named William Reed. Reed had belonged to a society that gave pensions to the widows of its members. The facts were these: she had been married once before, to a man named John Guest. Guest disappeared; seven years went by. People assumed he was dead. The plaintiff then married Reed. Lo and behold, Guest popped up again. Apparently, Mrs. Reed had had quite enough of Guest; she stayed with Reed. Guest, it seems, made no objection. Legally speaking, this woman's marriage to Reed was void. She was a bigamist. Her first husband was alive at the time she went through a marriage ceremony with Reed. But then Guest died; and, later on, so did Reed. After Guest died, she was free to marry Reed and make it all legal and proper. There was, however, no evidence that she did so—no evidence of a marriage ceremony. Still, the court awarded her the pension. It *assumed* a valid common law marriage. A marriage, said the court, may be "inferred" from the circumstances: here the parties "cohabited together as husband and wife"; they had the "reputation" of being married. That was enough.[13]

A later case, from Oklahoma in 1918, makes a similar point. A woman named Missouri A. Thomas claimed rights to the estate of John Thomas. John Thomas had been married twice. The first marriage produced a daughter; it was this daughter who objected to the "widow's" claim. After the first marriage ended, John married Missouri in the usual formal and ceremonial way. Later, they had a falling out and got divorced. Apparently, however, a few weeks after the divorce, the embers of love burst into flame again. John moved in with his ex-wife, Missouri, and they stayed together in a single household until the day he died. People in the community considered them a married couple. This fact, and their behavior, said the court, was "sufficient to warrant the presumption of a valid common-law marriage"; Missouri Thomas was John's widow and was entitled to a share of the estate.[14] Obviously, in this and many similar cases, the "marriage" began simply with cohabitation—with a "meretricious" relationship, as the courts put it ("meretricious" is legalese for illicit). But even so, as one commentator said, some "meretricious" relationships grow "insensibly into permanent unions"; it would be "sound public policy to accept the final compliance" rather than the "initial disregard of law."[15]

In most cases, courts used the doctrine of common law marriage to protect "widows" and children. Once in a while, though, the doctrine pointed in the opposite direction, as it did in a case from New York in 1850.[16] A man named George Messerve had a life interest in a trust that had been set up by his father. Under the terms of the trust, when George died, his share would go to his children. George had married a woman named Sarah Maria Young; and he had a daughter with her, Catherine Ann. Catherine Ann claimed the money; but the executors refused, on the grounds that she was illegitimate. Her mother, it turns out, had a somewhat checkered past. When she was about sixteen years old, Sarah Maria had become pregnant by a man named Richard Schenck. Richard was arrested, "under the provisions of the bastardy act," but never prosecuted. He and Sarah Maria lived together after the baby was born (the baby died less than a year later). Some people thought they were married. Later, when they split up, they executed a document, which they called a "separation agreement" and which described them as husband and wife. After the two broke up, Sarah Maria married George Messerve.

Clearly, if she was married—if she had had a common law marriage with Richard Schenck—then her "marriage" to George was no marriage at all; it was bigamy, and therefore invalid. Here was a case where a man and woman had lived together, openly; on at least one occasion they had said they were married; and some people had thought they were married. Normally, these facts would give a court every reason to say that they *were* married, in the common law way. But the result of such a ruling in this particular situation would be disastrous: it would make Catherine Ann a bastard and rob her of her inheritance. This the New York court refused to do. The evidence, said the court, was against the earlier union. Richard and Sarah Maria's relationship had been "meretricious." The marriage to George was therefore legitimate, and Catherine Ann was entitled to her money.

The case clearly bothered some of the judges: three of them dissented. One judge, who wrote a concurring opinion, remarked that a "life of illicit cohabitation" is a situation of "moral turpitude"; and "in all civilized societies" people of this sort are "excluded . . . from all intercourse with respectable people." So if two people are openly living together, the right thing to do would be to presume the "purity" of their relationship. The case at hand was different, however, because presuming the legitimacy of the first relationship would make the daughter of the second a bastard.[17]

These cases turn on money; they are fueled by land and money, and it is land and money that bring them into court. But sex, marriage, and cohabitation are not just ways to decide who gets a farm when somebody dies. They are close, intimate relationships; religious codes try to regulate them; social norms assess them, judge them, moralize about them. Morality is never far distant from these cases, even though morality does not drive them into the courtroom. In one 1860 case, in Georgia,[18] the issue was procedural: James Dupree and his wife, Uriah, filed a lawsuit against a man named Uriah Askew. The male Uriah was accused of mismanaging the estate of the female Uriah's father. The male Uriah interposed a technical objection. James and the female Uriah, he said, were not really married. James could not therefore be party to her lawsuit. James and his Uriah *thought* they were married, or once thought so: the marriage was performed by a certain A. Buckner, who claimed to be a "minister of the Gospel." But before the marriage, allegedly, Buckner had been "deposed from the . . . church," his credentials were revoked, and he was "excommunicated." Thus, said defendant Uriah to plaintiff Uriah, your marriage is invalid, and your supposed husband is no husband at all.

Judge Lumpkin, who wrote the decision, sided with the female Uriah. True, Buckner had no right to marry them, and the ceremony was invalid. But she and James (said the judge) had a lawful common law marriage. Of course, there was no evidence to support this. Lumpkin admitted as much; he had "never known," he said, "[o]f a self-solemnized marriage." But the doctrine of the common law marriage was a wise one, especially for "the female. . . . Her honor is saved, and this is worth more than everything, even life itself." After all, he said, the law of Georgia (at that time) allowed boys of fourteen and girls of twelve—"infants" (legally speaking)—to "enter into the binding contract of marriage," against the usual rule that the law will not recognize the contracts of "infants" as binding. The reason? At these ages "the sexual passions are usually developed"; and the law, in its wisdom, "to guard against the manifold evils which would result from illicit intercourse, declares even infants capable of forming this relation." Clearly, as far as Lumpkin was concerned, the common law marriage had the same salutary effect. It saved men and women from "illicit intercourse." That it did so by simply relabeling their "illicit intercourse" as "licit intercourse" did not seem to bother Lumpkin. But he lived at a time that was extremely concerned with appearances. What endangered society was not sinful intercourse per se, but sinful intercourse that thumbed its nose at the norms; sinful intercourse that flouted, attacked, and tried to undermine conventional morality. Conventional morality could survive any number of secret sinners. It could not survive open rebellion.

The common law marriage also saved the children. It gave them the farm and the money, which was no small thing. It preserved the reputations of their parents, and in this way saved the children from the horrific label of bastardy. Justice Strong, in an 1877 case in the United States Supreme Court, pointed out that marriage was "a thing of common right"; it was state policy to "encourage" marriage. Without common law marriage "the offspring of many parents conscious of no violation of law" would be "illegitimate."[19] Of course, we have no idea whether these parents were "conscious" or not of "violation of law." But that was a minor consideration.

Marriage as a Contract

The common law marriage was, as we said, recognized in the majority of the states. From the mid-nineteenth century on, however, it definitely had ups and downs—mostly downs. As we shall see, there were factors that worked against it from the late nineteenth century on. But that it existed at all speaks volumes about the social meaning of marriage. Legal sources, over and over again, refer to marriage as a "civil contract"—not a sacrament, not a gift of the state, but a contract, an agreement. Of course, as noted earlier, it was a most peculiar contract, a deviant contract. But the idea of its being a "contract" did touch on something real. Marriage rested on the will, the choice, the decision, of two people; the state was (as it were) on the outside looking in, and so was the church. And the basis of marriage was love—not family, not reasons of property or state, but love.

The actual "contract" may have been a fiction. But it was not fiction to imagine that marriage was a matter of free choice, of will, of actual agreement between a man and a woman; and, indeed, that it was ideally a reflection of powerful, romantic love.[20] To be sure, the *consequences* of marriage were not at all dependent on agreement. In any event, there was rarely if ever any real evidence of this agreement. How could there be? It had to be "proved" by reputation, inference, and suggestion. The doctrine meant, then, in practice, as we pointed out earlier, that if people were considered married in their community, if they behaved the way proper married people behaved, then they were assumed or presumed to be married, even without a ceremony or any evidence of one. It was the behavior, then, that cast a moral glow over a couple's relationship. If it looks like bourgeois marriage, if it acts like bourgeois marriage, if it feels like bourgeois marriage, then legally it *is* bourgeois marriage.

In a way, the doctrine thus pointed in two rather different directions. In one sense, it allowed people to form relationships entirely on their own, without state and church; it took informal relationships, relationships of commitment—and these were apparently common in society—and it legitimated them. It took away from these relationships the label of evil or sinful. The doctrine also had a number of subsidiary functions. As in the Georgia case, it cleaned up the mess made by failed ceremonial marriages. It also was a way to clean up the mess made by illicit sex: it gave the partners a chance to acquire legitimacy—to purge themselves of sin, at least in the eyes of the law. In a New York case in 1889,[21] a widower named Joseph Gall began a "criminal intimacy" with his cook, Amelia Stieb. He was nearly eighty at the time. Joseph was, in a way, a wonderful advertisement for men in their golden years, long before Viagra; and Amelia became pregnant as a result of this "intimacy." Joseph sent her to a doctor, who confirmed the pregnancy. Amelia gave birth to a daughter. Old Joseph supported her, bought her a house, installed her, her mother, and the rest of her family in the house, and visited frequently—staying overnight, sharing a bed with Amelia, and eating "at the same table." They acted like husband and wife; he did in fact call her "Mrs. Gall," and sometimes referred to her as "my wife." Eventually, he moved in on a permanent basis. With his "old acquaintances," however, he never mentioned his wife and continued to pass as a widower—perhaps, as the court remarked, because he was embarrassed by the fact that he had married his cook. When he died at the age of eighty-two, Amelia (who was pregnant again at the time of his death) claimed her legal share of his estate. She won her case. At first, the court noted, Joseph and Amelia's relationship had been "purely licentious"; but later, it had all the appearances of legitimacy. "The cohabitation, apparently decent and orderly, of two persons opposite in sex, raises a presumption of more or less strength that they have been duly married." In other words, whether they were actually married was a fact question, which the jury was entitled to decide, as they did, in favor of Amelia.[22]

The doctrine, in short, rescued the reputation, and the respectability, of women who were living informally with men—it safeguarded them, while it also preserved rights of property. The women were decent, not the type who lived in "criminal intimacy." At the same time, the doctrine defined the relationship as a marriage, a real marriage, a valid marriage, rather than something else, some halfway status, something between "criminal intimacy" and full marriage. In so doing, social norms (and the law) underscored a fairly traditional point: sexual and family partnerships were acceptable in marriage, and only in marriage. That the definition of marriage was bent out of shape a bit was unfortunate but unavoidable.

The Law of Divorce

Divorce has had a tangled history in the United States. The process of ending marriages has always been much more controversial than the process of beginning them; it has also been more complicated, legally speaking. "Family law" lawyers and specialists are, basically, divorce lawyers. You do not need a lawyer to get married, or to stay married; but in most societies, you need a lawyer, and usually also a judge and a court, to get divorced. Yet the social meaning of divorce depends on the social meaning of marriage. And the legal shape of divorce follows from its social definitions. Is marriage a sacrament? a mere contract? a special kind of contract? a partnership? a form of companionship? a status that is important because it leads to children? a major element of personal growth and self-realization? The answers to these questions are likely to determine what the working law of divorce will look like in any given society.

In the sixteenth century, Henry VIII broke with Rome partly on the issue of divorce. The king got his divorce, but the law in England nonetheless did not, for centuries, allow ordinary people to get a divorce. The divorce process was extremely cumbersome—and extremely expensive. If a man, say, wanted to divorce his wife, he first had to file suit for a legal separation. Then he had to bring an adultery action against his wife (a civil action for "criminal conversation"). After this, he had to petition Parliament for a private act dissolving his marriage.[23] Obviously, this meant that the mass of the public had no chance of getting a divorce. Divorce was very rare; only persistent members of the nobility, or of the very rich, had any hope of achieving it.

This situation lasted until 1857, when Parliament passed a divorce reform act. But even under this act, divorce was in practice restricted to the wealthy. Now divorce became a judicial proceeding, not a Parliamentary one. But the process was still far too expensive for the poor or the lower middle class. The new divorce court sat only in London—another barrier to most people in the kingdom. This inconvenience was not unintended. Quite to the contrary, it was exactly what the government wanted. It was generally felt that the moral fabric of English society would be in danger if the common man had access to divorce. This is what the elites—who drafted the law and voted for it—believed.[24] And divorce, in fact, remained fairly rare even after the law of 1857. There were only 573 petitions for divorce in 1895, and 609 in 1900; there were fewer than 1,000 a year until the time of the First World War.[25] The grounds for divorce, too, as we shall see, were very restrictive under this act.

Divorce was easier in the United States.[26] To be sure, in the first part of the nineteenth century, in many states, particularly in the South, the only way to get a divorce was to petition the legislature. (In one state, South Carolina, divorce was not available at all, and would not be until deep into the twentieth century.) The legislative divorce was, naturally, not particularly common. Still, to ask the legislature of, say, the state of Alabama to grant a divorce was much less of a burden than to ask the great parliament in London to grant a divorce; in fact, the statute books of some southern states are full of statutes granting divorces to particular couples. Between 1789 and 1835, for example, Georgia's legislature granted 291 divorces.[27] The statutes were usually very short and unrevealing: to take one example of many, a law of the state of Maryland, from 1847, simply declared that the marriage of Sarah Price and John Price was "forever null and void" and that they were "divorced a vinculo matrimonii."[28] But behind each statute was, of course, a story, with petitions, affidavits, and narratives drawn up to convince a skeptical crowd of legislators.[29] The legislatures would by no means rubber-stamp the petitions. In Virginia in 1841, Olympia Meridith hoped to divorce her husband, an abusive bounder named Moody Blood. Moody had been put in jail for receiving stolen property, leaving Olympia with her two children, Fleming Blood and Friendless Blood. But the legislature turned down her petition. She tried again two years later, and the legislature said no again.[30] During the period of legislative divorce in Virginia, men and women petitioned for divorce in roughly equal numbers; in no year did the legislature grant the majority of the petitions. Overall, until the system was abolished, only one out of three petitioners got the divorce.[31] In a few states in the South, divorce actions began in the courts, later to be confirmed by the legislature. This was the case, for example, in Mississippi until 1840.[32]

In the northern states, divorce was more freely available; here the road to divorce went through the courtroom, rather than through the legislature. Pennsylvania had a general divorce law in 1785, Massachusetts a year later. Under laws of the northern type, either a husband or a wife could petition the court for a divorce. The plaintiff had to be an innocent party, one who had been wronged by the other spouse. Each state had a statutory list of the wrongs that amounted to "grounds" for divorce. Typically, the list included adultery and desertion. In Connecticut, for example, divorce was available in court for "adultery; fraudulent contract; willful desertion for three years, with total neglect of duty"; also for "seven years' absence of one party, not heard of."[33] Some states were more restrictive than others. New York was a notable example of stringency. In New York, divorce was available only for adultery. In other states, besides adultery and desertion, cruelty was added to the list; and there were miscellaneous other grounds in this or that state—habitual drunkenness, for example, or conviction of a serious crime. In New Hampshire, it was grounds for divorce if one partner joined a "religious sect" that rejected marriage, and if that partner "refused to cohabit . . . for the space of three years."[34] This was aimed at the Shakers, who did not believe in sexual intercourse—a fatal blow to the typical marriage. Kentucky, too, allowed divorce if one party or the other became a member of a group that called for "renunciation of the marriage covenant" or forbade "husband and wife from cohabiting."[35]

A Double Standard

American divorce laws were, formally speaking, pretty much unisex. On paper at least, husband and wife had the same legal right to a divorce in the nineteenth century. In some other legal systems, the so-called double standard was part of the law itself. Under the English law of 1857, a man could divorce his wife on the grounds of adultery; but if a woman sued for divorce, garden-variety adultery on the part of her husband was not enough. He had to be guilty of a kind of aggravated adultery—"incestuous adultery, or of bigamy with adultery, or of rape, or of sodomy or bestiality," or adultery together with behavior sufficiently cruel as to entitle her to a legal separation, had she wanted one; or adultery joined with "desertion, without reasonable excuse for two years and upwards."[36] The Louisiana Civil Code of 1825 (Articles 136, 137) and earlier Louisiana codes had a similar distinction. If a married person was asking for legal separation (so-called divorce "from bed and board"), simple adultery was all a husband needed; but a wife could only complain about her husband's adultery if he was brazen enough to keep his "concubine" in their "common dwelling." No one should be fooled by the fact that most of the laws were formally unisex in the United States. The double standard was in full flower in the United States, just as it was in other countries. In some states, for example, well into the twentieth century, the *criminal* law of adultery made a distinction between husband and wife. In Minnesota, for example, a married woman was guilty of adultery if she had sex with a man "other than her husband, whether married or not." But a married man was only guilty of adultery if he had sex with a married woman.[37] If a married man had sex with a single woman (or a prostitute), this was not criminal adultery at all.

Socially, it was not difficult for a man to be forgiven if he had sex outside of marriage; for respectable women, this was impossible. Under the so-called unwritten law, a man who found out that his wife was unfaithful was free to kill his wife's lover; the deceived husband was almost never punished for this crime.[38] No statute book actually contained this "law"; but it was reflected in the behavior of prosecutors and certainly in the behavior of juries. The sensational trial of Daniel Sickles, in Washington, D.C., in 1859 is only one example. Sickles, a congressman, had a young wife, Teresa, who began an affair with Philip Barton Key (son of the man who wrote "The Star-Spangled Banner"). Sickles found out about the affair and shot Key to death on the streets of Washington. He was tried before a jury, which acquitted him.[39] The fig leaf covering this nakedly biased verdict was Sickles's claim of "temporary insanity." His lawyers argued that if a man found out his wife was unfaithful, the situation could quite easily drive him into a murderous rage. Whether this story actually persuaded the jury is another question. Probably they responded more to the other argument which Sickles's lawyers made: Key was sinful scum and deserved to die. In another famous nineteenth-century trial, Daniel McFarland was charged with murdering Albert Richardson. Richardson had had an affair with Daniel's wife, Abigail. Abigail divorced Daniel and began living with Albert. McFarland shot Richardson, who died two months later—after a "notorious bedside marriage of Albert to Abby."[40] Here too, at the trial in 1870, the lawyers drew a picture of a man driven insane (temporarily, of course), when his wife betrayed him. The jury set him free.[41] In the McFarland case, an ex-husband killed the man who broke up the marriage. Adultery was grounds for divorce; but a woman's adultery was also, as these cases show, grounds for murder. In other words, family law, including the law of divorce, in practice reflected the grim and unforgiving norms of Victorian morality.

Of course, it is only to us today that these norms seem so heartless and so biased. At the time, they seemed not only just, but essential. The traditional family, with its separate "spheres" for men and women, seemed part of God's plan. More to the point perhaps, it was the bedrock of society, the foundation on which everything else was built. Tamper with it, tinker with it, and you were threatening the whole fabric of social order. To people who thought this way, divorce was an evil, to be resorted to only in the most extreme cases; a toxic medicine, poisonous except in very small doses.

This was the official view, and probably the majority view. But divorce, like marriage, is an intensely personal affair. Divorce is the way to put an end to a shattered and unhappy marriage. Divorce is also a social phenomenon. What makes a marriage happy or unhappy is of course unique to each married couple: what turns them on or off, what's tolerable and intolerable. But happiness and unhappiness are also themselves social phenomena. They reflect what men and women expect from a marriage and what counts as a violation of the marriage vows, and also what counts as a disappointment in marriage, love, or sex. The law of divorce is affected, then, by the social definition of marriage. It reflects social expectations: what people want to get out of a marriage. Yet divorce is above all a *legal* institution. The demand for divorce is a demand for a legal status; nobody needs a formal divorce or a court order to skip out of a marriage, to pack one's bags and move out, or to move in with somebody else. But you do need a divorce if you want to remarry, legally and properly; and if you want to start a new and legitimate family—a family that can hold up its head in society and, perhaps more to the point, inherit your property when you die.

This means that a rise in the demand for divorce is not just a reflection of how men and women relate to each other, though of course it is certainly that. The economic facts of American life helped produce the demand—above all, the widespread ownership of land and other property. As pointed out earlier, the United States was the first middle-class country, the first country in which masses of families had title to a piece of land and therefore needed clear legal lines of ownership. Divorce, then, had important economic functions. As late as the first half of the nineteenth century, married women lost the power to control, sell, or buy real property when they married. The power was in their husbands. In 1812, the legislature of Maryland granted Anne Hoskyns a divorce from her husband, John Henry. John was a criminal, a forger; he had absconded, leaving Anne with three children—and a pile of John's debts. Yet under the law, as long as they were married, John Henry Hoskyns controlled her property, and that meant not only John Henry, but also his creditors. Divorce was invoked as a solution to the problem, as a way to get Anne's husband off her back.[42] Divorce in this case helped avoid a situation that people in the nineteenth century loathed: a blockage or obstruction to the sale of land. A woman could not sell land without her husband's consent; and how could you get his consent if he had deserted you? This was a problem for the wife—but also for the people who might want to buy the land.

Divorce law was also the gateway to remarriage; and through remarriage a man—or woman—could create a new, and respectable, family. Their children would be legitimate. The wife (or husband) could claim a share of the estate. This was not only an economic matter. The two could live in the community proudly, as married people, not as adulterers. In most states, open and notorious adultery was not only a scandal; it was also a criminal offense.[43] To be sure, divorce also carried a stigma in the nineteenth century. But the stigma of adultery was deeper and more indelible.

A Subterranean Demand

In the late nineteenth century, the divorce rate steadily rose in the United States. Behind this, no question, was a rise in the demand for divorce. According to U.S. government figures, there were 9,937 divorces in 1867, 25,535 in 1886, and by 1900, more than 55,000 a year.[44] These figures hardly seem startling, compared to the divorce rate at the end of the twentieth century. But the rate was staggering compared to England; and to many respectable people in the nineteenth century, the sheer number of divorces was an alarming development. For Roman Catholics, of course, divorce was forbidden; but the Roman Catholic church was a minority church in the United States.[45] For the Protestant majority, divorce, though not absolutely forbidden, seemed at best a necessary evil, a sign that something was seriously amiss in society. Divorce was dangerous. It could sap the vitality of the whole institution of marriage. Easy divorce was particularly bad policy. It encouraged the breakup of families. The danger was greatest, it was felt, among the "lower classes," who were the most easily "demoralized and corrupted" by divorce laws that were excessively lax.[46] Joel Bishop, the author of treatises on family law in the nineteenth century, put it this way: "Marriage . . . is the very highest public interest. *Prima facie,* therefore, each particular marriage is beneficial to the public; each divorce, prejudicial." If marriage were abandoned as a "permanent status" and became the "subject of experimental and temporary arrangements and fleeting partnerships," the result would be "the demoralization of society itself." Ideally, marriage should be "a union for life," according to Bishop. "Figuratively speaking," the two partners "should walk hand in hand up the steeps of life and down its declivities and green slopes, then lay themselves together for the final sleep at the foot of the hill."[47]

In Utopia, Bishop thought, there would be no divorce. But the United States was no Utopia. Divorce was needed, even though generally undesirable. Without divorce, there was the danger of something worse: if people whose marriages were totally shipwrecked could not divorce and remarry, these people would be "liable . . . to commit breaches of the rules of morality, either by promiscuous indulgences" or by entering into "alliances" that were not real marriages, resulting in "spurious issue."[48] Bishop here strikes what was probably the prevailing, orthodox line among respectable elites. Divorce should be possible but uncommon, and reserved for cases where one of the partners was guilty of some terrible offense against the marriage. Hence these elites, particularly religious leaders, fought any move to make divorce cheaper and easier. In the main, they were successful. Because of their efforts, although states tinkered with the formal law of divorce, its essence changed relatively little in the late nineteenth century. The laws were, for the most part, frozen and immobile.

Yet, even though the *formal* law of divorce was locked into place, and even though the strong moral objections to divorce created a legal stalemate, the quiet, subterranean demand for divorce continued. Men and women needed and wanted ways to get out of a dead or dying marriage. Everywhere the rule, solemnly stated by text writers and judges, was crystal clear: the law allowed no such thing as consensual divorce. Equally clear, it was an offense to manufacture evidence for divorce. As an old Georgia statute put it, "If the adultery, desertion, cruel treatment, or intoxication complained of shall have been occasioned by the collusion of the parties, and with the intention of causing a divorce . . . no divorce shall be granted."[49] "The policy of our law," said a Vice Chancellor of New Jersey in 1910, "disfavors divorce." If a man and wife "agree that one of them shall bring a suit for divorce against the other, and that no defense shall be made," that is "collusion"; and a divorce could not be based on collusion.[50] It had to be based on actual "grounds"—on an innocent partner and a guilty partner. If two civilized people simply felt their marriage was a failure, that it would be best to call it quits and start over, there was, in theory, absolutely nothing they could do. Or if both of them were offenders—if both of them had lovers, for example—there was also, in theory, no way out of the marriage. They were bound to each other, till death did them part. If one of them acted cruelly or otherwise misbehaved, but the behavior was not on the statutory list, here too, in theory, there was no escape from the bonds of matrimony. Marriage was presumptively for life—that was the mantra; and only if the strict requirements of the law were fulfilled was divorce a possibility.

But this was pure theory. The practice was totally different. In practice most divorces *were* collusive.[51] A careful reading of the sources reveals a real change, from about 1870 on, in the *living* law of divorce. Divorces became more common—and more fraudulent. Most of the time, court proceedings were essentially a sham. Most divorces were, in point of fact, plainly the result of a bargain, an agreement to end the marriage. They were divorces by consent. They were cut and dried—decided on ahead of time. This does not mean that husband and wife were equally eager, in these thousands of cases, to put an end to the marriage. We have no way of knowing whether this was so or not. Perhaps only the man wanted the divorce—to be free to marry his girlfriend, for example. No doubt this often happened. And perhaps the wife reluctantly gave in, or felt forced to do so. Whatever the case, nine times out of ten, husband and wife had come to some sort of agreement; they had settled their issues, as best they could, before stepping through the courtroom door.

In the typical case, it was the wife, not the husband, who actually filed the lawsuit.[52] Before the rise of the collusive divorce, when most divorce cases were probably based on real offenses against the marriage, men and women were plaintiffs in roughly equal numbers. But by the late nineteenth century, women were a clear and strong majority of plaintiffs. In the twentieth century, too, before no-fault statutes were passed, women were overwhelmingly the plaintiffs in divorce cases. In San Mateo County, California, for example, between 1950 and 1957, women were plaintiffs in 81.7 percent of the divorce cases.[53] There were a number of reasons why this was the case. In New York, for example, where adultery was the only grounds for divorce, it was less of a scandal if a wife accused her husband of adultery than if the husband accused his wife.[54] Also, if a woman hoped to get alimony, or custody of the children, practically speaking she had to be the "innocent" party. Typically, then, the wife would file and allege whatever was the best or handiest statutory grounds—cruelty, desertion, or adultery.

In states that allowed divorces for cruelty, cruelty tended to be the favored grounds. Desertion was popular as well. Except in New York, and other states where adultery was the only way, claims of adultery were avoided. Such claims were far too messy and rancorous. In San Francisco in 1919, women who sued for divorce alleged cruelty 40 percent of the time, desertion 31 percent, neglect 24 percent; adultery made a poor showing, with only 1 percent.[55] It is hard to imagine that adultery was so uncommon in San Francisco. In the typical case, the husband would play his part simply by doing nothing. He would not appear, nor file an answer. Thus, there was nothing to contradict the plaintiff's pitiful story; she usually had at least one corroborating witness, confirming the pitiful story; and the judge would simply grant the divorce. Judges were not naive; they knew exactly what was going on. For the most part, they said and did nothing. An occasional judge spoke out against the system; but most just went along quietly. Two authors who studied the system in one state (Ohio) around 1930 put it this way: only the "proverbial ostrich" burying its head in the sand could imagine divorce law actually worked as it was described "in the law books."[56]

There were other detours around strict divorce laws in the United States. The federal system opened one prominent door. Each state was sovereign; each had its own divorce laws. Under the Constitution, each state was supposed to give "full faith and credit" to the judgments of sister states. Thus, a valid divorce in an "easy" state could be recognized in all other states.

An "easy" state was usually easy in two ways: it would have a long list of "grounds," loosely interpreted; and it would have short residency requirements, so that birds of passage could flit in, get a divorce, and flit right out again. A number of states experimented with easy divorce in the nineteenth century. These were the so-called divorce mills. Indiana was a prominent example; so were South Dakota and North Dakota. But divorce mills had a hard time keeping themselves "easy." Criticism from those who disapproved of easy divorce was loud and persistent; in the end each "easy" state had to tighten its laws and shut down the business of granting divorce to their temporary guests. In the twentieth century, the main divorce mill was Nevada. This was a barren desert state, with few resources, few people, and even fewer scruples.[57] Easy divorce was good business; so was quick, easy marriage. "Wedding chapels" open day and night, ready to tie the knot for a trivial fee, flourished in Nevada. By the middle of the twentieth century, Nevada was easily the divorce champion of America. Its divorce rate for "residents" was more than fifty times the rate in New York (the state most stingy with divorce), and almost fifteen times the rate in California.[58]

The "migratory divorce" was not without legal difficulties. Under the "full faith and credit" clause of the Constitution, New York, for example, had to honor the divorce decrees of Nevada. This was the case, however, only if the decrees were valid—if, for example, the gay divorcee had legally taken up residence in Nevada. But what if the "residence" was a sham? Two notable decisions of the U.S. Supreme Court dealt with this issue, examining the tangled affairs of one O. B. Williams of North Carolina and his (alleged) new wife, a Mrs. Hendrix. Williams had a wife and four children; but in 1940, he left them and took off for Nevada. So did Mrs. Hendrix. After six weeks in the Alamo Auto Court—six weeks was all one needed for "residence" in Nevada—Williams and Hendrix each got a divorce and married each other. Back in North Carolina, they faced charges of "bigamous cohabitation." In the first case, the Supreme Court threw out the convictions for bigamy. North Carolina had to honor the Nevada divorce, if Nevada considered their marriage valid. But then they were tried again—same charge, but this time on a different theory. Now North Carolina argued that the residence in Nevada was phony—that Nevada had no real jurisdiction over the parties, because they had no real domicile there. Thus Nevada's action did not deserve "full faith and credit." This time North Carolina prevailed—and the Supreme Court affirmed the convictions.[59]

Cases of this type cast a shadow over divorces that came out of Nevada and other divorce mills.[60] Quick Mexican divorces were even more questionable. New York courts in the 1950s and 1960s sometimes did, and sometimes did not, recognize these divorces as valid, though in the end, in a 1965 decision, the New York court of appeals seemed to come down in favor of validity.[61] But most quick divorces, in Nevada and elsewhere, were never questioned—most of them were, after all, consensual; neither party was anxious to complain.

Divorce: A Dual System

Divorce had become what might be called a dual system. The official law and the law in action were radically different. In a sense, every field of law has some elements of a dual system; official law is never completely congruent with living law. But the gap is much greater in some fields of law, at certain times, and in certain places, compared to other fields, times, and places. A good deal of Italian traffic law could be described as a dual system. There are laws about speeding, parking, or staying in the proper lane; but no one seems to pay the slightest attention (at least, it looks that way to a visitor). Divorce in the nineteenth and early twentieth century, in the United States, is a classic case of a dual system. The texts of the statutes, the treatises on family law, and the appellate cases themselves give no clue to the real law of divorce, the working law of divorce, divorce as ordinary people experienced it—and ordinary lawyers and judges as well.

The reason for the dual system has already been hinted at. Divorce law was stalemated. There was no way to reform the law, or to move it in either direction. The law was frozen in time and space. Powerful, articulate groups opposed any reform that would make divorce easier, cheaper, and more available. The people who did want easier, cheaper divorce were diffuse and unorganized. There was no such thing as a lobby of unhappy husbands and wives. But there *were* unhappy marriages; and the demand for divorce was a social fact. What came out of this stalemate could, in fact, be described as a kind of compromise—a treaty between two warring sides, though it was never (of course) officially acknowledged. It was a dual system of a particular type: one side held the moral high ground and controlled the official law; the other side burrowed in the earth and undermined the system from below. There are many examples of similar dual systems. Prostitution is one example; pornography is another. Almost nobody in the nineteenth century defended prostitution openly, or praised pornography. But there was a huge subterranean demand for both. Prostitution and pornography flourished because there were so many customers. But the customers never won over—or even tried to win over—the custodians of community morality.

No one planned the compromise in divorce law; it simply evolved. No one was, or could be, particularly satisfied with it either. But the two sides were apparently rather evenly matched. Hence divorce law for decades was doomed to survive in its twisted, frozen shape, stuck fast in the nineteenth century. It kept its slogans and its high ideals deep into the twentieth century. The messy reality also remained the same. The great mass of people who actually wanted a divorce got what they wanted, though at a price—in money, and in subterfuge.

The men and women who denounced divorce, or easy divorce, were mostly sincere; they were trying to protect the family, trying to salvage the institution of marriage. But they were plainly wrong about the social meaning of divorce. In one important sense, divorce was no threat to marriage at all—it was, in fact, a sign that people valued marriage highly. One of the main aims of divorce was remarriage. Some people, of course, simply wanted to end a miserable marriage; but some had another, new marriage in mind. For this, of course, they needed a divorce.

The social definition of marriage changed radically in the course of the nineteenth century. In a traditional marriage, the husband was the head of the family, and the wife was subordinate; the law said so, and it was also largely true in everyday life. Divorce is rare in traditional marriages, partly because such marriages make so few demands on husbands and wives. Both remained mostly in their own world. She spends her days at home, with her children and with female friends and relatives. He goes off to the factory or the office. He and she lead largely separate lives. If she makes a good home, raises the children, cooks his dinner, stays out of trouble, and is reasonably compliant in bed, what more can he ask for? And if he treats her with a certain amount of respect, has a decent job and brings home some money, never beats her, drinks in moderation, stays away from other women, and is not too demanding in bed, what more does she have a right to ask for? Of course, there were plenty of brutal, drunken, unfaithful, uncaring husbands—men who fell short of even this modest ideal. Wives had few remedies in traditional marriage. They were supposed to put up with what fate had dealt them; and mostly they did.

But marriages were changing; the way men and women related to each other was also changing. More and more, companionate marriage was becoming the ideal. Men and women were supposed to be partners, friends. The process of change was slow and gradual; it affected different families, and different types of families, in different ways; it also varied by region, class, religion, and occupation. But companionate marriage began to compete seriously with traditional marriage in the nineteenth century. To be sure, ideals of romantic love, partnership between men and women, and an increased economic role for women were not phenomena that suddenly fell from the sky in the twentieth century. The process was gradual. But by the twentieth century it was clear that middle-class marriage had changed in nature. Marriage had new and different burdens. It was, among other things, responsible for "fulfilling the emotional and psychological needs of its members." Family life now was expected to "provide romance, sexual fulfillment, companionship, and emotional satisfaction."[62] Modern marriage, a sociologist wrote in 1931, rested on compatibility, congeniality; the "complexity of modern life" made marriage "incomparably more difficult" than before. Both men and women were looking for "harmonious companionship" in their marriage; and this was not easy to find.[63]

This shift, of course, was only partial and relative. Father was still supposed to put bread on the table, and Mother was supposed to take care of the children. In most marriages, the husband was still very much in control. The two "partners" were certainly not equals when it came to scrubbing the floors, choosing careers, taking care of the kids, or making major decisions. And in many families—poor families, rural families—issues of food and shelter filled up so much psychological space that there was no time or energy left for "fulfillment." And, as noted earlier, the changes were at every point uneven, contested, and problematic.[64] But even small changes in the direction of companionate marriage had a powerful effect on what people expected to get out of marriage. Many women certainly wanted a new role in the family; and to some extent they got it. At common law, under the doctrine of coverture, married women in essence had no independent control of their property. The husband was manager and director of the family assets. From about the middle of the nineteenth century on, however, married women's property laws took away most of the disabilities of coverture.[65] Not many wives, of course, got true equality inside the family—in the bedroom or the living room. But probably many did get more true companionship. And some men, too, came to want a different kind of wife, someone to share more of his life and to play a bigger role than darning his socks. The terms of the contract were slowly changing. Husband and wife were intertwined in more complicated ways. But all this imposed new and tougher burdens on the institution of marriage. It became harder for a marriage to satisfy him—or her. And when a marriage failed to give people what they had come to expect, it was only natural for one or both parties to want out, to want a chance to start over—to want, in short, a divorce.[66]

Divorce had become, in essence, consensual. This adjective—"consensual"—of course has to be taken with a grain of salt, as we pointed out. A woman who discovers that her husband is cheating, who feels that her situation is intolerable, might very well agree to a divorce, or even demand one; but this is not what people usually think of as consensual. William J. Goode, writing in the middle of the twentieth century, thought that husbands wanted to escape from a marriage more often than wives. Wives often said they were the ones who first suggested divorce; but the husband might be making himself "so obnoxious" that the wife "is willing to ask for and even insist upon a divorce."[67] The man always had more freedom to go off and do his own thing, and the wife was much more tied to home and children. In most cases, she had more to lose than her husband did. But men lost too in divorce: they lost contact with their children, and they might lose economically as well. This was, naturally, more of a problem for the poor than for the rich.

Nevertheless, by 1900 divorce had become much more common in American society. Ordinary people, working-class people, were now to be found in the divorce courts. Divorce was no longer a monopoly of the middle class and the elite, or even of those who owned a farm or a bit of property. A study of divorce in Los Angeles, California, for the period 1890 to 1920 confirms this point: divorce had lost its connection with the middle and upper classes.[68] A study of divorce in northern California between 1850 and 1890 also found a great many blue-collar men in the divorce sample.[69] Divorce had worked its way into the ranks of plumbers, carpenters, and laborers; men of this sort appear sometimes as plaintiffs, more often as defendants. Other countries experienced a similar trend. In England, for example, in 1871, manual workers accounted for only 22 percent of the divorces, while 54 percent came from the upper class; recall that the law of 1857 aimed to make it hard for working-class people to get divorced. But by 1951, 69 percent of the divorces involved manual workers, and the upper classes made up only a small percentage of divorcing couples.[70] It is reasonable to assume that divorce, as it became more widespread, lost a good deal of its stigma. It was less reasonable to consider divorce a sign of immorality or a badge of disgrace when it had become an everyday affair.

Yet morality was still an important factor in the divorce rate—especially with landless urban workers and artisans, who usually had little or no property. For men and women in this group, divorce may have been more a matter of propriety than of property. To start over in a new relationship, with stability and legitimacy for the adult and for the children, a person needed a proper divorce. Odd as it may sound, the rising divorce rate was a tribute to the power of traditional, monogamous marriage. Many people in society worried about divorce—about the causes of divorce in particular. But marriage itself, and remarriage, were the ultimate causes of divorce.

Divorce became generally more acceptable. It was a way out of an unhappy marriage, and a way into a better one. That thousands of people wanted divorce was a social reality. The law technically stood in the way; but the law was ineffective. Most couples who wanted a divorce were, legally speaking, not eligible to obtain one; but the law was not a serious obstacle, at least for people above the poverty line. Divorce took money, effort, and a lawyer—and some genteel perjury as well; but it could be done.

In short, in the nineteenth century the law of marriage and divorce was dynamic, restless, moving, shifting character and form over time. It responded to an equally restless and changing social order. Marriage came to have a different, deeper meaning for many people, and this deeper meaning fed a growing desire for a way out of an unfulfilling union. The formal law of divorce was locked in a stalemate, but it could be managed and manipulated; and so it was.

3

Marriage and Divorce
in the Modern World

As described in the last chapter, American family law changed dramatically over the course of the nineteenth century. The changes in the twentieth century were, if anything, even more far-reaching. They involved the very conception of marriage in society.

Common law marriage probably reached its high point sometime around the middle of the nineteenth century. In the latter part of the century, it was in decline. The decline continued into the twentieth century. In 1900, about half the states recognized the common law marriage as valid. By the end of the twentieth century, less than a dozen did.[1] Early in the twentieth century, Illinois abolished common law marriage; in each decade more states followed suit. Minnesota abolished common law marriage in 1941; Florida in 1967; Idaho only in 1995.[2] The laws of all these states now require a formal, ceremonial marriage; the couple must get a marriage license ahead of time, and a clergyman or judge must perform the marriage. Even in those states where common law marriage survives, it tends to have very little importance. In short, common law marriage has virtually disappeared as a social phenomenon. It pops up once in a while and is probably not entirely useless. If, for example, a couple thought they were married, but for some technical reason the marriage was invalid, the doctrine can save the marriage, the inheritance, the children. But most people who live together do not know anything about common law marriage and have no idea whether their state recognizes it, or have some completely erroneous notion of what it means. Hence it makes little difference whether it survives in official law or not. Almost everyone, even in the states that preserve common law marriage, thinks of marriage in the usual terms: a marriage license, then a wedding ceremony. It usually also involves a celebration, with flowers, a white dress and veil for the bride, good food for the guests and lots to drink, then a wedding cake and dancing far into the night; or, at a minimum, it involves a more or less dignified procedure in front of a local judge or justice of the peace.

The State Steps In

This trend away from common law marriage seems, on the surface, to contradict the main line of development in family law. The common law marriage, after all, was a contract, an agreement between two people. Marriage was (in theory) a civil contract; and the common law marriage was the most contractual kind of marriage there was. The whims and wishes of the couple were paramount. They were married because they wanted to be married, because they exchanged private vows with each other (or were supposed to). They themselves controlled entry into marriage, with all its legal rights and obligations. Their families had no say in the matter; church and state had even less. This type of arrangement would seem to fit best the demands of modernity, with its stress on the individual, its downgrading of status and ceremony. Nonetheless, the common law marriage is in terminal decline.

The reasons are hardly mysterious. First of all, the modern world is increasingly bureaucratic. It is a world of records and documents. The common law marriage produces no records. It shows up nowhere in the state's great registries. In the early nineteenth century, when records were sparse and poor, common law marriage had a positive impact: it helped establish rights to property. By 1900, record-keeping had improved enormously, statistics were routinely gathered, and the common law marriage had become a nuisance. It was a hindrance, not a help, to the orderly disposition of land and other forms of wealth. It was a fertile source of legal uncertainty. This was especially so with regard to pensions and other benefits. As Mary Richmond and Fred Hall put it in 1929, common law marriage was an "anachronism." A common law marriage was an "unrecorded" marriage; it lacked any "permanent, official record"; it was "nebulous . . . confused and undocumented."[3] It created all sorts of problems in inheritance cases and in other death claims; under workers' compensation laws; and with regard to state pensions and Social Security.[4] It was also a nuisance in divorce proceedings, in prosecutions for bigamy, and in many other situations. Over 100,000 soldiers in the American army during the First World War claimed common law wives and children—a huge headache for the Bureau of War Risk Insurance.[5] Otto E. Koegel, an official of the United States Veteran's Bureau, speaking in 1921, declared that the bureau was, in effect, "the largest court of domestic relations in the world." Koegel, author of a treatise on the subject of common law marriage, was scornful of these alleged marriages: most, he said, were nothing but "meretricious relationships." He added that "very few, if any, of these persons really believe they are married."[6] Indeed, almost all of them believe "that common-law marriage and living in adultery are synonomous [sic] terms."[7]

There was another strong reason for the decline and fall of common law marriage. It frustrated the state's control over marriage. Marriage was the gateway to reproduction. Married people had children; unmarried people, generally, did not (or were not supposed to). In the late nineteenth century, the state began to concern itself with the issue of reproduction. It began to voice an opinion about who was fit to be married and, more significantly, who was not; which people were supposed to have babies, and which ones were not.

It was in the late nineteenth century also that abortion became a serious criminal offense. Before 1860, some states did not regulate abortion at all. The public, and the law, also drew a sharp distinction between early abortion—abortion before "quickening" (the stage of pregnancy when the mother feels life stirring and moving)—and abortion later on in the pregnancy. Thus, a Connecticut statute, as of 1821, made it a crime to administer "any deadly poison . . . with an intention . . . to murder, or thereby to cause or procure the miscarriage of any woman, then being quick with child."[8] But the situation changed after the middle of the century. Between 1860 and 1880, state after state passed laws restricting abortion or banning it altogether. Before this time, many abortionists plied their trade more or less openly. The infamous "Madame Restell" (Ann Lohman) had gotten rich from peddling her "female monthly pills" and providing a luxurious place for her female clients.[9] Ultimately, Madame Restell was hounded and threatened with prison; in an act that in a way symbolizes the success of the campaign against abortion, she slit her wrists and bled to death in the sumptuous bathroom of her mansion.

When abortion became illegal, this did not mean, of course, that no more abortions took place; they simply went underground. The situation in England, where abortion was illegal, was similar to that in the United States—abortion was common, clandestine, and dangerous.[10] In both countries, abortion was taboo. The campaign against abortion may seem at first to be unrelated to laws regulating marriage; but in fact, the two were strongly related. It was widely believed that middle-class married women were shirking their duties as mothers and killing their unborn children. This belief fueled the drive against abortion and provided it with a good deal of its energy and bite.[11]

A whirlwind of social change swept over the country in the late nineteenth century. A nation of farms and farmers was turning into a nation of factories, mines, and big business. The population was shifting from farms to towns, and from towns to cities. The cities themselves were growing dramatically. Vast numbers of immigrants were pouring into the country. These newcomers were different from the earlier immigrants. They came from southern and eastern Europe, not northern Europe, for the most part, and they were Catholic, Jewish, and Orthodox, rather than Protestant. The old order seemed to be vanishing almost overnight. A kind of panic overtook respectable people of traditional

American stock. In the late nineteenth and early twentieth centuries, they worried about the joint effect of a falling birth rate and a rising tide of immigrants. Every ship that landed in New York harbor disgorged a cargo of hungry immigrants, who swarmed into the slums of New York and Chicago and Philadelphia; in time, they also produced a bumper crop of babies. Meanwhile, those women who were Americans of long standing, women of "good stock," were having fewer and fewer children. They used birth control (another sign of social decay); and, worst of all, they bought the "female pills" that Madame Restell was selling, or the nostrums of other sellers; they took whatever measures they could in order to abort their unborn children. As one writer put it in 1874, abortion was one reason why there were so few "native-born children of American parents"; the country, he said, was "fast losing" its "national characteristics."[12]

There was also, of course, a strong moral and Christian element in the campaign against abortion. Abortion and contraception were condemned as evil practices; they perverted the purposes of marriage. They were labeled as sinful because they encouraged lust.[13] Anthony Comstock, the purity crusader, denounced those "articles of diabolical design" that were so "cunningly contrived to minister to the most degrading appetites"; and a doctor, N. F. Cook, announced that all means of "preventing offspring" other than abstinence from sex were "disgusting, beastly, positively wrongful, as well as unnatural, and *physically injurious*."[14] But the campaign was not solely a matter of religion or traditional moral values, important though those elements were. The state, in making abortion criminal, was trying to improve the bloodline of the population. It was trying to increase the crop of good, healthy, American babies—babies born to solid, respectable married women who were doing their duty as wives and mothers. Unless something was done, only inferior people, the dregs of society, along with the incredibly fertile immigrants, would make babies, and the nation would lose its soul, its energy, its moral fiber.[15] In England, too, there were worries about the birthrate. Here too, the fear was that the lower orders were doing all the breeding, while the better sort were not. This could make respectable English people a sort of endangered species.[16] In the United States, the falling birthrate was so alarming among members of the middle class that this class almost seemed to be committing what Theodore Roosevelt in 1903 called "race suicide."[17]

Marriage and reproduction had become important issues of public policy. The state simply had to insert itself into the marriage question. It had to regulate who married; and this meant that it had to regulate *how* they married. From this standpoint, the common law marriage obviously would not do. The new study of eugenics provided the state with strong support for its movement to regulate marriage. It gave a scientific veneer to campaigns to control the supply of babies, and to encourage the birth of healthy babies in moral families.[18]

Immigrants were not the only dangerous breeders. It was also important to control sex and reproduction among degenerates, criminals, and the mentally retarded. Pathology, people had come to believe, was inherited—passed down from generation to generation. Bad seed reproduced in kind. In the 1870s, a man named Richard Dugdale visited jails in New York and was amazed to discover a group of blood relatives among the prisoners. This aroused his curiosity. He did some research and then claimed that all of these miscreants were the descendants of a single man, himself the bastard son of a man Dugdale called "Mr. Juke." Dugdale published his findings in 1877. In his book about the "Jukes," Dugdale argued that there were "dangerous classes" in society, groups of misfits and criminals who multiplied like "rats in their alleys" and threatened "to overwhelm the well-bred classes of society."[19] There is good reason to believe that Dugdale exaggerated his case and that his book was, in fact, junk science;[20] but it made a loud noise at the time. Later, in the twentieth century, Henry Herbert Goddard, director of research at a New Jersey institution for the "feeble-minded," made what he considered a similar discovery. His family from hell was the family he called the "Kallikaks." They all descended from the bastard child of a soldier and a retarded woman at the time of the American Revolution. The "Kallikaks" were a long line of prostitutes, alcoholics, criminals, and other degenerates. Goddard recommended sterilization for families of this sort, an operation "almost as simple in males as having a tooth pulled" and not much more serious for women.[21]

"Findings" of this sort fed into popular consciousness and strengthened the hand of the eugenics movement. Indiana in 1907 was the first state to pass a sterilization law. As the preamble to this law solemnly stated: "Heredity plays a most important part in the transmission of crime, idiocy and imbecility." California passed a sterilization law in 1909; under this law, a state prison inmate whose behavior and record gave "evidence" that he was a "moral and sexual pervert" was a candidate for "asexualization."[22] Soon a fair number of American states had laws that allowed or mandated sterilization for criminals or the mentally defective. These laws were not dead letters. Up to January 1921, according to one report, 2,233 persons had been legally sterilized in the United States. Most (1,853) were men; but a substantial number (1,380) were women. Almost all the men underwent vasectomy; but 72 men had been castrated. Most of the victims of these various procedures were supposed to be feeble-minded or insane; only a few were "criminalistic." California was the state that led the pack in sheer number of sterilizations (about two-thirds).[23]

The late nineteenth and early twentieth century was also the age of indeterminate sentencing laws. Under an indeterminate sentencing law, when a defendant is convicted of a crime, the judge sets only a minimum sentence—often a year. During that year, prison authorities have a chance to watch the prisoner, assess him, and decide whether he is fit for society or whether he is rotten stuff, to be kept in prison almost indefinitely.[24] States passed indeterminate sentencing laws for all sorts of reasons, and the laws had all sorts of consequences. But one aspect, not usually noticed, is worth mentioning here. A man kept in prison a very long time on an indeterminate sentence is not going to marry and have children. Hence indeterminate sentencing laws, in their own small way, contributed to the eugenic cleansing of society.

The sterilization laws had their enthusiasts, but not everybody joined in the chorus of praise. Some critics were dubious about the whole "science" of eugenics. Some felt sterilization was too drastic an intrusion into people's lives. One commentator decried the attempts "to regulate everything on the face of the earth" and wondered whether soon there would be laws telling people "upon which side we must sleep and the kind, quality, thickness, and texture of our underwear, not to speak of the length, breadth, and thickness of our pajamas."[25] Some courts were bold enough to strike down sterilization laws. This group did not, however, include the country's highest court. In 1927, the Supreme Court was asked to decide whether sterilization laws violated the constitution, in a Virginia case, *Buck v. Bell*.[26] Carrie Bell had been raped, and then gave birth to a baby girl. Carrie and her mother, Emma, were both said to be feeble-minded; it was assumed the child was also feeble-minded. The state wanted to sterilize Carrie Bell. Oliver Wendell Holmes, Jr., who wrote for the Court, felt that the statute expressed a wise policy. Bad blood was a danger to society. Society had a right to protect itself from inferior people. In his famous words, "three generations of imbeciles are enough."[27]

If the courts—or most of them—could uphold sterilization laws, they certainly were not about to balk at laws that made it difficult for "degenerates" to marry; and in fact they did not. State control of marriage was a response to a need felt in society—at least a need felt by many elites. Unfettered marriage and reproduction were dangerous to society. In the late nineteenth and early twentieth century, many states passed laws to prevent unsuitable people from marrying.[28] A Connecticut statute of 1895 was apparently the first: no man or woman could marry if he or she was "epileptic, imbecile, or feeble-minded." Nor could such people live together "as husband and wife" if the woman was "under forty-five years of age"—a clear sign of what the law was actually about. Violations of the statute could be punished by up to three years in prison. It was also a crime for a man to "carnally know" a woman under forty-five who was "epileptic, imbecile, feeble-minded or a pauper"; an epileptic man was not allowed to "carnally know" a female under forty-five; and women under forty-five were not to "consent to be carnally known" by any man who was epileptic, imbecile, or feeble-minded. Here too the punishment could be severe: as much as three years in prison. Under a 1905 Indiana law, if a man had been in the poorhouse within five years, he was not entitled to a marriage license, unless he could show that he could support a family; and no license was to be given if either party had an infectious disease. A Washington state statute of 1909, applicable to women under forty-five and to men who married such women, barred marriage for any "common drunkard, habitual criminal, epileptic, imbecile, feeble-minded person, idiot or insane person . . . [persons] with hereditary insanity, or . . . afflicted with pulmonary tuberculosis in its advanced stages, or any contagious venereal disease." A 1913 Wisconsin law provided that all "male persons" who wanted a marriage license had to have a physical examination and produce a certificate that they were "free from acquired venereal diseases." The law was challenged in court on the grounds that it infringed on the "inalienable right of marriage" and interfered with "religious freedom." The Supreme Court of Wisconsin, however, upheld the statute.[29]

What of the fact that the Wisconsin statute singled out men and did not ask women to get a certificate or prove they were free of disease? Chief Justice John B. Winslow admitted that women who "marry and transmit a loathsome disease" were just as dangerous as men; but "the great majority of women who marry are pure, while a considerable percentage of men have had illicit sexual relations before marriage." And, in general, the "transmission of the so-called venereal diseases by newly married men to their innocent wives was a tremendous evil"; thus the legislation was clearly justified as a matter of public policy in restricting marriage as it did.[30] As Chief Justice Winslow's attitude makes clear, gender stereotypes played a powerful role in the drafting of these laws.

For whatever reason, however, few of the state laws had real teeth in them. As of about 1930, only a handful of states actually required a medical certificate. Many states considered and rejected the idea of demanding a medical certificate before a license could be issued. Many states had laws that purported to keep the unfit from marrying, though without a certificate. Slightly more than half the states, as of 1930, had provisions that banned marriages of people with epilepsy or venereal diseases or tuberculosis, or some or all of these. New Jersey specifically mentioned "chancroid in a communicable stage," and Wyoming had a similar clause in its law.[31] Virtually every state had a law on the books that forbade marriage for the "feeble-minded."[32] There were various ways of phrasing this prohibition: people "incapable of consenting for want of sufficient understanding" or those who were "imbecile or feeble-minded," an "idiot or lunatic," or similar language.[33]

Whether marriages that violated these norms were void (that is, whether they had no legal existence at all and could be totally set aside) or whether they were simply "voidable," or gave grounds for divorce, proved to be a difficult legal question. In a Connecticut case from 1905, a woman complained that her husband (and father of her child) was epileptic, knew it, and hid this fact from her until after they were married. The court held that she was entitled to a divorce, but that the marriage was not totally void. The court did add that the law against epileptic marriages was a good idea. After all, it was "common knowledge" that epilepsy was a "disease of a peculiarly serious and revolting character, tending to weaken mental force, and often descending from parent to child."[34]

Were these various laws effective in preventing the "unfit" from marrying? Probably not. This seems obvious enough in states that did not require a doctor's certificate. In Washington state, for example, an applicant could simply file an affidavit, declaring that he was "not feeble-minded, imbecile, epileptic, insane, a common drunkard," or "afflicted with pulmonary tuberculosis in its advanced stages, nor with contagious venereal disease."[35] This was hardly a significant hurdle. Even in states like Wisconsin, which asked for a certificate, many doctors considered the whole business a "farce" and "a joke." A man could always find a corrupt or careless doctor willing to help him out. Most men, according to one doctor, "go to their own family physician, have a good laugh, tell a story or two, and the doctor signs the certificate without even looking at the patient's tongue." Other doctors in Wisconsin disagreed; they felt the law was effective; it kept some diseased men from getting married; just knowing about the requirement was a deterrent: "at least it stops people with active lesions from marrying at that time."[36] Moreover, there was considerable skepticism about these laws among eugenicists, at least as far as the "feeble-minded" were concerned. These people, it was felt, had no moral sense, and little sense at all; laws would not be much use in keeping them from breeding.[37] Nonetheless, the ideology behind the various laws is clear and consistent. And obviously, the very existence of common law marriage doctrine was at variance with this ideology.

This is as good a place as any to mention laws against miscegenation.[38] These laws were, after all, another example of state control over marriage. A kind of eugenic motive was at least one reason (though not the only one) for these statutes. The main reason was no doubt to bolster white supremacy. But there was considerable talk about the genetic dangers of interracial marriage. When blacks and whites had sex, their children were "mongrels"; this went against the natural order, against God's plan, and it produced an inferior breed, which weakened the genetic stock of the country.[39] Whatever the motivation, all the southern states, and many states elsewhere in the country, outlawed marriage between whites and blacks. In Arkansas, for example, "all marriages of white persons with negroes or mullatoes" were declared to be "illegal and void."[40] In many states, such marriages were also criminal acts. Any sexual relations between whites and blacks were also illegal. Under Alabama law in the late nineteenth century, if a white person and a black person "intermarry or live in adultery or fornication with each other," they were liable to a prison term. In 1881, for example, Tony Pace, a black man, and Mary J. Cox, a white woman, were indicted, convicted, and sentenced each to two years in prison for "living together in a state of adultery or fornication." The U.S. Supreme Court upheld their conviction in a short, crisp decision.[41] There was no unlawful discrimination, according to the Court, since the law fell equally on blacks and whites. The ban on miscegenation, indeed, reached the point where in 1913 thirty of the forty-eight states had some sort of law on the subject. And the definition of miscegenation tightened, too: in Virginia, for example, the law once defined a person as black if he or she was one-quarter black or more; but by 1910, a "colored person" was someone with "one-sixteenth or more of negro blood," thus moving quite a few people out of the white category into the black category; and in 1924, the statute went even further: it adopted the so-called one-drop rule. Any traceable African ancestry was enough to make a person nonwhite.[42]

Some states, especially on the West Coast, prohibited a different kind of miscegenation. These were states with sizable populations of Chinese and other Asians and a history of virulent prejudice against them. These states added marriage between whites and Asians to the list of forbidden unions. In Oregon, for example, any marriage between a white and a person with more than one-quarter of "Chinese blood" was void.[43] California threw in for good measure "members of the Malay race." A few southern states also banned marriage between whites and Asians. Mississippi, hardly a hotbed of Asian immigration, made it illegal for a white person to marry a "person who shall have one-eighth or more of Mongolian blood."[44]

In short, for the reasons mentioned, the state developed a keen interest in controlling marriage (or, rather, the birth of children). The movement away from the common law marriage was clearly linked to these developments. Otto Koegel told the Second International Congress of Eugenics in 1921 that the doctrine should be abolished; otherwise "defectives" who wanted to marry could simply go to a state where common law marriages were valid, say the right words, and ignore the laws that tried to keep them from marrying.[45] Common law marriage was thus a threat to the eugenics movement. Wisconsin was one of the states that in 1913 had a law to prevent "defectives" from marrying, but Wisconsin at the time also recognized common law marriage. Lawyers were quick to point out that a couple did not actually need a marriage license to get married. Coexistence of a eugenics law and common law marriage was, in the words of one jurist, "ridiculous." Informal marriages apparently proliferated in Wisconsin after 1913.[46] According to one newspaper account, published in 1914, Julius Kroke, the Register of Deeds of Dane County (Madison, Wisconsin's state capital, is in this county) offered to "record common law marriage contracts for 10 cents each." This would save a young couple the $3 fee for the medical certificate.[47] It is no wonder that Wisconsin abolished the common law marriage in 1917.[48]

The Triumph of Marital Choice

The development of state control of marriage was important; but it did not weaken the trend away from traditional marriage and toward companionate marriage. In this development the idea of free choice of marital partners made its most important contribution. More and more people conceived of marriage as a real partnership, a union of interests, desires, and ways of life. This mindset eventually weakened, and even destroyed, the rules against contraception and abortion; here too the primary goal was to allow men and women to choose—in this case, to choose whether they wanted to have children, and if so, how many.

As for miscegenation, these laws, needless to say, are no longer on the books. They were doomed by the civil rights movement and, more broadly, by society's commitment to equality and multiculturalism. The northern states were the first to abolish their laws against interracial marriage. A flock of states changed their statutes after the Second World War. In 1948, the California Supreme Court declared void the section of the Civil Code that forbade marriages between whites and nonwhites.[49]

Times were definitely changing. The Supreme Court outlawed school desegregation in 1954 and in later cases extended this decision to all forms of segregation. In *McLaughlin v. Florida* (1964), the Supreme Court reviewed a criminal conviction under a Florida statute on interracial sex. The statute made it a crime for any "negro man and white woman, or any white man and negro woman, who are not married to each other," to "live in and occupy in the nighttime the same room." Another section of the Florida code made it a crime for any "white person and negro, or mulatto," to "live in adultery or fornication with each other." The Supreme Court invalidated the "same room" law and overturned the criminal conviction without "expressing any views about the State's prohibition of interracial marriage."[50] Still, it was clear which way the court was heading. The final move came three years later, in *Loving v. Virginia* (1967).[51] Richard Loving was a white man who had grown up in Virginia and married a black woman, Mildred Jeter, whom he had known since he was a child. The couple got married in Washington,

D.C., and then returned to Virginia. In Virginia, it was a crime for a white person to "intermarry with a colored person." They were arrested, convicted, and sentenced to a year in jail. The sentence was suspended, however, on condition that the Lovings leave Virginia and stay away.

They did leave, for Washington D.C. But later, they decided (with help from the ACLU) to fight to overturn the judgment against them. The trial judge held against them: "Almighty God," the judge felt, "did not intend for the races to mix." Virginia appeal courts upheld the law, with a lot of talk about "racial integrity," "racial pride," and a "mongrel breed of citizen." But the U.S. Supreme Court unanimously voided the statute. They ignored Virginia's arguments (including the claim that the only people who intermarry are "people who have a rebellious attitude toward society, self-hatred, neurotic tendencies, immaturity").[52] In the Court's view, the law was nothing but a device to "maintain White Supremacy," which was true enough. Significantly, too, the Court talked about the "freedom to marry." No state could control a marriage choice in the name of a racist ideal. But there was also in the shadows the idea of marriage, sex, and personal life as the ultimate, uncluttered domain of individual choice.

Medical control over marriage and reproduction also basically disappeared in the twentieth century. Rules to keep epileptics, paupers, or people with low IQs from having children dropped out of the statute books. The doctor's certificate survived in many states, but not for eugenic reasons. The point was to prevent men who had syphilis and other such diseases from infecting their wives and passing the disease on to their children. This was the theme of *Ghosts,* the powerful play by Henrik Ibsen; at the end of the play, the son goes blind because of disease he inherited from his father. Doctors generally agreed that venereal disease was a major cause of blindness among children. "Social diseases" produced many other harmful effects. And it was "outrageous and revolting" that a guilty spouse should infect an "innocent wife or husband."[53]

The terror evoked by these insidious plagues, from the late nineteenth century on, was an important element of public policy. The terror was a significant prop in campaigns of the early twentieth century against vice, debauchery, prostitution, and the red light districts of America's sinful cities.[54] It is not surprising, therefore, that medical tests for VD outlasted other forms of testing imposed on people who wanted to get married. The Colorado statute, for example, as of the middle of the twentieth century, required a doctor's certificate before a couple could get a license to marry. The medical examination had to include "a standard serological test for syphilis, made not more than thirty days prior to the date of issuance" of the license; and the doctor had to certify that the applicant is either "not infected with syphilis, or other venereal diseases," or at least was not infectious. The Connecticut law required the couple to submit to a "Wasserman or Kahn or other similar standard laboratory blood test" and get a doctor's statement similar to the one demanded in Colorado.[55]

Today, even these laws have largely vanished. As of 2003, most states—thirty-one out of the fifty—have absolutely no requirement of a medical test, or a certificate, or anything else. Oklahoma, however, still wants a doctor's certificate, based on a lab test, to make sure neither bride or groom have syphilis; so does Massachusetts.[56] Virginia, worried about people who might be HIV positive, rather timidly hands out to the loving couple an educational kit that tells them about AIDS; but nobody has to read this material, or pay any attention to it. A few states want tests to show immunity to rubella.[57] In Indiana, the couple has to sign an "acknowledgment" that they received information about "dangerous communicable diseases that are sexually transmitted and a list of test sites for the virus that causes AIDS," but nothing else is required.[58] In Arizona, people who apply for a marriage license have to state that "they understand that information on sexually transmitted diseases is available from the county health department on request" and that they know that "these diseases may be transmitted to their unborn children."[59] But nobody is forced to *do* anything.

The typical state statute insists on a marriage license; but this is a fairly simple form, listing names, addresses, ages, and the like, and basically nothing more. The majority of the states still want married people to have at least some minimal amount of mental competence. A few states have language about "idiots," "imbeciles," or "lunatics." In the District of Columbia, for example, the marriage of "an idiot" or a person "adjudged to be a lunatic" is "void." Most states have for the most part dropped this offensive kind of language in favor of something more tasteful. No marriage license, for example, in California, can be issued if "either of the applicants lacks the capacity to enter into a valid marriage." In Maine, people cannot marry if they are so "impaired by reason of mental illness or mental retardation" that they lack "sufficient understanding" to make decisions about "property or person." Tennessee and Mississippi have the sensible provision that a marriage license should not be issued to somebody who is drunk at the time. In California, no license is to go to either a drunk or someone high on a drug.[60] About fourteen states, however, seem to have no requirements about mental state at all. At one time, the state of Nevada made money by specializing in quick, cheap, and easy marriages. It still does a roaring business in marriages. But nowadays marriage is cheap, easy, and quick in every state.

Sterilization is also, in large part, a thing of the past.[61] A society like Nazi Germany was committed to getting rid of people they considered human trash, including the mentally retarded. The Nazis sterilized huge numbers. But the United States went to war against the Nazis, and the Nazi way of thinking seemed increasingly wrong as the twentieth century progressed. In *Skinner v. Oklahoma* (1942),[62] the Supreme Court dealt a serious blow to American laws on sterilization. Skinner had been convicted for such crimes as armed robbery and stealing chickens. He was ordered to undergo a vasectomy, under the applicable Oklahoma law. Skinner objected; and the Supreme Court found the Oklahoma statute unconstitutional. The decision did not go so far as to outlaw all sterilization laws. But the Court found a fatal flaw in the Oklahoma law: embezzlers and people convicted of political crimes were exempted from sterilization. This distinction violated the Equal Protection clause of the Fourteenth Amendment. But it was clear that the Court found sterilization laws extremely offensive. The right to have children was a fundamental right, according to the Court, and restrictions on it had to be carefully considered. By implication, marriage must also be a fundamental right. The *Skinner* case was an important precursor of the "privacy" cases, which are discussed in Chapter 5. In general, this kind of sterilization law fell into disuse in the late twentieth century; fourteen of the statutes were repealed in the 1960s and 1970s. The few that survive are (apparently) hardly used. In 2002, the governor of Virginia, Mark Warner, issued a "formal apology" for a program that had sterilized about 8,000 residents of the state between 1924 and 1979. The governor of South Carolina, who called the program "shameful," also apologized; then North Carolina and Oregon joined in; finally, in 2003, the governor of California added his voice, saying to the victims that the people of the state were "deeply sorry for the suffering you endured."[63]

The state, in short, has largely given up the struggle to control the right to have babies. Marriage laws today are about formalities, license fees, and the like; restrictions on marriage have generally disappeared. Having babies is a choice that is up to the individual—and so is the choice *not* to have babies. The rules against contraception have disappeared. Abortion has become a (much disputed) constitutional right. It is still the case that poor people and immigrants have many babies while the middle class woman has only a few babies, or one, or even none. The birthrate is still a matter of concern. In Europe—West and East—the birthrate plunged to record lows in the late twentieth century. Italy, Spain, Germany, Estonia, and other countries face a future in which their populations are likely to shrink. This threatens to become a genuine crisis for the welfare state, with its early retirement and generous benefits. There are cries of alarm and policy suggestions of various sorts. Immigration, and the demographic makeup of countries like Sweden or France, are politically embattled and controversial. But the age of eugenics is over, probably for good.

Breach of Promise

The changing meaning of marriage is well illustrated by the fate of a peculiar type of lawsuit: the action for breach of contract of marriage. In the nineteenth century, if a man was engaged to a woman and one of them broke off the engagement for no good reason, the other was entitled to sue, asking damages for breach of contract. Marriage was, as we said, a civil contract. Once the two parties had agreed to marry, they had made a contract; and this contract, like all other contracts, was binding on both of them.

Of course, marriage was, and is, no ordinary contract; and the action for breach of promise was no ordinary lawsuit. In theory, the breach of promise suit was unisex: either partner could bring it. But in practice, only women did. As an Alabama judge put it in 1846, "a just regard for public morals" had "long since confined the action alone to the female sufferer."[64] Scholars, patiently mining the records, have found a male plaintiff here and there; but such cases were always rare. An English study found that women were 97 percent of the plaintiffs in English cases. The few men who sued usually lost.[65] In many, perhaps most, reported cases, the real complaint was not simply that the man had jilted his fiancée. The real claim was that the woman had given up something precious—her virginity, or her best years on the marriage market—on the strength of the broken promise. In some cases, the woman had borne a child out of wedlock. If she was a respectable, middle-class woman, this meant that she was "ruined." Prospects for a decent marriage were dim.

Theoretically, it made the woman's case weak, not strong, if the couple had indulged in sex, and especially if the woman had a baby out of wedlock. After all, a woman who "immorally yields to her seducer and bears a child" had no claim to sue him for the "wrong; because she participated therein with him." But this was just talk. The living law was quite different. In the actual case law, intercourse and childbirth made jilting a woman "a much heavier offense," to be "followed by heavier damages, than if the conduct of the parties toward each other had . . . been upright"; and the majority of the cases so held.[66] Behind these cases, then, was the image of an innocent and foolish woman or girl, seduced and abandoned by a cad who had (falsely) promised to make her his wife. She had given in to him because she loved him; and he had also professed his love. Romantic love, after all, was almost an excuse for sex before marriage. As Karen Lystra has argued, romantic love "purified sexuality and affirmed its moral standing" in Victorian days. The "unvarnished logic of the heart" was a challenge to the "long-standing taboo against premarital intercourse."[67] The woman's conduct was thus excusable; and the cad, for his part, had not only "ruined" the woman he had slept with; he had also lied to her and betrayed her: his pretended love was a cheat, a ruse, a lie.

There is a certain tension between the law of breach of promise and the formal doctrine underpinning common law marriage. In a common law marriage, the man and the woman became validly married as soon as they exchanged words of agreement to marry, in the present tense. By *considering* themselves married, they became in fact married. But what if the words were in the future tense? If the couple said "Let's get married soon"—or "tomorrow," or "next week"—then (according to the texts) they were not yet married. They became married only when they had sex. This rather strange idea was expressed in a Latin phrase, *per verba de futuro cum copula* (words of the future, plus copulation). But this seems to be pure theory. The courts (and society) never recognized any such thing. Sex was never part of the definition of marriage. Of course, married people do have sex; but sex was supposed to happen after marriage, not before; and having sex never in itself made a marriage a marriage.[68] As one author put it, a doctrine that required "two persons to fornicate a number of times before they create a legal status" would be "absurd."[69] If, in fact, a promise plus sex equaled marriage, then the breach of promise cases would make no sense: the promise had not been breached, and in fact, plaintiff and defendant were legally married. Joel Bishop explained the matter this way: if the two people are "under an agreement of future marriage" and "have copula," which is only "lawful" for married people, then they are presumed to have "transmuted their future to present promise."[70]

This strikes the modern reader as a bad case of hairsplitting. The social distinction between the two situations was, however, reasonably clear. The common law marriage cases covered situations where the man and woman lived together; the issue was, were they married or not? The breach of promise cases came out of situations where the two were most definitely *not* living together; here the question was not whether they were married, but whether they had been engaged to be married (regardless of any possible sexual relations). What is interesting is that breach of promise cases were often successful, and sometimes produced sizable damage awards. Clearly, in some cases at least, juries were very sympathetic to the jilted woman; and they forced the man to pay through the nose for his folly or his injustice.

But this cause of action was controversial almost from the very start. To some legal scholars, and indeed to many ordinary citizens, breach of promise was grossly unfair to the male defendants. They, not the women, were the victims. The women were blackmailers or gold diggers. They preyed on gullible and wealthy men. English literature from Dickens on was merciless in its treatment of the breach of promise lawsuit.[71] Dickens savagely satirized a breach of promise suit in the *Pickwick Papers* (1836). Gilbert and Sullivan heaped scorn on these suits in their operetta *Trial by Jury.* A decent women, people said, would never wash her dirty linen in public. Nor would she want a loveless marriage. An alliance without love, an English critic wrote in 1879, is "a curse which has no equal on this earth." If a woman forces marriage by threatening to sue for breach of promise, she is perpetrating a great evil. She is encouraging "desecration of the nuptial bed."[72]

All this scorn and derision was actually undeserved. In terms of the norms and manners of the time, many of the cases seem justified: the women plaintiffs had been victimized, cheated, lied to, robbed of opportunities.[73] In any event, women continued to bring these cases, often successfully, throughout the nineteenth century and into the twentieth century as well. In the 1930s, a strong campaign to get rid of breach of promise laws arose.[74] A number of states abolished this cause of action—for example, Pennsylvania in 1935, Massachusetts in 1938, California in 1939, Illinois in 1947. The Illinois statute began by reciting that breach of promise actions had been "subject to grave abuses" and were "an instrument for blackmail."[75] The cause of action limped on in other states, but it was increasingly uncommon. In England after 1920, fewer and fewer cases were reported, tried, or discussed in the newspapers.[76] A law commission report published in 1969 recommended abolition; the existing law, said the report, gave "opportunity for claims of a 'gold-digging' nature."[77] In 1970, Parliament did get rid of breach of promise. In the debates, the usual arguments were made: gold diggers were preying on foolish men, marriage should be totally voluntary, and so on.[78] The statute left the door open for claims to return gifts conditioned on marriage. A man who jilted his fiancée, then, not only escaped punishment; he even had the right to get back the engagement ring.[79] In some places, breach of promise lingered on: a case in British Columbia in 1972 awarded $2,250 to one Mrs. Tuttle, a divorced "lady in her mid-fifties" who devoted fifteen years of her life "to a hit-and-run artist," a bounder who ended up marrying another woman.[80] In the United States, however, by 2000, breach of promise was almost completely gone.

Why did the law change direction? Despite the drumbeat of criticism, jury behavior attests to social support for breach of promise actions. Certainly, this kind of lawsuit *could* be an instrument of blackmail or extortion. In other instances, however, it most definitely was not. In nineteenth-century England, working-class women used breach of promise as a weapon against men who had betrayed and abandoned them, sometimes after long engagements. In one Massachusetts case from 1945, the plaintiff, a woman who had been strung along (she said) for years by her employer and who had submitted to his "embraces" complained of the emotional harm he had done; he had also robbed her of the chance to meet "honorable" men.[81] She was trying to make an end run around local law, since Massachusetts had abolished breach of promise. She lost her case; but if what she said was true, her boss had in fact done her serious social and emotional harm.

But the most spectacular and well-publicized cases were those in which young women sued foolish, older, and wealthy men. These were the cases that gave breach of promise its bad name. In Kentucky in 1893, Madeleine Pollard brought a case against a congressman, W. C. P. Breckenridge. She was twenty-eight; he was fifty-six. She claimed a long affair with Breckenridge, who promised to marry her (she said) when his wife died. Instead, he married somebody else. Breckenridge admitted the affair, but not the promise. Miss Pollard, moreover, had not been a spotless dove when they started their affair, or so he said. But a jury believed her story and awarded her $15,000—an enormous sum for the day.[82]

To men like Congressman Breckenridge—though not to the members of the jury—cases like this were scandalous and unjust. But what doomed the lawsuit, perhaps, was the diminishing value of chastity. Chastity lost a lot of its cachet in the twentieth century. Surveys of college students on qualities they valued in a mate give chastity an increasingly poor grade. Out of a list of eighteen traits, men rated it tenth in 1939; by 1996 it was down to sixteenth; for women, it was tenth in 1939 and seventeenth in 1996. (In first place in 1996 was "mutual attraction, love.")[83] The sexual revolution and the rise of cohabitation devalued chastity. The whole idea of breach of promise now seemed hopelessly archaic. A middle-class woman of the year 2000, engaged to be married, who had sex with her fiancé, could hardly claim she had been ruined for life. Women had entered the workforce, women were voting and serving on juries; they were moving toward formal equality with men. Underlying breach of promise cases was an image of women as delicate, dependent creatures, sexually naive, modest, easily upset, and incapable of earning their keep without a man. This image was more and more out of step with the facts of life in the twentieth century. In addition, by the middle of the century, the ethos of marriage was different from the ethos of marriage in the previous century. Marriage was an intensely individual choice. Marriage involved two people who loved and desired each other. Nobody should be dragooned into a marriage he or she does not want. Moreover, not being married was not as devastating for a woman as it had been. A middle-class woman without a husband was no longer a useless appendage, a spinster, an "old maid." She no longer seemed pathetic, ridiculous, useless, a desiccated and aging figure cut off from the fulness of life. A man should be free to break an engagement, if he changed his mind. If he did, he was not necessarily a cad, a bounder, a heel.

Along with breach of promise, the old actions for "criminal conversation" and alienation of affections, and the criminal action of "seduction," went into the dustbin of history. These were based on old stereotypes—that women were sexually passive; that they could be seduced, but were not sexually aggressive in their own right. These actions also assumed that the husband was the dominant figure in the family, and that he and he alone was entitled to enjoy his wife's sexual favors. This gave him, as the court in *Gasper v. Lighthouse, Inc.*, a 1987 Maryland case, put it, "a well-recognized property interest in both his wife and his marriage."[84] Daniel Gasper and his wife, Nicole, had been having marriage trouble. They turned to a firm called Lighthouse, Inc., for marriage counseling; and Lighthouse assigned Don Derby to be their counselor. For Daniel, this turned out to be a big mistake. Don Derby ended up having sex with Nicole, who then divorced her husband. Daniel sued Derby and the company for breach of contract, negligence, infliction of emotional distress, malicious interference with the marriage, and anything else he could think of. The court threw the case out. This was an action for alienation of affections or criminal conversation, thinly disguised as something else. But Maryland had abolished actions for alienation of affections and criminal conversation. The only "basis" for the negligence claims was "Derby's cuckolding activity," and this was no longer legally sufficient.

As a reading of the laws of Maryland, the decision is perfectly reasonable. But it is striking that not a word in the decision expresses sympathy for Daniel—quite the opposite. For the court, it seems clear (reading between the lines) that Nicole was free to have sex where and when she wanted, to marry and divorce as she wanted. The old rules were dead and buried, and their normative world had been buried with them.

Similarly, in a 2000 Massachusetts case,[85] Gilbert Quinn and his son Michael brought a lawsuit against Joseph Walsh. Walsh had had an affair with Susan, wife and mother, respectively, of the plaintiffs. This affair (father and son claimed) had, as one of its purposes, to "injure Quinn." Gilbert and Susan's marriage broke up; and the Quinns sued Walsh for inflicting "severe emotional distress" on father and son.

The court would have none of it. This was an action for alienation of affection and criminal conversation under some other name. The legislature had abolished these causes of action. On the issue of "emotional distress," the court said there could be recovery only when the conduct of the defendant was "extreme and outrageous . . . utterly intolerable in a civilized community." The adultery in this case might be "reprehensible," but it did not cross the line between the merely reprehensible and the "extreme and outrageous." Adultery simply did not reach those depths of iniquity. Clearly, the country had traveled a very long distance since the seventeenth century, when adultery was (in theory) a crime that could bring you to the gallows.

Divorce: The "Silent Revolution"

In the first half of the twentieth century, on the surface at least, the dual system in divorce law was still thriving in the United States. The vast majority of divorces were in fact collusive; they resulted from a deal between husband and wife. (Whether the deal was really "consensual"— that is, a bargain between equals, between two people who both wanted a divorce—is, as we noted before, another question.) Collusive divorces were, strictly speaking, illegal, as we pointed out. But the official law was a living lie. In Illinois, for example, if the court found that the parties colluded, "no divorce shall be decreed," according to the statute. This was (as noted) standard doctrine. But according to a study published in the 1950s, almost all divorce cases in Illinois were actually collusive—they came about as a result of "agreement by the parties to the divorce as such." The "testimony" in these cases was usually cut and dried. The typical plaintiff complained of cruelty: her husband beat her, slapped her, abused her. As the author of the study remarked sarcastically, the "number of cruel spouses in Chicago . . . who strike their marriage partners in the face exactly twice . . . is remarkable." To back up her story, the plaintiff almost always brought along her mother or a sister or brother.[86]

Deep into the twentieth century, the formal law stubbornly insisted that an agreement "between husband and wife that suit shall be brought and no defense entered" was unacceptable; and such a case had to be dismissed. The "policy of our law favors marriage, and disfavors divorce," as a New Jersey judge put it in 1910.[87] In Indiana as late as the 1950s, according to the law, if the defendant failed to make an appearance, the judge was supposed to notify the prosecutor, and the duty of the prosecutor was to enter and defend the case; this was also to happen if the judge suspected any sort of collusion. But these were empty strictures. In practice, almost all cases in Indiana were still uncontested, no defense was made by anybody, the prosecutor never intervened, and plaintiffs could have their divorce virtually "for the asking."[88] In New York, where adultery was the only practical grounds for divorce, a bizarre form of collusion was commonplace. The husband would check into a hotel. A woman hired to play his lover would join him in the room. Both of them would take off some or all of their clothes. A study of 500 divorce cases conducted in the 1930s actually counted how often the man was nude (23), in a nightgown (8), in "B.V.D. or underwear (119)," or in pajamas (227). The woman was nude more often (55 times); in a nightgown 126 times; in a "kimono" 68 times. At this point of undress, a maid would arrive with towels, or a bellboy with a telegram. Suddenly, a photographer would burst into the room and take pictures. Then the man would pay the woman; she then thanked him and left. The photographs would be shown in court as "evidence" of adultery.[89] In England, too, adultery was the only grounds for divorce before 1938; and, as in New York, hotel evidence of this phony type was used in many cases.[90] There were occasional scandals and crackdowns, but the system always went back to normal, after some decent interval.

In the nineteenth century, the British government had been less complacent about collusion than the states. Divorce was socially unacceptable, especially for the lower orders. In 1860, only three years after the divorce law was passed, a new statute created the office of the Queen's Proctor. This officer had the duty of sniffing out collusion and protecting the interests of society in divorce cases. The point was to prevent consensual divorce. On the whole, the experiment did not succeed.[91] The rigid class system of the British did provide some support for a tough regime of divorce; but slowly, the same forces that overwhelmed American divorce overwhelmed the British system as well.

What seems clear is that everywhere in the developed world there was a tremendous, pent-up demand for divorce—a powerful force that simply had to find an outlet. Change or reform remained difficult, if not impossible; respectable society (and legislatures frightened of some of their voters) simply did not permit "easy" divorce. The result was the dual system—collusion and migratory divorce. Another outlet for the divorce demand, at least in New York state, was annulment. In New York, the law, as we have seen, was unusually severe, allowing divorce only for adultery. As a result, New York became the annulment capital of the United States. An annulled marriage, legally speaking, never existed. It was dead from the start because of some grave impediment or fraud. In most states, annulments were much less common than divorces. They were used mostly by Roman Catholics, whose church did not recognize divorce. In San Mateo County, California, in the 1950s, 12 percent of the petitions to end a marriage were petitions for annulment; in the period 1890–1910, only 1 or 2 percent of such petitions in Alameda County, California, were petitions for annulment.[92]

But in New York the situation was entirely different. Annulments were exceedingly common. The New York statute allowed annulment of a marriage if the "consent" of one party was "obtained by force, duress, or fraud" or if "one of the parties was physically incapable of entering into the marriage state" or was a "lunatic."[93] There was nothing unusual about this statute. But in most states, the courts interpreted annulment laws rather strictly. Fraud was not easy to prove. Joel Bishop, writing in the late nineteenth century, found annulment cases "inherently" embarrassing (and "not numerous").[94] It is one thing to want to get rid of a spouse, quite another to accuse that spouse of fraud (or even worse, of total impotence or frigidity). In New York, however, the courts stretched the concept of "fraud" almost beyond recognition, and in general they opened up the legal grounds of annulment to an astonishing degree. By 1950, in ten counties in New York, there were more annulments than divorces; for the state as a whole, there were two-thirds as many annulments as decrees of divorce.[95] To be sure, the appellate courts were not always willing to grant annulments in dubious cases. The case law was quite involute and complex.[96] Loretta Coiley Pawloski failed to get an annulment for fraud against her husband, Alex John; she claimed he lied about his name and told her he was "German" when in fact he was Polish. Loretta "did not care much for Polish people." They had been married over twenty years. This "fraud," even if proven, did not "go to the essence" of the marriage contract, said the court.[97]

Still, it says something that Loretta even *thought* she had a chance at annulment. In most states, her claim would have gotten exactly nowhere. And in many other cases, the New York appellate courts were more willing to discover "fraud" and other impediments. In a 1923 case, James Truiano told Florence Booth, a schoolteacher, that he was a U.S. citizen; in fact he was not. The court granted an annulment.[98] And a young man was able to get an annulment in 1935, when he claimed that his (foreign) wife married him only to get his money, as part of a "scheme" of European "nobility" to "inveigle" wealthy Americans into marriage. The man, said the court, was "unaccustomed to dealing with the workings of a shrewd and cunning European mind"; he had been "deceived and defrauded." The marriage was duly wiped off the books.[99] Most annulment cases, one must remember, were never appealed. They began and ended in the trial courts. They were just as consensual as the thousands of divorces in other states. The New York annulment statistics speak for themselves on this point.

Contemporary Chile is another jurisdiction where annulments have been terrifically and abnormally common. Chile, until 2004, was the only major Western country that still did not recognize absolute divorce. (In that year, the legislature finally enacted such a law.)[100] Annulment was an obvious escape hatch. People used all sorts of tricks and stratagems people used in their quest for an annulment. In both Chile and New York state, the official law said one thing, and the ordinary lower-level courts did something quite different. Both jurisdictions were trapped in a situation of historic stalemate.

The stalemate, however, came to an end in New York, and in the United States in general, in the second half of the twentieth century. Up to that point, official reform was slow and difficult. But underneath, the dual system was simply rotting away. Divorce became more and more common. Its stigma slowly evaporated. As a judge in Chicago put it around 1950, most people thought divorce was nobody's business, except that of the man and woman in question. Getting a divorce was, or should be, like getting a marriage license: a couple was "entitled to a marriage license for a certain fee" and a blood test, and nothing else. Why not make getting a divorce equally easy? This judge thought "Hollywood" was to blame for the change in attitudes, for the loss of "scandal and shame."[101] This was surely giving Hollywood too much credit (or blame). Movie stars got divorces, of course, but the movies themselves were quite skittish on the subject; indeed, for a while in the 1930s and 1940s they almost never dealt with divorce at all.[102] The judge might even have been somewhat off base in his reading of general public opinion. But there is no doubt that the winds were shifting; even the official law began to evolve, though in a rather gingerly way. New Mexico was bolder than most states: from 1933 on, its divorce statute specifically listed "incompatibility" as grounds for divorce.[103] "Incompatibility" means basically that two people do not and cannot get along. As far as traditional divorce law was concerned, this was rank heresy.

New Mexico was unusual. But in a fair number of states, the law began to ease the path to divorce in a different way. Divorce became available, even without "grounds," if the couple had been separated for a specific number of years—from two to ten, depending on the state. By 1950, about twenty states had a provision of this sort. In Arizona, Idaho, Kentucky, and Wisconsin, the period was five years; in Rhode Island, it was ten; in Arkansas and Nevada, it was three years; in Louisiana and North Carolina, two years.[104] These statutes, too, were heretical. They plainly recognized that some marriages were dead and gone. It was only decent to give them a proper burial and let people get on with their lives. In fact, in many of these states few couples took advantage of this device. Why wait two, five or ten years when a few harmless lies could bring about a divorce right away?[105]

In many states, a spouse was entitled to a divorce if the other spouse had become "incurably insane" or the like. Sometimes the statute required actual confinement in an insane asylum—for five years in Vermont and Kansas.[106] A spouse also commonly had the right to a divorce if the other spouse was in prison on a felony charge. These seem fairly obvious grounds; but in fact they contradicted the theory of traditional marriage—the promise to cleave together in sickness and in health; in good times and in bad. Cancer or heart disease were never grounds for divorce. Why then insanity? or imprisonment, for a crime not committed against the spouse? Neither of these was technically desertion. But from the standpoint of the sane spouse, or the spouse not in prison, the marriage was a hollow shell and a daily frustration.

There were a few cracks in the armor at the level of appellate courts. In California, a 1952 case, *De Burgh v. De Burgh*,[107] was an important sign of oncoming change. Daisy and Albert De Burgh were suffering through what was obviously a rotten marriage. Albert beat her, bragged about his other women, was often drunk, was lavish with waiters but stingy with Daisy. This was her story. His story was different. He claimed she was spreading lies about him; she was trying to ruin him in business and wreck his reputation, sending letters to partners and associates, accusing him of "dishonesty and homosexuality." Under standard legal doctrine, if both parties were cruel or otherwise at fault, there could be no divorce. The Superior Court, accordingly, denied the divorce and dismissed the case. The California Supreme Court reversed. The family, wrote Justice Roger Traynor, "is the core of our society," and the state should "foster and preserve marriage." But when a marriage "has failed, and the family has ceased to be a unit," the couple should be able to end it through divorce. The evidence in the case showed a "total and irremedial breakdown of the marriage." Traynor sent the case back to trial; the trial judge was instructed to "determine whether the legitimate objects of matrimony have been destroyed" and whether the marriage could be "saved." Theoretically, the judge had the power to deny the divorce; but Traynor's words made that very unlikely.

In the last third of the twentieth century, what Herbert Jacob has called a "silent revolution" finally destroyed the dual system.[108] The "silent revolution" refers to the passage of no-fault divorce laws. Jacob called this revolution a "silent" one because, though it seemed like a radical change, it was accomplished with little discussion and even less controversy. It was as if no-fault crept into the law like a thief in the night. Technocrats drafted the laws, and they were adopted almost without serious debate. A system that had lasted a century vanished in the twinkling of an eye.

Socially, if not legally, the old system had simply rotted away. In the age of individualism and the sexual revolution, in the age of the enthronement of choice, people felt there was no point saving marriages that no longer satisfied either husband or wife or both. They had a right to a divorce whenever the marriage "just didn't work out." Demand for recognition of this social fact finally overwhelmed the forces that held traditional views. And, of course, nobody ever really liked the collusive system. It was corrupt, dirty, and expensive. It demeaned everybody involved in the process—lawyers, judges, and the parties to the divorce themselves.

What came out of California was the so-called no-fault divorce. No-fault divorce is not consensual divorce; it goes far beyond that. It is really unilateral divorce, divorce at will, divorce when either partner, husband or wife, wants a divorce and asks for it. Under a no-fault system, there are absolutely no defenses to an action for divorce. There are no longer any "grounds" for divorce. No-fault reconstructs divorce in the image of marriage; marriage and divorce become parallel, legally speaking. For a marriage to take place, two people have to agree to get married. Breach of promise has been abolished. Both the man and the woman have a veto, then; each one has a right to back out of marriage, up to the very moment when someone pronounces them man and wife. In movie after movie—*The Graduate* is one of the best known—somebody in fact does pull out in the very shadow of the altar. Under no-fault, this veto power continues after marriage. Either partner can decide if the marriage goes on or comes to an end. Either one can break the marriage off, at any time, for any reason—or for no reason at all. This is the practical meaning of a no-fault system—the way it actually operates.

The first no-fault divorce law took effect in California in 1970. The old "grounds" for divorce were eliminated, except for two: total insanity, and "irreconcilable differences, which have caused the irremediable breakdown of the marriage."[109] Interestingly, the experts and jurists who wrote the reports and drafted the law never intended a no-fault system. They wanted to get rid of the old dual system; they wanted to clean house, eliminate hypocrisy and fraud, end the dirty business of collusion, and allow consensual divorce—divorce by mutual agreement. This was already the living law, and they wanted to make it official. They never intended to make divorce easy or automatic, and certainly not unilateral. Marriages were a good thing, they felt; and if at all possible, marriages should be saved. They wanted, for example, a system of marriage counseling. They wanted the courts to mend sick marriages and, if possible, cure them. Their notion was to give more power and resources to family courts; couples in trouble could find help, advice, and perhaps a certain amount of therapy.[110] Herma Hill Kay, a scholar and expert in family law active in the reform movement, suggested remodeling family court in the image of juvenile court. Husband and wife would meet with a counselor; they would explore together whether the marriage could be saved. An important role would be played by "professional caseworkers," psychiatrists, and "experienced supervisors." There would be no "coercion." Ultimately, the court would decide whether "the legitimate objects of matrimony have been destroyed."[111] None of Kay's proposals, as it turned out, would actually stir into life.

Still, the original California law, taken literally, contemplated something other than what actually happened. The law asked a question of fact: are there "irreconcilable differences," and has the marriage completely broken down? Presumably, it would be up to a judge to decide this factual question. But almost immediately the law came to mean something radically different. It took on a life of its own. Divorce became simply automatic. Judges never inquired into reasons; they never actually asked whether a marriage had "irretrievably broken down," or broken down at all. They merely signed the papers. What is more, the no-fault "revolution" swept the country. State after state adopted a no-fault statute—or, more accurately, a statute that turned out to mean no-fault. The details varied from state to state, but almost everywhere no-fault made its mark on the statute book. Some states, like California, were "pure" no-fault states—in Rhode Island, for example, divorce was to be "decreed, irrespective of the fault of either party, on the ground of irreconcilable differences which have caused the irremediable break-down of the marriage."[112] In some states, the legislature simply added no-fault to the list of "grounds," even though this was in a way illogical, since no-fault meant that the grounds were no longer important.[113] Utah and Tennessee, for example, added "irreconcilable differences" to their list. In Ohio, what was added was "incompatibility, unless denied by either party."[114] But in most states, divorce became automatic, just as in California. Either party could end the marriage. Judges never did any looking, questioning, or counseling. They became a rubber stamp, nothing more.

To be sure, tough issues of property rights and custody of children remained to plague family law. Many hotly contested cases turned on these issues. They provide plenty of business for divorce lawyers. But the divorce itself was no longer something to fight and contest. No-fault is the epitome of what used to be called "easy" divorce. In fact, divorce is almost never easy, psychologically speaking. But no-fault made the legal part of it much less painful—and cheaper, too. This is especially true if the duration of the marriage was short, no children were born, and there either was no money to divide or no argument about how to divide it. Divorce can even be, for some people, a do-it-yourself project. Nowadays one can buy books that tell readers how to get rid of a spouse in ten easy lessons, without paying for the time and services of a lawyer.

Changes in sexual mores, in the social meaning of marriage and divorce, and in the relationship of men and women underlay the no-fault movement. These factors were more or less common to all developed countries. All of them have moved in the same direction. Some countries in Europe and Latin America—those that are strongly Catholic by tradition—resisted divorce altogether. Italy, Spain, and Ireland for a long time had no laws allowing absolute divorce at all (they did recognize legal separation, however). Gordon Ireland and Jesus de Galindez surveyed divorce laws in the countries of the Western hemisphere just after the end of the Second World War.[115] At that time, there was still no such thing as absolute divorce in Argentina, Brazil, Chile, Columbia, and Paraguay. Divorce had had a long history in some of the republics of Latin America; in others it had come only later—in Uruguay, for example, in 1907, and in Bolivia only in 1932. With the exception of Chile (where absolute divorce, as we saw, was not legally available until 2004), every Latin American country by 2000 had provisions for breaking the bonds of matrimony. Brazil adopted a divorce law in 1977. Strongly Catholic countries in Europe, too, eventually came to adopt divorce laws, though often in the teeth of furious opposition. Italy began to allow divorce in 1970; Spain did so in 1981, after the end of the Franco regime. Divorce is now available in Ireland as well.

Moreover, many countries have modified their laws along paths roughly similar to that of the United States. Brazil, as mentioned, had no divorce at all until 1977; and its first divorce law was quite restrictive (for example, no one was allowed to get divorced twice). In 1992, however, a more modern, consensual divorce law was enacted.[116] In some countries—France, for example—divorce by mutual consent has become available, along with a no-fault system (if the couple had a long-time separation). Germany in the late 1970s adopted a no-fault system; divorce is available whenever the marriage has simply broken down. Sweden, too, has a no-fault system.[117] Most countries have not gone to the same extreme as the United States. But even so conservative a state as Switzerland has liberalized its divorce laws. A new law, in force as of 2000, allowed for divorce by mutual agreement of the parties; and either party can ask for divorce after four years of separation. The law in Austria is quite similar: a couple can get a divorce after six months of separation, if both declare that their marriage has broken down.[118] In England, despite waves of reform, it is still the law as of 2003 that a divorce is allowed only if a marriage has "irretrievably" broken down. In practice, however, as Stephen Cretney has put it, "divorce is readily and quickly available if both parties agree"; and even if one does not, the marriage is basically over. After all, there is no point "denying that the marriage has broken down if one party firmly asserts that it has."[119] Divorce rates have also risen in almost all Western countries. The ropes that bind married people together have gotten weaker; for millions, they are altogether gone.

The divorce epidemic reflects and reinforces a peculiarly modern conception of marriage. Marriage is seen as an individual matter, a personal matter. It is a reflex of what has been called expressive individualism—a form of individualism that "holds that each person has a unique core of feeling and intuition that should unfold or be expressed if individuality is to be realized." It is the belief that the "meaning of life" is "to become one's own person."[120] Marriage is a status that people choose—and unchoose, according to how much it does to help them in the pursuit of happiness. The motives, aims, and expectations people bring to marriage are also intensely personal. Thus the changes in the laws reflect a view in which, as Mary Ann Glendon has put it, "an individual's primary responsibility is assumed to be to himself." Marriage is a "relationship that exists primarily for the fulfillment of the individual spouses. If it ceases to perform this function, no one is to blame, and either spouse may terminate it at will."[121] In her book *The Divorce Culture*, Barbara Whitehead put it this way: a "psychological revolution" has given rise to "expressive divorce." The "revolution" has in fact redefined the family. Once the "realm of the fettered and obligated self," the family had become a "fertile realm for exploring the potential of the self, unfettered by roles and obligations." Divorce was now the servant of the new self and the new family. Divorce was no longer a pathology, but a "psychologically healthy response to marital dissatisfaction."[122]

All this may seem obvious. It is, however, in striking contrast to the way people talked about marriage in the past; and it fits in rather poorly with the slogans, still often heard, that marriage is the basis of society, that marriage is the glue that holds everything together, and so on. As we will see, there is a great deal of concern—panic even—about the condition of marriage; and there have been some attempts (feeble perhaps) to remedy the situation. But whatever the speechmakers and politicians say, for most people in modern society, marriage is no glue and no foundation, but a status that does or does not meet their personal needs. This does not mean that they are cavalier about marriage or divorce. People do not marry glibly and frivolously; nor do they end their marriages that way. Divorce is usually a traumatic experience, a confession of failure, a source of misery and pain, even when people honestly believe that it is best for them. That no-fault divorce leads people to treat marriage like a piece of clothing to be worn, used, and discarded is a myth. Millions of people believe that, for them, marriage is worth the agony and the effort.

Under no-fault divorce, each spouse has the choice, unrestricted by law, to stay or to go; but in fact the right to stay is contingent on the other partner in marriage. In a regime of choice, one person's choice may collide with, interfere with, or contradict another person's choice. Modern divorce law resolves the conflict by giving higher priority to the spouse who wants to go. The relationship, in short, has to be mutually satisfying. This is true of all relationships in modern family law—marriage, marriagelike relationships, even relationships of parents and children. "Choice" is what you choose for yourself; but you cannot choose for anybody else. When your choice depends on somebody else's choice and that somebody else disagrees, your choice gives way.

This is the essence of what we might call "expressive divorce." It is intensely personal—like expressive marriage. The sheer wealth of modern Western societies in part explains the rise of the "expressive divorce." In middle-class countries of Europe, North America, and elsewhere, most people—factory workers, secretaries, computer programmers, electricians—have cars, color television sets, paid vacations, and a social safety net. They may have to work hard for these goods, but in the end they have enough money, and time, to spend part of their lives in the pursuit of happiness. And they pursue it with a vengeance. They want fun, sex, the fulness of life; they want a family, too, but in the context of an expressive marriage. And if this marriage fails, they want an expressive divorce. The inexorable march of divorce legislation tells the story more graphically and solidly than any public opinion poll. Nothing seems able to stand in the way. The Catholic Church continues to tell Catholics they cannot get a divorce, but Catholics do it anyway. Even the local priests can sound halfhearted on this point; they know that the faithful do not go along. No Catholic country any longer fails to provide for divorce, now that Chile has finally defected.[123]

There has been much discussion of the actual impact of no-fault. Do divorce rates go up under no-fault? A study of the German divorce law published in 1988 suggests strongly that the answer is no. The divorce rate rose after the new law was enacted in Germany; but it had been rising before no-fault, and there was no sign that the new law led to any change in the curve. The new law did not incite couples to rush out and break off their marriage.[124]

Has no-fault divorce hurt women economically and socially? This is a harder question to answer. Women by the millions in most developed countries are part of the labor force. They work before, during, and after marriage. They may earn less than men; but they do earn. The welfare state has also helped women to become more independent economically. Like men, they are entitled to benefits—for unemployment, for child care, old age pensions, and so on. All this has an impact on women who want a divorce, or are forced into one. Many women with jobs or careers feel they can live on their own, without a husband. In a more negative sense, men are encouraged to *think* women can earn a good living for themselves. If so, why should the men pay alimony? Support payments for divorced wives have declined in the United States.[125] A divorced woman with custody of the children can expect some child support, and a share of the property (if there is any), but very often nothing more. For this and other reasons, some feminists feel that no-fault has made women worse off than before. But the evidence is mixed and inconclusive.[126] There is also, as we shall see, a lot of controversy over the effect of divorce on the children. Nobody thinks divorce is good for kids; but exactly *how* bad it is for them is disputed. A wretched, abusive marriage is not good for children either.

No-fault divorce swept the United States in short order and made its mark elsewhere as well; but it has also provoked a good deal of criticism.[127] We mentioned the charge that no-fault has made things worse for women. Conservatives of all religions are also suspicious of no-fault. They feel it makes divorce too easy; and easy divorce, they assume, leads to decay or dissolution in family life. There has been a certain amount of legal backlash against no-fault in the United States. A Louisiana law of 1997 created a new form of marriage, "covenant marriage." A couple now has a choice: ordinary marriage or covenant marriage. If you choose covenant marriage, you give up the right to a no-fault divorce and you agree "that the marriage . . . is a lifelong arrangement."[128] This sounds very strong, very durable. Are the two really bound for life? The answer is no. They can get a divorce, but not a no-fault divorce. A partner in a covenant marriage has to have grounds for divorce, just as in the old days: adultery, desertion, physical or sexual abuse, or a felony conviction.[129] He or she also has the right to end the marriage after a substantial period of separation. And the parties in a covenant marriage have to undergo marriage counseling before divorcing. Some other states have considered covenant marriage, or something like it; and Arizona and Arkansas have adopted their own versions.[130] In Arizona, as in Louisiana, loving couples can "solemnly declare" their marriage to be a covenant, lasting as long as life itself. Here too, it is possible to get a divorce for adultery or desertion, or after a one-year separation, even for those in a covenant marriage. And the covenant marriage can also be dissolved if "husband and wife both agree."[131]

So far, in Louisiana at least, there are not many takers. A study of covenant marriage published in 2001 was bad news for the backers of covenant marriage.[132] Less than half of the public in Louisiana even knew this form of marriage existed. Hardly anybody knew any couples who actually had a covenant marriage. Most people thought covenant marriage was a good idea, but that it wouldn't work. When people applied for a marriage license, about two-thirds of the clerks never mentioned it; only 29 percent offered any information about it. Most of the clerks in fact had poor understanding of the law. Some clerks thought the law was a good idea; others thought it was a sham, or "bullshit," a "waste of time," or a useless "feel-good" law. Very few couples, the clerks said, seemed interested in trying it. So far, then, in these early returns, covenant marriage is hardly a roaring success.

these conflicts—the institutions that decide the undecidable and answer the unanswerable questions.

Who Is a Mother?

The question "Who is a mother?" comes up less often than the question "Who is a father?" It is usually pretty obvious who a mother is, biologically speaking. Of course, the state can, and does, take children away from unfit mothers, or those whom it considers unfit mothers. There is also nowadays the issue of surrogate motherhood.[109] A woman who signs a surrogacy contract has agreed, usually for money, to get pregnant, carry the child to term, and then give up the baby to the couple who paid her. Biologically, the surrogate mother in the typical case is a real mother: it is her egg, her womb. Contractually, she is bound to abandon her claims to the baby. Is this contract legal? The issue has come up a number of times, most notoriously in the "Baby M." case in 1988.[110] William and Elizabeth Stern paid Mary Beth Whitehead $10,000 to carry a baby for them. William provided the sperm, and Ms. Whitehead supplied the egg and the womb. But when the baby was born, Ms. Whitehead refused to go through with the agreement. She felt too attached to her little girl; she just "could not part with" her baby. A long and somewhat sordid struggle followed; at one point, Whitehead took the baby and fled to Florida to get away from the Sterns and their legal demands. Ultimately, the conflict ended up in court. The crucial decision, by the New Jersey Supreme Court, was in some ways a compromise. The contract, said the court, was illegal under New Jersey law. Surrogacy "totally ignores the child; it takes the child from the mother regardless of her wishes and her maternal fitness; and it does all of this . . . through the use of money." Mary Beth Whitehead, after all, was the biological mother; and she had done nothing that (without the contract) would have allowed a court to terminate her maternal rights. She was neither unfit nor abusive. The surrogacy contract could not be enforced, said the court; and thus it had no legal bearing on the ultimate question: Who gets to have and raise "Baby M."?

Some cities have adopted a "Community Marriage Policy," a somewhat different tack in the struggle to make marriages last and discourage divorce. This consists of (voluntary) guidelines "for premarital preparation" administered by the clergy. The goal (which one can hardly quarrel with) is to give people tools, ideas, and information that will help them have a healthy and happy marriage. Another goal is to reduce the divorce rate: the ministers who signed on to this policy, in Grand Rapids, Michigan, for example, hoped to cut the divorce rate 10 percent in five years and 25 percent in ten years. They also aimed to "promote chastity outside of marriage and faithful marital relationships."[133] It remains to be seen whether this will happen.

Covenant marriage may be a sideshow, a mere blip on the screen; or it may be another turn of the wheel. Its proponents are eager and dedicated. They feel that the country is in danger, and that the family must be saved at all costs. They are also optimists. But they are also somewhat naive, and unaware of the history of divorce law. As we pointed out in this chapter, there was a kind of no-fault divorce *before* no-fault divorce; certainly there was a *form* of consensual divorce, without grounds. This was part of the living law. The divorce laws may have been a burden and an obstacle, at least to people without much money. But divorce was readily available, although you would never know this from the statute books. All it took to get a divorce was a little cheating and lying or a trip to Nevada, if you could afford it. Is history going to repeat itself in Louisiana?

Covenant marriage is based on the idea that easy divorce breaks up families, that divorce is evil in itself, and that divorce makes families disintegrate. This is a very dubious notion. It confuses cause and effect. It is family breakup, misery, and disappointment that causes divorce, not divorce that causes family breakup, misery, and disappointment. Divorce is a legal status. If divorce becomes cheap and easy, more marriages will end in divorce rather than separation and desertion. Perhaps more couples will get divorced instead of just living apart. But a happy couple, walking hand in hand, is not going to rush out and get a divorce even if divorce is available at fire-sale prices (or even free) and as easy as falling off a log.

In theory, easy divorce might even lead to more marital happiness. People find it easier to get out of bad marriages and into good ones. Unfortunately, the evidence, such as it is, does not bear this theory out. The percentage of happy marriages in the United States declined between the 1970s and the 1990s.[134] Why should this be so? Surely because of powerful cultural trends, which have driven individuals to want more and more self-satisfaction, more joy out of life, more sex, more deep emotional fulfillment. When these fail to materialize, the result is divorce—or a miserable marriage. The roots of divorce, like the roots of satisfaction and emotional health, lie deep in the social structure; and no law reform can get at these deep and powerful roots.

Partners

Since families no longer arrange marriages, young men and women have to do the job themselves. They have to search for a mate wherever they can—in school, at the workplace, in church, in social clubs, or elsewhere. Finding Mr. Right or Ms. Right is not easy. There are companies and services that are only too willing to help. A whole industry of intermediaries has sprung up. Some traditional societies had matchmakers; but they generally worked with families, not with isolated, lonely individuals. The wonders of technology are today's matchmakers; people can use "a modem, phone line, or advertisement" to "bring potential partners together."[135] In many cities and countries, lonely people place ads in newspapers, describing themselves and hoping to attract a partner for love, friendship, marriage, sex, or all of the above. These newspaper "personals" are anonymous. Identity is hidden behind a number or a code. The man or woman who places an ad can screen the answers and decide whom to meet and whom to ignore. The texts of these ads are hardly objective—every man is handsome, charming, and interesting, every woman warm and attractive—but they are in a way significant social documents. People usually list their habits and hobbies, their likes and dislikes. They usually give their age, race, and ethnic background. They talk about their favorite music, whether they do yoga, what kinds of food they like to eat. I pull the following, almost at random, from the local Palo Alto (California) newspaper: a man describes himself as "very outgoing" and "open-minded"; he is looking for a woman who is "nice" and "communicative," for "conversation, parties, movies, cafes, possible romance." A woman who calls herself "playful," who is "passionate about music, ideas, great books, good movies, lively conversations and beautiful places," confesses to a love for "hiking, biking, Tuscany, volunteering, kids (none of my own)." She is "warm-hearted," full of "joie de vivre," and needs a "bright, kind-hearted soulmate, 37–50."[136]

These ads have appeared in local newspapers and magazines at least since the early 1970s. As Theresa Montini and Beverly Ovrebo put it, the ads reflect the "common cultural belief that there is a perfect partner for any given person," that fate can bring "two *unique* persons together."[137] Though the ads mention age and sex, sometimes race and sexual preference, they emphasize personality, good points (sometimes a bad point or two), hobbies, interests, and ways of life; only occasionally do they touch on such matters as religion and family background. There is always the implicit message that the writer of the ad is a special, one-of-a-kind person. And although each person is a unique package of traits, desires, and talents, the prevailing belief is that somewhere out there this unique person can find someone who matches, someone who fits like a glove fits a hand or a key fits a lock. The underlying ethos of these "personals" is the ethos that underlies the modern conception of marriage: the coming together of two unique paths. People have to be meant for each other; they have to match—not necessarily in some mystical, astrological way, but in terms of their unique composition, their unique personalities.

This is no American exclusive. There are ads of this sort in many countries. A businessman in Berlin, Germany—a man of heart, with an "infectious joy of life"—is looking for his "dream woman," who "speaks Italian" and is tall and slender, between thirty and fifty (he is in his sixties), a woman of "passion" and elegance, so that they might "enjoy life together." Another German man is seeking a sweet, attractive woman "to release me from my loneliness."[138] How often the bait catches suitable fish is hard to say; but thousands of these ads appear every day, all over the world. Sometimes, they must work; so too of Internet dating. In the social section of the *New York Times* at the end of 2002, we read about a fifty-year-old man, a divorced owner of an art gallery in the city, who got his new wife from an on-line dating service. Her ad was "clever, yet self-effacing. . . . Funny and funky." They chatted on-line. He was "Escher-Guy," she was "laffqueen." A year later they were married.[139] These on-line services have multiplied enormously. According to one source, some 40 million Americans were "visiting at least one online dating service" in August 2003.[140]

The people who place ads or surf the net do not specifically want to get married. They are looking for relationships, for romance, for "soul-mates." They are looking for sex, too, though this is not usually openly expressed, at least not in the newspaper ads.[141] They are surely looking for company, for human contact, often for something deep, permanent, long-lasting. In the Palo Alto newspaper referred to earlier, a man who was (he said) as cute as a "koala bear" used the bear theme to express his longing for intimacy and commitment: "Bear with me, I won't bear to be without you. Bare your heart and soul, and I'll bare mine. Possible co-hibernation, possible cubs."[142] Much of so-called reality TV, so popular at the beginning of the twenty-first century, plays on similar themes: dating, finding mates, relationships, lovers, husbands and wives. What makes the search so pressing, and so difficult, is the weakness of traditional ways of finding mates and the awesome burden of expressive individualism.

In contemporary times, too, the line between types of relationship has blurred considerably. A pillar of traditional marriage was its monopoly of legitimate sex. But the sexual revolution has gone a long way toward destroying this monopoly. Even among the hopelessly traditional, the nexus between marriage and sex has eroded in many Western countries. Yet there is a general hunger among most people for something deeper and finer than casual sex. There is a hunger for "relationships," which the personals, and even reality TV, clearly exploit.

"Cohabitation" is a modern term for a relationship that was once called "living in sin." Until fairly recently, if a man and a woman lived together unmarried, it was not only a moral offense and a cause for scandal; it was actually a crime. In the United States in the nineteenth century, most states made adultery and fornication crimes, especially if "open and notorious."[143] The phrase "open and notorious" is significant. It was not only (or even not primarily) the act itself—the sin—that the law was to punish; it was being "open and notorious," that is, flouting respectable society and thumbing one's nose at traditional norms and values.[144] To be sure, there is not much information about enforcement of these laws; what little we have suggests that very few people were actually prosecuted for this kind of crime. And the institution of common law marriage relabeled and legitimized relationships that would otherwise have violated the taboo.

Socially, the norm against sex outside of marriage was strongest for the bourgeois middle class. In respectable society, a sexually active person was a social pariah. Sex was for married people. Of course, the double standard was strong: men, with their supposedly violent sexual urges, could be forgiven for breaking the rules at least once in a while. If good girls were unavailable to satisfy these urges, there was always a copious supply of bad girls, many of whom used their badness as a profession. Prostitution was illegal; but it was tolerated in the late nineteenth and early twentieth century to an astonishing degree. Cities had "red light districts." These were more or less immune from crackdowns, often because the brothel owners paid bribes to politicians and police officers. In Philadelphia alone, a vice commission report in 1913 claimed that there were hundreds of brothels and "disorderly saloons" in the city and estimated that 3,700 women in Philadelphia sold sex for a living, not counting "kept women" and "casual prostitutes."[145] All of these women had customers, who might have preferred more respectable women but found none available.

In an amazingly short time during the twentieth century, the taboo against premarital sex, in developed countries, all but disappeared. (It remains quite strong, of course, in traditional societies, especially Muslim societies).[146] In Europe and North America it is extremely common, and even the norm, for couples to live together before marriage, or instead of marriage. Some members of the older generation may grumble; but most accept the new order of things. In parts of the American south, and in other areas of the country where pockets of traditionalism and deep religious fervor exist, schools and churches continue to preach the doctrine of chastity before marriage. From the 1970s on, there was something of a "counter-movement against sexual hedonism."[147] Chastity is still, in a way, official policy. The U.S. government hands out money to the states to promote chastity (this is called "abstinence education").[148] Magazine articles have reported what they claim is a movement to bring back chastity—they call it the "new virginity." In the United States, the number of high-school students who had never had intercourse went up 10 percent between 1991 and 2001; and there are even what *Newsweek* magazine has called "renewed virgins"—kids who were once sexually active and who then gave up sex for born-again chastity.[149]

A good deal of enthusiasm, even genuine ardor, lies behind this campaign. Still, on the whole, it seems to be a losing battle. There are blips here and there, zigs and zags in the statistics; the fact remains that huge numbers of young people—including high school and college students—have active sex lives. Most of them see nothing wrong with this. Why not take advantage of nature's gift of puberty and an active sex drive? For most young people, the chastity crusade is ineffective. It can also be positively harmful if it prevents or inhibits schools from teaching kids about birth control or sexually transmitted diseases.

Cohabitation, of course, is more than sex before marriage. It is a more complicated sharing of lives; it is, in short, a *relationship*. But the two phenomena are obviously related. There is little doubt that a sexual revolution has actually taken place. Unlike the French or Russian revolutions, it is hard to pinpoint a date when this revolution broke out. Behavior (and attitudes) change gradually; when it comes to sex, the change takes place quietly and surreptitiously, behind closed doors. The very term "sexual revolution" is older than one might think. Sociologist J. P. Lichtenberg, in a book published in 1931, spoke of the "modern sexual revolution."[150] The famous Kinsey reports on male sexual behavior (1948) and then on female sexual behavior (1953) caused an enormous stir because of one loud and deliberate message: the sexual revolution had arrived. Kinsey tried to show—in bold, blatant figures—that adultery was epidemic, that practically all men masturbated, and that "crimes against nature" were everyday occurrences. Kinsey's statistics were bitterly attacked (and probably deserved the attack).[151] Yet research on sexual behavior in general in the last half of the twentieth century reaches conclusions not very different from Kinsey's. In the United States, attitudes and behavior have rocketed away from the dictates of traditional morality. By the 1970s, according to Julia Ericksen, "sexual intercourse outside of marriage was just a normal part of becoming an adult."[152]

The United States is certainly not the only country with a sexual revolution. Premarital sex is common in most of the developed world. The number of couples who live together without bothering to get married now runs into the millions. In Germany, for example, at the beginning of the twenty-first century about 11 percent of all couples—about 2 million couples—were joined in nonmarital partnerships.[153] Many of these couples will eventually get married. In fact, many couples see cohabitation as a stage on the road to marriage. In France, for example, only a minority of young people "save themselves" for the honeymoon; they move in with their beloved long before then. Cohabitation, according to Claude Martin and Irene Théry, "is nowadays the normal way to begin a partnership" in France. In the 1960s, 16 percent of "cohabiting unions" in France began "outside marriage"; in the 1990s, this figure had reached the astonishing level of 87 percent.[154] The same trend can be observed even in some of the less well-off European countries. In Bulgaria, for example, Velina Todorova reports that a majority of young people surveyed in 1999 "stated that they did not prefer marriage as a form of cohabitation."[155]

Nonetheless, significant differences remain between various European countries. In southern Europe—in Greece, Spain, and Italy—cohabitation is less common than in the north. In 1981, according to one study, only 2 percent of the population lived in a "non-nuclear" household (indeed, only 3 percent lived alone).[156] Very likely, the figures have increased since then. In the Nordic countries, cohabitation is positively rampant. Partly these differences between countries result from whether it is customary for young people to leave home, married or not. Getting one's own place is less common in the southern European countries. In Spain in 1994, 79 percent of men aged twenty to twenty-nine who were not married lived with their families of origin. The corresponding figure for the United Kingdom was 36 percent; for France, 41 percent. At the same time, within the family, even in southern Europe, young people probably have more independence nowadays than they had in the past, whether they live at home or not. They may be, in short, little better than boarders in the house. They tend to have their own room; they come and go as they please; they have a great deal of personal privacy.[157] Once again, affluence makes a big difference. Money buys space; and space buys privacy. But if money makes it possible to buy privacy, it does not create the *taste* for privacy. That has deeper, wider roots.

As cohabitation became more common, it was bound to affect the law. In the United States, all issues somehow end up in court. With regard to cohabitation, *Marvin v. Marvin* (1976) was a key case.[158] The defendant, Lee Marvin, was a famous movie star. He had what could be considered an "open and notorious" relationship with Michele Triola, who even called herself Michele Marvin. After a number of years, the couple had a falling out, and Michele left Lee Marvin's home. She then brought a lawsuit against him. She claimed she and Lee Marvin had an agreement: she would live with him as his "companion, homemaker, housekeeper and cook," and she would give up her own career. In exchange, he allegedly promised to "share equally any or all property as a result of their efforts." His "efforts" as a movie star, of course, produced a great deal of money.

Lee Marvin refused to pay. In court, his lawyers cited a long line of cases in which courts refused to enforce "immoral" contracts—agreements to render "meretricious sexual services." These contracts were unenforceable because they were "against public policy." The trial court agreed and dismissed Michele's claim. The California Supreme Court, in a startling and pathbreaking decision, reversed. First, the court brushed off the earlier cases as not really relevant. An agreement involving sex was not illegal, even if sex was an element, so long as sex was not the *sole* object of the contract. "Adults who voluntarily live together and engage in sexual relations," said the court, are still "competent to contract respecting their earnings and property rights." They cannot agree to exchange sex for money; that would be "prostitution." But in other respects, they can "order their affairs as they choose"; and the courts will enforce their agreements.

The court could have stopped there. But in an outburst of frankness, it went further. Times have changed, said the court. Many young couples live together without the "solemnization of marriage." Cohabitation in itself, but also as a kind of trial marriage, was "pervasive" in society. The "mores" of society had "changed so radically" that the court did not wish to "impose a standard based on alleged moral considerations that have apparently been so widely abandoned by so many." So saying, the state Supreme Court overturned the trial court's decision and sent the case back for a full hearing, in which Michele would have a chance to prove her case.

Marvin v. Marvin created a minor sensation. It was widely reported in the newspapers. It was the subject of TV talk shows, editorials, cartoons, letters to the editor. Dozens of lawsuits followed in other states, inspired by the California decision—and reports (not always accurate) of the case in the media. The results were mixed. Some states seemed to agree with the California case and its outcome. A case in 1986, in Arizona, concerned a woman named Judith Carroll, who lived with Paul T. Lee for fourteen years; the couple then went their "separate ways." He ran an auto repair shop; she kept house ("cleaning, cooking, laundry, working the yard") and sometimes helped him at the shop "with billing and bookkeeping." They had a joint checking account. She also sometimes worked as a photographer. They never got married; they never even considered marriage seriously. Judith sued for "partition" of real and personal property. The Arizona court took her side, citing *Marvin v. Marvin* with approval. There was no good reason not to let Judith sue. The "meretricious relationship" could be separated from the "implied agreement" to provide homemaking services, said the court. In a 1987 Connecticut case, the court pointed out that the state had revised its laws to

"decriminalize sexual activities between unmarried consenting adults."
Hence there was no "basis" for failing to recognize that "contractual
rights may develop in the course of a cohabitation that includes a sexual
relationship."[159]

But not all states welcomed the *Marvin* doctrine with open arms.
Some rejected it out of hand. This was true, for example, in Illinois.[160]
Victoria Hewitt had lived with Robert Hewitt for fifteen years; they had
three children together. She had become pregnant in college; Robert (she
said) told her that they were married, that they didn't need a ceremony,
and that they would share "his life, his future, his earnings and his property." They called themselves husband and wife; they lived a "conventional, respectable and ordinary family life"; but they never had a
ceremonial marriage. The court seemed afraid that the *Marvin* doctrine
might hurt the "institution of marriage." Perhaps the "increasing numbers of unmarried cohabitants and changing mores of our society" had
reached the point where Illinois ought to recognize, again, something
like common law marriage. But, as the court pointed out, the legislature
of Illinois has foreclosed that possibility: it had abolished common law
marriage. Victoria and Robert had no formal contract or agreement.
State laws about marriage (and divorce) rested on policy that made it
impossible (the court said) to recognize and enforce Victoria's claims.

The Illinois court was swimming against the tide. Perhaps it knew it,
since it admitted that "mores" had changed. In general courts and legislatures accepted the idea, the spirit, behind the Marvin case. Times had
changed. Cohabitation was no longer outlawed. Some courts, however,
seemed worried about fraud and trumped-up claims. The solution here
was to ask for more formality. Under a Minnesota law, for example, partners who cohabited were free to enter into an agreement; but courts
would only enforce an agreement "written and signed by the parties."[161]
Courts and legislatures wrangled about the precise legal consequences,
and the ghost of the common law marriage hung over the case law; but
stigma for men and women who lived together without getting married
had drained out of the system like water from a tub.

Some countries have gone further in recognizing the rights of people in "relationships." In Sweden, for example, unmarried partners with some kind of commitment to each other can enjoy many of the privileges and obligations of regular marriage.[162] In Canada, too, the law is moving in this direction. John Miron and Jocelyne Valliere of Ontario lived together with their children, but never married. John was injured in a car accident. Jocelyne had an insurance policy that covered her and her "spouse." The company refused to pay. John, said the company, was not really a spouse. The Canadian Supreme Court felt otherwise. Denying the claim, it said, violated basic rights guaranteed by the Canadian Charter. Denying the claim here would be discriminatory, and might impair the "essential dignity and worth of the individual." Moreover, people "involved in an unmarried relationship constitute an historically disadvantaged group." They deserved special constitutional consideration.[163] Of course, drug addicts and embezzlers are also "historically disadvantaged groups." At one time, John and Jocelyne would have been considered more akin to these groups than to (say) oppressed natives or Chinese-Canadians. But in Canada too, times have changed.

Indeed, several Canadian provinces have given important rights to unmarried partners through judicial decisions.[164] Even in the United States, a number of cities, institutions, and private corporations have extended medical benefits to "domestic partners."[165] The issue is complicated by the related issue of long-term, committed partners who happen to be men living with men or women living with women. Most unmarried couples, however, consist of one woman and one man. In late 2002, the American Law Institute (ALI), which drafts model laws and then tries to convince states to adopt them, strongly recommended an increase in the rights of "domestic partners." The ALI defined "domestic partners" as "two persons of the same or opposite sex, not married to one another, who for a significant period of time share a primary residence and a life together as a couple." The ALI suggested that domestic partners, when they split up, should be entitled to "compensatory payments," more or less like alimony; and a fair division of property.[166] The law is indeed inching in this direction.

Cohabitation of course is both a modern and a premodern custom. It is exceedingly common in Scandinavia, where young people apparently find marriage a ceremonial nuisance. The Scandinavian countries are by world standards extremely rich. In many poorer countries, cohabitation is a kind of paupers' marriage; thus, in much of Latin America, poor people, especially in impoverished rural districts, frequently cohabit. Many people simply cannot afford a regular marriage. In some countries, including Paraguay, Panama, Mexico, and Ecuador, legal provisions grant property rights to people in "uniones de hecho" (unions in fact if not in law). In Turkey, after Ataturk stuffed the Swiss Civil Code (in translation) down the country's throat, only civil marriages were recognized. Most people in Anatolian villages, however, continued to marry in the same old Moslem way. These marriages were, strictly speaking, legally worthless; but the government chose to enact a whole series of "amnesty" laws, which allowed Turkish couples to register, thus saving their children from the status of bastards. Millions of children were legitimated in this way.[167] "Modern" societies, however, for reasons already explained, have almost uniformly tried to insist on bureaucratic marriage, marriage that leaves a mark, a record, a statistic.

Cohabitation, not surprisingly, reminds lawyers and judges of the old common law marriage. Some courts, looking at the case law, have even felt that the doctrine is coming back to life, like a ghost or a zombie. The Illinois court specifically tried to exorcise this demon by flatly turning down the *Marvin* doctrine. Law and custom have indeed blurred the distinction between cohabitation and common law marriage, but critical differences do remain. The common law marriage, after all, was a full, valid marriage. It automatically carried with it all the rights and duties of marriage. And marriage has always been an either-or affair. You were either married or not married. If you were married, certain consequences followed. Unless you were one of the rare couples with an antenuptial agreement, the law fixed your rights and duties. Cohabitation, by contrast, allows the parties to customize their relationships. How many actually do so is another question.

What exists now in many states and countries is a complex and flexible situation: a continuum of sexual relationships, from one-night stands to full-blown marriage, with any number of intermediate positions. The traditional family—husband, wife, and children—is distinctly in the minority in some countries, and has been for some time. In Britain, for example, in 1985 only 28 percent of the households consisted of families that were made up of husband, wife, and children. The rest were people living by themselves, unmarried couples living together (some with children), one-parent families, married couples with children (though not necessarily *their* children—some were children of prior marriages, stepchildren, or foster children), and families that included other relatives, often meaning the old folks.[168] Of course there is nothing new about most of these arrangements—there have always been single-parent families, and in the nineteenth century, when so many parents died young, many children were brought up by relatives, or even by strangers. But "open and notorious" cohabitation on the scale of the early twenty-first century definitely marks a change in family life. Millions of people seem to be seizing the right to customize relationships.

Sexual Freedom and the Pull of Commitment

Law and custom in the United States stress the element of *choice. Marvin v. Marvin* was, strictly speaking, a contract case. The court asked: was this a valid contract, and, if so, what exactly were its terms? In one sense, this is all the case decided. But this would, I think, be a rather flat and unrealistic reading. The "agreement" in cohabitation cases is as shadowy and presumptive as the "contract" in the old cases on common law marriage. What the California Supreme Court sensed was that the two people in the case had made a life together, had become some kind of life partners. And if two people live together for years, decades, a lifetime, something gets built up, something grows, matures, and hardens—something permanent, something that deserves legal recognition.

Some countries, as we noted, give substantial rights and recognition to couples who cohabit. But everywhere, simply moving in with somebody does not give you any rights. Commitment is still a key concept. In some countries, the legal distinction between marriage and cohabitation has diminished almost to a whisper—but only for committed couples, for "domestic partners." In the United States after *Marvin,* some commentators assumed, rather hysterically, that almost any kind of sexual relationship—anything beyond a furtive grope in a hotel room—risked the creation of legal rights. But this was never the meaning of the case, and this was never in the cards. Sexual mores, to be sure, have changed enormously—in ways that are repulsive to many traditionalists and that go against the teachings of many religions. Yet the principle of monogamy has shown remarkable strength. Even under the most "advanced" legal arrangements, a line is drawn between commitment and noncommitment, between couples who have some sort of loyalty to each other and those who have "open" relationships or no deep relationship at all. There is, as Stephen Parker puts it, an official "ideology" that one form of family is and ought to be dominant; and the tendency of the law is to "differentiate *marriage-like* cohabitees . . . from others."[169] You no longer have to get "married," in some countries; but you must still take some definite step—cross a threshold, register, undergo a ceremony, execute a document—*something* to indicate a deep desire to share a life.

Is this inconsistent with the trends in the law of marriage and divorce? Both marriage and divorce have gotten easier. Under no-fault, any partner can say good-bye and head for the door at any time, for any cause (or none at all). Is it a contradiction to build up the legal rights of people who are not married at all? But in fact, the changes on the whole have moved in a parallel direction. In a no-fault system, one has total control of personal choices; but property and custody are another question. The same is true of committed relationships. Each "domestic partner" holds the key to the apartment, so to speak; either one has the right to move on or move out, marriage or not. The question is: with what consequences? Are there property rights in joint earnings? And what about the children?

In the contemporary Western world, there is an extraordinary amount of sexual freedom. Almost all forms of sexual behavior between consenting adults are legal, including same-sex behavior. The laws against adultery and fornication have either disappeared or are moribund.[170] Chastity is fighting for its life. But "marriage" in the broadest sense is far from dead. The deep hunger for commitment remains. Even the lonelyhearts ads bear witness to this point. Men and women who place these ads are looking for much more than sex. They are looking for meaning, for emotional attachment, for commitment.

So marriage, in the broadest sense, survives. And the magic number for a marriage is two, not three or six or seven. The sexual revolution has hardly increased the thin supply of free-love communes. Marriage and commitment are for *couples*. This is equally true of the much discussed issue of gay marriage. Gay marriage is a particularly tender and sensitive subject in the United States. It has been more or less validated in some European countries, and recently in Canada. At this writing, there are steps in this direction in the United States—along with a strong backlash (more on this later). The very *idea* of gay marriage has been greeted in some states with the welcome one might give to bubonic plague. But gay and lesbian couples go through ceremonies and profess their love; their ceremonies are even recorded in the solemn pages of the Sunday *New York Times*. Some essential core of marriage, or the idea of marriage, remains alive and vital in Western societies. Traditional marriage, to be sure, has lost its monopoly. It now has to share its privileges with cohabitation, and even with same-sex relationships. It is no longer the exclusive gateway to legal rights.

Of course, marriages and quasi-marriages are not just household, or bedroom, arrangements. They often produce children. There can be, and are, many families without children; there are marriages and quasi-marriages that cannot produce children (marriages of elderly people; most same-sex marriages). But children are at the core of most families, whether the parents are married or not. Children are also important objects of legal attention. The law relating to children, like the law relating to the family in general, has been transformed in modern times. Some of these transformations are the subject of the next chapter.

4

Who Are Our Children? Adoption, Custody, and Related Issues

In English, "children" is a word with two meanings. First of all, it refers to very young people; everybody in a kindergarten class is a child. But it also refers to offspring: the seventy-five-year-old son of a hundred-year-old woman is the woman's child. This double meaning is also found in many other languages (for example, *das Kind* in German). At one time, parental control over children continued as long as the children lived; for example, as mentioned earlier, parents arranged their children's marriages. In those aspects of law that deal with children, there has been a strong, long-term trend toward emancipating the child from its father and from the family in general. The emancipation is absolute for adult children. Adults are under no duty to obey their parents or to take account of them in any way; even the duty to support aged and infirm parents has been evaporating. The state has largely taken over that duty. Older people, retired people, get government pensions in Western countries (in the United States, this is called Social Security). More and more, elderly people tend to live alone or, at any rate, not with their grown children. Adult children also more and more tend to leave the nest. In the United States (though not in many other countries) if an adult male of, say, thirty still lives at home with his mother and father, people consider it somewhat unusual or even peculiar.

Obviously, babies and young children cannot be emancipated. Their parents must manage their lives—feed them, watch them, train them. But even here the law more and more recognizes the child as a distinct individual. It punishes abusive or neglectful parents. It can take children away from a bad family and give them to a good family. It has the ability to act "in loco parentis," as the phrase goes—in place of the parents. In effect, children have legal rights as against their own mothers and fathers. If the children are too young to do it themselves, the state enforces these rights. Also—and this is a critical point—the state has taken over education. It teaches children what they need to know, at state expense. Laws make school mandatory up to a certain age.[1] The state, not the parents, decide what the child will learn, and how the child will learn it. Even for those few children who are home schooled—that is, children whose parents teach them and who do not go to state or private schools—many states require parents to cover certain material, or to file reports with some state or local agency. It also provides curriculum for private and religious schools. What children learn is, to be sure, often a source of conflict.

The general changes in family life we have seen over the past century are relative changes. The authority of the family is weaker than it was, but it is still extremely strong. The state can take a child away from the family; but it does so for the most part reluctantly, and only in extreme cases. This reluctance is, if anything, growing: the days when children could be snatched from the homes of members of Native Americans and given to white families are over. Law and society clearly recognize that in general the rights of parents are sacred. The government has no right to tell parents how to raise their children; the parents, not the state, decide what church to attend or not attend, whom their kids can play with, what clothes they wear, what food they eat. Parental rights are constitutionally protected.[2] Family life and family relations are still, as they always were, central to most people. Modern times have revolutionized the family and changed its shape. New forms of family life have emerged. But nothing has actually replaced the family. Parents have less control over their children (parents of teenagers often feel they have none at all); but parents are still at the center of their young children's lives. Even for millions of older children, parents are a powerful influence on their lives;

and for many parents, children (and grandchildren) are the very core of their existence.

The law that deals with children is complex and has many facets. In this chapter, we will deal only with a few that seem particularly germane to our thesis. We start with the law of adoption.

Adoption

The English common law did not recognize any such thing as adoption. Essentially, in fact, no child could be legally adopted in England; the situation changed only in 1926, when Parliament enacted the Adoption of Children Act.[3] In English law, "children" meant children of the blood, and nothing else. In this regard, the common law stood apart from many other legal systems. In many systems, adoption was recognized as a way to guarantee that a family with no blood children would not die out. Adoption was a well-known feature of ancient Roman society. French law recognizes two forms of adoption. "Simple" (or limited) adoption allows a family to adopt even adults, in order to carry on the family name or for some similar purpose—uncles can adopt nephews, cousins can adopt cousins. Besides limited adoption, there is another kind of adoption: full adoption, or *adoption plénière*, the more familiar kind. Under full adoption, it is always young children who are taken into the family, and the adopting parents are usually childless. Indeed, until 1923 adults were not adoptable in this way at all; and until 1976 parents with children were not allowed to adopt (this was also once the rule in other countries—for example, Switzerland). In Brazil, too, under the 1916 Civil Code, couples with children were not eligible to adopt legally, nor were people under the age of fifty (presumably because they just possibly might have children of their own.)[4] Rates of adoption vary from country to country. Adoption is still rather uncommon in France. French society—like English society at one time—seems to place enormous emphasis on actual blood lines. The United States, by contrast, has four times the population of France but ten times as many adoptions.[5]

Adoption in the United States was altogether lacking throughout the colonial period and into the nineteenth century, just as it was lacking in England. The first true American adoption law, it is often said, was passed in the state of Massachusetts in 1851. But if we look carefully, we can find traces of adoption even before 1851. Certainly, the terms "adopt" and "adoption" were known; and arrangements that were functionally very similar to adoption existed even in the colonial period.[6] Children were commonly bound out as apprentices, for example, which meant that from a fairly early age they were living in somebody else's household.

Other practices came closer to the modern idea of adoption. A number of state legislatures passed private laws that were in effect adoption laws—laws making this or that child someone's heir, or changing the name of a child. Often these were illegitimate children whose father was acknowledging them and taking them into his home; sometimes they were orphaned relatives.[7] There were about 100 of these private laws passed in Massachusetts between 1781 and 1851; in Vermont, a small state, there were over 300 petitions for adoption between 1804 and 1864.[8] The statutes were brief and to the point. To take one example: in Kentucky, the legislature passed a law in 1845 permitting Nancy Lowry to "adopt . . . her step son, Robert W. Lowry, Jr. . . . as her own child, who, in all respects, shall stand in the same legal relation to her as if she were his mother in fact." Robert could inherit from her if she died, "as if he were her own personal issue, born in lawful wedlock." A few states apparently began to generalize the practice. A Mississippi statute of 1846 empowered local courts to change names and also, "upon application of any person, to make legitimate any of their offspring, not born in wedlock." After the court order, the child would be "legitimate and heir or joint heir of the person petitioning." The courts could also, for "sufficient reasons shown," make "any other person the heir" of the person petitioning. This was, in short, a general adoption law in everything but name—the word "adoption" never appears in the statute. A Texas statute of 1850 provided that anybody who wished to "adopt another" and make that person an "heir" could do so by filing a statement in the "office of the clerk of the county court," stating that he or she was adopting this person as a legal heir. Once this was done, the child was a legal heir.[9] But the Massachusetts law was a more elaborate statute, and the first one that required some sort of formal procedure for adoption.

After 1851, there was a strong movement to create adoption laws, more or less on the model of Massachusetts. State after state enacted its own adoption statute. By the end of the century, adoption was universally recognized in the United States; and this is of course still the case. Adoption laws reject the classic common law understanding that blood relationship is crucial, and that people are joined by blood or marriage or not at all. The laws reflect a more fluid and contractual notion of the family. Some of the early statutes were almost nakedly contractual. Under the first Missouri law (1857), the procedure for adopting a child was not much different from procedures for buying or selling a cornfield. Under the statute, if any person "shall desire to adopt a child, as his or her heir" it was to be done by a deed, "executed, acknowledged, and recorded . . . as in the case of conveyance of real estate."[10] In 1917, Missouri enacted a more modern adoption law; instead of a deed, adoption now required a court proceeding; the judge was to decide, "after due hearing," whether the adoptive parents were "of good character" and "of sufficient ability to properly care for, maintain and educate said child," and if the "welfare of said child would be promoted" by the adoption.[11]

This was the trend in the law. More and more, the rules and procedures expressed the idea that the welfare of the child was the paramount interest that these statutes protected. But not entirely. The adoptive parents had rights and interests as well. The same Missouri statute just mentioned, echoing considerations found in marriage and divorce laws, gave the adoptive parents the right to back out. They were entitled to annul the adoption if, within five years, the child developed "feeble mindedness or epilepsy or venereal infection as the result of conditions existing prior to the time such child was adopted." Other states had similar provisions in their laws.

What accounts for the flowering of adoption laws? Adoption, as a legal status, had a definite economic meaning. Adoption was important in

American society (and, later, in other societies) because of its relationship to inheritance and property rights. Adoption was useful for that vast
army of American families that owned a farm, a house, a plot of land in
town, and maybe other assets. This is similar to the point made earlier
about common law marriage and about divorce. The private adoption
laws of the early nineteenth century often mentioned specifically the
right to inherit. The pioneer Massachusetts statute stressed this point.
The statute created a legal procedure for adoption and provided the
adopted child with the right to inherit. It was, however, a rather narrow
right. The child inherited from the adopting parents. Beyond this, the
statute was silent. In some states the issue was resolved rather differently.
New York's adoption statute of 1873 specifically provided that the
adopted child did *not* inherit from the adopting parents. But this provision was sliced out of the statute in 1887.[12]

In general, under all adoption statutes, the adopted child inherits
from the adoptive mother and father. In early statutes, the child also
inherited from birth parents; gradually, adoption came to represent a
sharper break with the past. Law and practice have vacillated, however,
on whether the child also inherits from other relatives in the adoptive
family. If a grandfather—the adoptive father's father, say—dies without
a will and the adoptive father is dead, does the adopted daughter of
the grandfather's son inherit? If the "natural born" son of the adoptive
parent dies, does the adopted child inherit from the brother? The answer
at first was maybe. Some states allowed rather broad inheritance rights;
others did not.[13] Also, does the adopted child inherit from its own blood
relatives? In a number of states, the answer to this question was yes. Under a Texas statute of 1931, when a child was adopted, even though "all
legal rights and duties between such child and its natural parents" were to
"cease and determine," this did not "prevent such adopted children from
inheriting from its natural parent." An adopted child "shall inherit from
the adopted as well as its natural parents."[14] But in other states adoption, as the California statute puts it, "severs the relationship of parent
and child between an adopted person and a natural parent," and for all
purposes.[15]

Suppose a person was the beneficiary of a trust, enjoying its income for life; after the beneficiary died, the property was to go to his or her "children" or "issue" or "heirs." Would this include an adopted child? Strictly speaking, this is a question of interpretation: What was in the mind of the person who set up the trust? If the text gave no clear answer, courts generally refused to include adopted children. This was the thrust of statutes and case law alike. This question, and other questions of inheritance, were contested well into the twentieth century.[16] As of about 1930, there was still considerable vacillation in the laws of the various states. In a number of states, the adopted child still could not adopt from adoptive uncles, aunts, or grandparents; and if the statutes were silent on this point, courts tended to hold against inheritance.[17] But more recent law is quite different. Unless a will, trust, or other document specifically excludes adopted children, these children inherit as if they were children of the physical body. In other words, the law now tends strongly to treat adopted children and "natural" children exactly the same—at least with regard to property and inheritance.

It must be remembered that adoption is a legal status. Nobody needs a court decision or a formal document to take a child into a family, feed it, raise it, and love it. Informal "adoption" was the norm in England and the United States before adoption laws were passed. (In upper-class families, guardianship was one way to provide for orphans.) Informal adoption is still very common in third world countries. In Brazil, for example, in the vast slums of the big cities, children often move from household to household—raised now by a relative, now by a neighbor, particularly when a mother or father is too poor to give them what they need. In these cases, the original family does not really "abandon" the child, no matter how the situation looks to middle-class professionals.[18]

Demographic change has had an important effect on adoption and adoption practices. In the nineteenth century, divorce rates were low, but families disintegrated at a high rate nonetheless. It was the angel of death, not the divorce courts, that produced "broken homes." Orphans were in plentiful supply. Women died giving birth; plagues and accidents carried off fathers and mothers alike. The children left behind were often raised by aunts, uncles, or grandparents. Those who had no relatives to take them in were often sent to orphanages. In the nineteenth century in the United States, many children were sent out of the big city (chiefly New York) into the countryside, to be taken in by farm families. This would be better for these children, it was thought, than life on the mean streets of the city, or in institutions. The farm families rarely adopted these children legally; in many cases, they were little better than servants, cheap labor for the farm. And not all of these children were orphans; some were the children of destitute, often immigrant, parents. In the second half of the nineteenth century, some 90,000 children were placed out by the Children's Aid Society, an organization founded by Charles Loring Brace. Brace's activities were not universally applauded. Many of the children came from Catholic families; the farms they were sent to, and the agencies that sent them, were resolutely Protestant.[19]

This brings up the dark side of adoption. In theory, adoption is an arrangement in which nobody loses: the child gets a good home, the birth parents get rid of a burden or an embarrassment, the adopting parents get the child they want so badly. The guiding principle, as in the law of child custody generally, is the best interests of the child. But it is not always easy to decide what these "best interests" demand. In practice, custody decisions have often been open to serious abuse. These decisions, like so many others in the legal system, are strongly influenced by social norms and prejudices. Courts and social workers tend to define a child's "best interests" in terms of middle-class notions and values. In most situations, there is no conflict: nobody would argue that children who are beaten, tortured, burned with cigarettes, or left to starve are not better off with somebody other than the parents who treated them this way. But there are many marginal situations; and the poor, the socially deviant, and the culturally distinct tended to lose out, in ways that we would now define as unfair, or worse. Charles Loring Brace thought of himself as a noble humanitarian; today we are not so sure he was. The problem has been particularly acute, and the abuses particularly blatant, in the case of children of native tribes, or black children whose parents are poor. Mothers who cannot afford to raise their children, single mothers, women in trouble, have in effect often been forced to give up their babies, who are given to "better" homes.[20] Whatever the legal theory, the best interests of middle-class adopting parents have often trumped the best interests of the birth parents, or perhaps even the best interests of the child.

Adoption laws generally claim to protect the rights of the birth parents, and especially the birth mother. Her consent is necessary for ordinary adoptions. The weak point is the reality of this consent. Social and family pressures can be intense. Families often badgered unmarried mothers to give up the babies and avoid the shame of a bastard child. Poverty and destitution could drive a mother to the same decision. In the United States, as well as in other countries—Australia is a prime example—possibly the worst historical scandal was the way the state dealt with children of native peoples. They were often removed—sometimes kidnapped—from their homes. They were then delivered to boarding schools or foster homes and, eventually, to respectable white families. The point of the boarding schools in the United States was to "civilize" the natives—to teach them how to be, in effect, white, and to get them to unlearn their own languages, religions, and customs.[21] A congressional report estimated that between a quarter and a third of all Native American children were adopted as babies, and almost all of them were given to non-Native families.[22] (Congress passed a law in 1978 that was designed to prevent this from happening).[23] In Australia, between 1910 and 1970, somewhere between one in three and one in ten indigenous children were removed by force from their homes and families. Even as late as 1973, a native boy was kidnapped and sent a thousand miles away to live with a white family.[24] A 2002 movie, *Rabbit-Proof Fence,* told the story of some Australian children, whose fathers were white, who were forcibly removed from their native mothers and sent to boarding schools. The movie was based on actual incidents. Another sad and powerful movie, *The Official Story* (1985), dealt with the children born to political prisoners ("los desaparecidos") in Argentina. These children were given to families of the politically powerful, to be adopted. What all these tragedies have in common is devaluation of the birth parents. In the case of Australia and the

United States, in the days before plural equality, no doubt many people honestly believed they were doing these children a favor. They were taking them out of "primitive" conditions and uncivilized homes and giving them a chance for a better life among people who could give them advantages beyond the reach of their birth parents. These policies were part of a more general policy of assimilation, which meant in practice the destruction of native customs, religions, and languages.

Mainstream adoption in the middle of the twentieth century was quite different from nineteenth-century adoption. Middle-class people were living longer. Death in childbirth had become a rare event. In the age of antibiotics, plagues and epidemics took a more smaller bite out of the population. The supply of orphans dried up. Adoption at one time primarily involved children whose parents were dead or too poor or desperate to keep them. In the twentieth century, adoption became more and more the destiny of children whose parents, for whatever reason, did not want them or were unable to resist social and legal pressures to give up their children. It was frequently the destiny of babies born to teenage, unmarried mothers. And the adopting parents, in many cases, were strangers, not relatives or neighbors. They were childless couples who wanted a baby and could not produce one themselves.[25] A study of adoption in Washington state documents the changes in the practice of adoption. In the 1930s, of birth parents who gave up their babies, 22 percent did so because the babies were illegitimate, 19 percent because the family was breaking up, 13 percent because the parents were poor; by 1970, illegitimacy accounted for 89 percent of the relinquishments of children, and the other motives were insignificant. In the 1930s, 9 percent of the birth parents were widows who could not support the children and 14 percent were widowers who had no way of taking care of the children. In the 1970s, the widowers had disappeared entirely, and the widows had almost disappeared; 85 percent of the birth parents were single women.[26]

More recently, the nature of adoption has changed again, in response to changes in social norms and in demography. For one thing, the birthrate has continued to spiral downward—especially in Western Europe, but generally in all developed countries. Many countries—Italy,

Germany, France—face the prospect of shrinking populations. There are fewer babies generally, so there are fewer babies available for adoption. Moreover, by the late twentieth century illegitimacy had lost most of its stigma. A young middle-class woman who found herself pregnant would in an earlier time have been desperate to get rid of the baby; many hid their pregnancies, gave birth secretly and quietly, disposed of the baby to some agency or a private party, and then tried to get on with their lives. There are still women who feel this way; and in France, women have the right to give birth anonymously (the mother will be listed on the birth certificate as "X").[27] In most Western countries, however, this prime source of adoption babies—young mothers giving birth secretly—has all but vanished. In 1970, in the United States, some 89,000 babies were adopted by strangers. By 1975, this figure had dropped to 48,000. For many years thereafter, it remained more or less constant.[28] In the late 1990s, the figure began to balloon; and the number of adoptions doubled between 1995 and 2001, partly because the government offered money to help move children out of foster care and into adoptive homes.[29] Today, childless middle-class couples who wish to adopt are fairly desperate; they are willing to pay good money to get a baby. It would probably surprise these couples to learn that at one time the flow of money often went the other way: mothers paid people to take their babies off their hands. A study in Chicago in 1917, carried out by the Juvenile Protective Association, unmasked the scandalous behavior of the "baby farms." These organizations were charging money to take babies; the babies were supposed to be resold to adoptive parents. The study found "shocking abuses." Unscrupulous doctors and hospitals "took advantage of the unmarried mother willing to pay any amount of money to dispose of her child."[30] These baby farms made a profit from a "grisly calculus": most babies, in the days before reliable bottle-feeding, simply died when separated from their mothers. Add to this filthy conditions and poor care, and it is no surprise that most babies in baby farms did not survive. Allegedly, up to 80 percent of all babies admitted to one Baltimore baby farm died within weeks. Basically, nobody cared.[31]

All this seems like ancient history. As the demand for adoption increased, these newborn babies became valuable commodities. The adoption rate swelled in the twentieth century, then crested, and began to fall in the latter part of the century. Not that fewer couples wanted to adopt. It was the shortage of babies: particularly, in the United States, a shortage of the most desirable babies—white, middle-class, and newborn. In adoption practice, the ideal is to "match" children to their adoptive parents in race, background, and religion (as if babies have a religion). But all this is not so easily managed nowadays. Parents consequently are more willing to consider adoption across race and ethnic lines—even across national boundaries. In a fluid society, a society committed to plural equality, and a society that no longer punishes interracial marriage, white folks with black children no longer seem quite so extraordinary. The global market in babies is also flourishing. Desperate couples cast about for places with a better supply. After the Second World War, Americans found children to adopt in countries devastated by the war—Greece, for example, or Germany. After the Korean War in the early 1950s, Americans adopted flocks of Korean children.[32] Parents also turned to other poor countries. Latin America was a prime source in the 1970s. Russia and China are important sources today. American parents now commonly fly off to Bolivia, Romania, or China, bringing home children from these countries—legally or otherwise. It is estimated that there are between 15,000 and 20,000 such adoptions each year.[33] Some of these children are orphans; others come from very poor families. A study of Latin American birth mothers who gave up their children found that they were typically young (fourteen to eighteen years old), jobless (or beggars or prostitutes), with no education, and from bad homes themselves. In China, some parents were giving up excess daughters. Some Korean birth mothers were unmarried women, facing the stigma of illegitimacy. Many of these women were destitute; and some of the Korean children were mixed-blood children left behind by American soldiers.[34] The United States, of course, is not the only country where childless couples go abroad to find a supply of children. The leader in the field, in fact, is Sweden; it has the highest ratio of international adoptions to population of any country.[35]

By the 1970s, some white couples were choosing a once unthinkable answer to the problem of the shortage of babies. They were taking children of other races, mostly black, mostly American born. The practice became embroiled in controversy. Originally the objection came from other whites. Race mixing was taboo in many states. Under Texas law, for example, no white child could be adopted by a "negro person, nor can a negro child be adopted by a white person."[36] There were also some biased white judges who simply refused to allow such adoptions to take place.[37] A related issue arose in custody cases when, for example, a divorced white woman awarded custody of her children marries a black man or has a relationship with a black man and the father tries to get custody, claiming that an interracial household is unsuitable.[38] Generally speaking, in the late twentieth century the courts have rejected this notion; race could not be taken into account in this way. The Supreme Court also weighed in on the question. Linda Sidoti and her husband, Anthony Sidoti, were divorced in Florida in 1980; Linda got custody of their little daughter, Melanie. A year later, Anthony tried to get custody; Linda was "cohabiting with a Negro, Clarence Palmore, Jr., whom she married two months later." The trial court gave custody to the father. Despite "strides" in race relations, the judge said, little Melanie was sure to "suffer from . . . social stigmatization." The Supreme Court reversed this decision unanimously: "Private biases may be outside the reach of the law, but the law cannot, directly or indirectly, give them effect."[39]

The Sidoti case was decided in 1984. By this time, the situation had reversed itself. Objections to adoption across race line were coming from blacks, not from whites. The National Association of Black Social Workers condemned transracial adoption in 1972; they labeled it a kind of cultural genocide.[40] To put black children in white homes would cut them off totally from black culture. Sometimes this was true; sometimes not. Some white parents of black children tried hard to expose their children to the world of black America. Whether these attempts were successful—or useful—is another question. These adopted children live lives quite different from the lives of children growing up in a black community. Two authors who studied the problem found it was just "not realistic for a black child in the United States to have two racial identities." Identifying "with the human race" was simply no substitute.[41]

Many of these children surely feel ambiguity, imbalance; many feel that they vacillate between two worlds and do not quite fit into either.[42] Yet on the whole, children adopted across race lines claimed to be happy with their adoptive parents. They were surely better off economically than with their birth parents. Most did not show much interest in finding their biological parents. The overwhelming majority criticized the attitude of the black social workers: one black female called the statement "a crock—it's just ridiculous . . . I am fully comfortable with who I am."[43] Of course, this woman had grown up in a white family; the damage (if it was damage) had already been done.

There were other arguments, too, against transracial adoption—for example, that it reinforced stereotypes. It perpetuated the idea that black mothers were bad mothers and that white mothers were better. In this way, the argument went, black-white adoption propped up white supremacy.[44] The furor over black-white adoption more or less died down after a while. Perhaps it was simply the pressing need for homes for black children that overcame the objections. The Multiethnic Placement Act of the 1990s, a federal statute, waffled a bit on the issue; but it did state that an agency that "receives Federal assistance" was not to discriminate in placement decisions "on the basis of the race, color, or national origin of the adoptive or foster parent, or the child"; the statute was, however, repealed a short time later.[45]

The black social workers were asserting racial pride—and, perhaps, the right of black children to *their* racial pride. That pride would be hard to maintain if black children were to grow up in a white neighborhood with a white family, white friends, and whiteness all around. These children would be lost to the black community. Yet (so the argument went) these children had a right to align themselves with the black community, black culture, black heritage. Native American tribes have taken much the same attitude. And so have many ethnic whites, and religious groups as well.

The argument assumes a distinct black culture in America—and a distinct Navajo culture, a Jewish culture, an Irish Catholic culture. To a certain extent, this is surely true. The *experience* of growing up black, or Jewish, or Navajo, is surely different from the experience of growing up white, or Catholic, or Italian-American. But exactly how different is it? The unspoken premise is that the differences are deep-seated, precious, and fundamental. Another premise is that there are such things as cultural rights. Identity groups have a right to perpetuate themselves, to foster their cultures, to fight against assimilation.

No one can deny some of the cultural differences. There is a Navajo language, and it is totally different from English. There are also native religions and native customs. In the age of plural equality, these differences get far more respect than they once did. In the Indian Child Welfare Act (1978),[46] Congress tried to make amends for the scandalous and tragic events of the past. Native American children were not to be torn from their families and homes. Tribes had the right to transmit language, religion, and culture to their young. The preamble to the act mentioned the "alarmingly high percentage of Indian families" who had lost their children in the past. Children were a "resource," vital "to the continued existence and integrity of Indian tribes." It was official policy, according to the law, to promote "the stability and security of Indian tribes and families" (though the statute also aimed to protect "the best interests of Indian children"). Rules for placement of children were to "reflect the unique values of Indian culture." The act gave Indian tribes "exclusive" jurisdiction of custody cases involving children living on the reservation. Tribes also had the right to intervene—subject to the objection of birth parents—in cases of termination of parental rights or of foster-care placement that took place off the reservation, if the parents were Indians.[47]

There has been a fair amount of litigation under this act, and one rather prominent Supreme Court case. In this case, a Choctaw woman, pregnant with twins, left the reservation in Mississippi and gave birth to the children elsewhere. The father was a Choctaw man. They had never married. Both parents signed a consent form in state court, authorizing the adoption of their children by non-Indians. The Choctaw tribe objected; and the Supreme Court, reading the Indian Child Welfare Act quite broadly, decided in favor of the tribe. The statute, said the Court, gave the tribe a right superior to the state of Mississippi to decide where the twins should live, and with whom.[48]

This was clearly a decision steeped in the ethos of plural equality—as, indeed, was the statute. The statute spoke of the "integrity" of tribal culture—an idea that would have astounded most people in the nineteenth century. This culture included, or could include, what Rachel Moran has called "alternative definitions of family."[49] Case and statute are evidence that official culture (and to a good extent, popular culture) has embraced a multicultural ideal and has decisively rejected the ethos of assimilation. The melting pot is gone. Or rather, it is a different sort of melting pot. There is no longer the belief that, say, Chinese-Americans, blacks, Jews, and Armenian-Americans have to learn to conform to the culture and norms of, say, white Presbyterians of British descent. Also, in a culture of choice, there is more and more a right to choose your roots, your heritage, and to insist on your own uniqueness and the uniqueness of your culture.

But what is culture? It is not something genetic. It is far more malleable than most people imagine. The great-grandchildren of slaves—or Africans—and the great-grandchildren of Jews from Polish villages, or Chinese workers on Western railroads, descend from cultures that were vastly different from each other, and from "American" culture as well. But today, these great-grandchildren are thoroughly American. They dress American, talk American, act American, listen to American music, watch American TV. However much they value their "roots," they are part of a single, overwhelming, pervasive American culture, an almost suffocating presence that surrounds them, influences them, and makes them what they are.

A "multicultural" society is ethos and theory. Reality is quite different. In actual fact, assimilation is rampant and almighty. It destroys everything in its path. Television and the media are so powerful, so pervasive, and so uniform that they threaten to crowd out every last pocket of diversity. The California condor is not the only endangered species in America. The Amish with their horse-and-buggy culture, the speakers of

Gullah dialect or the French of the Louisiana bayous, the surviving frag-
ments of the native Hawaiian or Cherokee language: all these are seriously endangered. Most of the native languages are trudging down the
dusty road to extinction; many of them are already gone. Young people
speak English. They watch TV in English. Minority cultures hang on by
their fingertips; tradition has foundered on the reefs, and the survivors
cling to little bits of wreckage bobbing in the sea. Law and culture recognize a person's right to choose an identity, to hold on to minority forms
of living; but basically, it is simply too late. Minority cultures and identities have in many ways already vanished. They have all become at best
dialects of one huge cultural language: the language of modernity, of
contemporary mores, the ethos of McDonald's, cable TV, popular music, and the Mall of America. Mass culture—the culture of daily life
in America—has overwhelmed these minorities. Nothing can resist the
power of mass society. Regional cuisines, like regional dialects, either
disappear or go national.

In part, the very passion for holding on to cultures and identities bears
witness to the looming danger. Minority cultures and identities cannot
automatically survive. They have to be fought for and defended. Yet the
multicultural ideal is politically and socially powerful. And it is far from
meaningless. It is meaningful that the President might greet his Muslim
constituents on Ramadan and his Jewish constituents on Hanukkah;
that he appoints blacks to his cabinet, and that a Chinese-American
woman in 2003 is Secretary of Labor. In a sense, it is precisely *because*
there is so much assimilation that multiculturalism becomes possible.
True multiculturalism—true diversity—is not an option in any modern
society (or in fact in any society). Our "multiculturalism" means, first,
that we recognize variations (in religion, skin color, cuisine, accent), but,
second, that we consider these variations fairly unimportant. Multiculturalism of the modern Western type could not tolerate something *essentially* different—the habits of Amazon headhunters, for example; and
it has a terrible time coping with a truly fundamentalist form of Islam.

Identity politics appeals to an ethos of rampant individualism. This
includes the individual's right to make choices among a wider menu of

identities. Identity is not necessarily something immutable and inborn. More and more, it is something a person supposedly chooses for him- or herself. The "supposedly" is important. Whether or not people *can* make such choices, practically speaking, is another question. Well-off white middle-class people have more "choice" than, say, poor black people in this society; this is true, for example, of decisions in family matters— whether to keep a child or give it up for adoption; whether to get an abortion; and so on.[50] A person's race is not a matter of choice. A person who is part Italian-American and part Armenian-American can decide to stress one part or the other; but an African-American person of mixed blood does not have this option. Other people will define this person as black, whatever he or she wishes.

Yet it is also true that people *think* they have choices, and that they *should* have choices. How real these are depends on the situation. A black child reared by black parents in a black community cannot decide to be white. That depends not on the child, but on the white community. It is the (majority) white community that defines what it is to be white or black. That community, too, decides how much it will allow "black people" to blend into white society. The same can be said about the Hispanic minority. Yet the rigidity of racial definitions, and the resistance to "race-mixing," is much less pronounced than it was a century ago, or even fifty years ago. Moreover, the *perception* of choice is, as I said, an important social fact, whatever the realities. An African-American woman does have the right to decide for herself when she grows up whether she wants to be a black separatist or to assimilate as much as society will allow; or to try something in between. She has to decide whether to pivot her life around issues of race or focus on something else entirely (feminism, baseball, religion, stamp collecting, jazz, orthopedics). Children adopted across race lines have the same rights, perhaps more so. Children of mixed races have been insisting lately that they should have the right to decide which genetic strain they will push to the head of the line. And, of course, *all* children claim rights of individual choice, in lifestyle and other issues. That much is taken for granted.

Confidentiality and the "Best Interests of the Child"

Adoption became a formal, legal status in the late nineteenth century. Under the early laws, adoption was a matter between the two sets of parents. The court, to be sure, ratified the agreement; but otherwise the state did not play any particular role. Only later did the state insist on a more formal, professional process.[51] Adoption over the course of the twentieth century became more complicated, more enmeshed in legal business. A Minnesota law of 1917 was an important milestone. It required a state agency to investigate the situation before allowing a child to be adopted. The agency had to make sure the child would have a "suitable" home. This law also called for sealed records in adoption cases.[52] Adoption records were to be confidential—kept away from the prying eyes of the public (though not kept secret from the child who was adopted).[53] Even in the 1920s, however, adoptions were still largely informal, except for the court proceedings themselves. Studies in two states, Massachusetts and New Jersey, found that two-thirds of all adoptions were carried out without the involvement of an agency.[54] But the states later began to tighten the screws. In Illinois, under a 1967 statute, a state agency or "licensed child placement agency" had to investigate the adoptive parents and check on their "character, reputation, health and general standing in the community"; their "religious faith," and that of the child, were also relevant; and, in general, the agency had to decide whether the prospective parents were "proper persons to adopt the child."[55]

The trend was, in short, to focus on the child; and this meant controlling the process more rigorously. Baby-trading or -selling was to be outlawed. Some states insisted that only authorized agencies, with a license from the state, could legally place a baby for adoption. The states also quite generally insisted on secrecy. No one, except the people immediately involved, had any business finding out where the adopted child came from or who the birth parents were.

A person who truly believed some of the articles of faith of eugenics—who believed, for example, that bad people passed down their inclinations genetically from generation to generation—would tend to be wary of adoption. They would suspect that the child of defectives would grow up to be defective, whatever the home life of the adoptive parents. Obviously, social workers and others who believed in adoption resisted this notion. They would tend to stress the importance of a good home over the importance of heredity. Eugenics did leave a mark on adoption practice, however. It led social workers and agencies to use and recommend psychological tests to assure adoptive parents that their new children were sound.[56] And it probably also influenced the notion of "matching"—the insistence on placing children with families who were pretty much the same as the child, in brains and background. If intelligence was an inherited trait, it would be best if an adoption agency avoided putting the child of dumb parents into a family of brilliant people. A sound home environment was good for children, of course; but heredity was a complication, and it could not be ignored.[57] The Minnesota law of 1917, mentioned earlier, had a kind of "lemon law" for adopting parents, as did the Missouri law previously mentioned. As in Missouri, adoptive parents in Minnesota could ask a court to "annul" an adoption if, within five years, the child developed "feeble-mindedness, epilepsy, insanity or venereal disease," provided this was due to conditions existing at the time of the adoption and the adopting parents were not aware of the blemish. Eight states had provisions more or less of this type around 1930; and a similar law was passed in California in 1937.[58]

Once a child was adopted, many states insisted on secrecy and sealed records. They wanted the child's prior history wiped off the face of the earth. It was as if the child had come from nowhere and from nobody. One reason for this secrecy was to wipe out the stigma of illegitimacy. Even the birth certificate was doctored in some states; under an Illinois law, the adopting parents could ask for a new birth certificate, one that carried their names instead of the original names that appeared at the time of the child's birth.[59] Adoption in Illinois thus created a new family, and destroyed—obliterated—the old one. No doubt this was what many adopting parents wanted. Mother Nature had played a trick on them, robbing them of the chance to make babies. Adoption gave them the chance to create a family nonetheless. But underlying the legal norms—

of secrecy, faked birth certificates, and the rest—was the notion that a family was in essence a biological unit; at the heart of it was what Barbara Yngvesson has called a "mystical commonality" of mother and child. The secrecy and rewritten birth certificates expunged the birth mother; in this way, as Yngvesson puts it, the adoptive family became a real family, the adoptive mother became a real mother, just as if the family was one that biology had created. The policy of matching babies and families fits in with this conception—the careful way in which social workers and agencies "map adoptive parent onto adoptive child."[60] For the mothers who gave up their children, of course, adoption was often a way out of a difficult situation. It let them hide the dark secret of illicit love, sex, and birth. Sometimes, too, it was a way to give their baby a chance in life that the birth mother or father could not provide.

As in family law in general, the welfare of the child became, in theory at least, the central issue in adoption. Children were not commodities. They did not "belong" to their parents. State agencies had to control the process of adoption, to make sure that these rootless children were placed in good, solid homes; they were not to be bought and sold like cattle. But state caution came up against the great hunger of childless couples for babies. Especially in strict states—states that tried to control the adoption process tightly—a kind of black market in babies developed. There were frequent scandals about baby-selling and the lawyers and others who arranged illegal adoptions. The black market developed because of the high hurdles adoptive parents had to jump over. There were more parents looking for babies than babies of the kind they wanted; official agencies probed and poked about in the lives of couples who wanted to adopt, investigating their habits, checking up on their income, judging the quality of their marriage, and so on.[61] Unlike the lucky people who could produce babies at will, adoptive families had to meet demanding standards. To many childless couples, this seemed tremendously unfair. In defense of the system, one could point to a certain symmetry. Although it is true that anybody who is fertile can have or make babies, nobody has an absolute right to keep and raise children. The state can take children away from bad homes: homes with drunken mothers or fathers; homes that reek of destitution and neglect; homes with filth, cockroaches, and general decay. Children coming out of such hellish homes have a right (according to the theory) to something much better, and the state has an obligation to make sure that these children reach a safer haven in life.

What children need, most people believe, is a real family—a warm, loving, caring, and prosperous family. Not an orphanage. Not foster care, which is (sometimes perhaps unfairly) reviled. Public policy today strongly favors adoption. The Adoption and Safe Families Act, a 1997 federal law, embodies this policy. When President Clinton signed this bill, he also proclaimed a National Adoption Month and announced his "commitment to adoption as a new beginning for thousands of children."[62] Adoption holds up a model: the traditional, two-parent, loving, middle-class family, with stability and permanence. But adoption stands in opposition not only to foster care, but also to the policy of keeping children with their "real" parents as much as possible, even when these parents fall far short of the American dream or the American ideal.

But what of the children in the era of individual choice? Young children have no say in the matter of family; but when they grow up, they behold a whole garden of options. They can, if they wish, get a kind of no-fault divorce from their parents. This is easy to do in this society, even for children who live with their birth parents. Adopted children have this option too—and, now, more and more, they have another choice, a choice that children who live with birth parents do not have.

This is the option to search for, and find, birth parents. Adoption law, in the period after the Second World War, built a wall of secrecy around the adopted child. Adoption records had long been "confidential"—that is, not public. But they were open to the adopted child. That situation changed. The birth was to remain a mystery—even from the person who was born. The child's birth certificate was, more likely than not, a lie. For everybody's sake, the child's origin had to remain a mystery—one that neither the adopted child nor the birth parents could solve.[63] Some adoptive parents even kept the fact of adoption secret from their adopted children. (Most parents, however, did tell their children sooner or later—often with the sentimental story that they "chose" this baby, just like the way mom and dad had chosen each other.)

This period of maximum confidentiality did not last very long. There soon developed a powerful movement to break through the wall of secrecy. Thus now we have so-called open adoption, where the child and the adoptive parents stay in touch with the birth mother. The birth mother may even be treated almost as part of the family. Most adoptions in the past, of course, were not the least bit open. And some adopted children began to search for their "real" parents, and to demand the right to do so. They wanted the public authorities and the agencies to cooperate, even to help them in their search. This desire to search became a kind of social movement in the late 1960s and early 1970s. A leader of the movement was Florence Fisher, who published a book called *The Search for Anna Fisher* in 1973, the story of her quest for her birth mother. Fisher founded an organization called the Adoptees' Liberty Movement Association to lobby for changes in the laws about sealed adoption records.[64]

Social movements, even small ones, never come out of nowhere. What lies behind this one? Birth parents are not just people who have sex and make a baby; they are also pools of genes. Their baby may go to a new home, may call new people mom and dad; but this child carries in every cell the mark of the biological mother and dad. Adoptive children's keen interest in knowing their biological inheritance, their revolt against the wall of secrecy, may be connected to a more general trend toward transparency in government. This is the trend that lies behind the Freedom of Information Act; and the various civil rights movements, grounded as they were in a "vision of egalitarian, participatory democracy," were also something of a revolt against authority and hierarchy. Rights consciousness extended to adopted people as well.[65] A Colorado law of 2000, breaking sharply with the norm of secrecy, gave as one reason the right of adopted children to "make informed medical decisions, determine genetic consequences of certain medical and reproductive decisions, and enjoy the benefits relating to knowledge about one's family history."[66]

The medical motive is genuine enough. As time goes on, more evidence piles up about the genetic element in disease. Genes and chromosomes matter a great deal; and family history is often quite relevant on health issues. Adopted children who lack access to their background are genetic orphans; they feel a need to know what secrets may be locked up in their genomes. The adoptive parents may need this information too. Parents who adopt may learn only later, to their horror, about some awful inherited disease that their child is subject to. In the United States, some adoptive parents have gone so far as to sue adoption agencies, claiming the agencies knew about certain diseases or defects of the child, but kept the news to themselves. Some courts have allowed such suits against agencies, if it can be shown that the agency knew the truth about a child's medical condition and lied about it. In the leading case, *Burr v. Board of County Commissioners of Stark County* (1986), an Ohio county welfare board told Russell and Betty Burr that little Patrick, then seventeen months old, was a "nice big, healthy baby boy," born at a local hospital, that Patrick's mother could not care for him, and that his grandparents were "mean" to him. In fact, the child that the Burrs adopted was retarded, had hallucinations, and was ultimately diagnosed with Huntington's Disease—a death sentence. The story about the parents and grandparents was fabricated; the mother was in fact herself a mental patient, described as "bovine," and of low intelligence. An appeal court affirmed a judgment for a quarter of a million dollars. Adoption agencies are not "guarantors" of the children they place, said the court; but in this case, the agency's fraud and lies deprived the Burrs of "their right to make a sound parenting decision."[67]

A person's desire for "roots," for identity, for a sense of past is also a powerful factor in this movement to rip away the curtain of secrecy. An adopted child can feel cut off from a long chain of history, isolated from the ancestral line, separated from places and people that are part of the child's physical inheritance. The search for background, for ancestors, is a current fashion—and not only for people whose ancestors came over on the *Mayflower* or who might boast of an earl or a prince in the bloodline. The ancestors might have been peddlers, pirates, or slaves; whoever they are, we want to know as much as we can about them. This hunger for identification, for finding one's group or one's "roots," may seem at first out of place in this age of expressive individualism. But modern in-dividualism does not imply a sort of free-floating rootlessness. It means the urge to develop every aspect of the self; and this implies knowing the self, a curiosity about the self, a passion to explore one's past as well as one's future. It means finding an answer to the question "Who am I?" For many adopted children (and many not-adopted children) knowing who they were, where they came from, is extremely important information. It helps the job of self-definition, self-understanding, self-realization. It is for millions of people incredibly interesting to trace one's family back into the darkness of history, to solve the mystery of one's remote origins.

Adopted children, in the age of closed adoptions, were a special case. Their roots—even roots as recent as their own birth—were hidden. For many of them, the mystery cried out to be solved. Not all these myster-ies, however, could be solved; nor were the solutions always neat and sat-isfying. The search may have been particularly important, or difficult, for African-American, Asian, or Latino children raised by white, Western families. These children became aware at an early age of the discordance between their "roots" and the home they lived in. As we saw, some adopted children were looking in earnest for their roots by the 1970s. To be sure, most adopted children did not, in fact, feel the need to search; and those who did were sometimes disappointed. Some no doubt enjoyed learning their "heritage," and perhaps became part of a new or enlarged family. Others found only pain and disillusionment, estrange-ment and crushing rejection.[68]

Adopted children who search for their roots are almost certain to find out what they must have suspected: they were born illegitimate. To be sure, by the late twentieth century in the developed countries, this did not matter very much. Illegitimacy had lost most of its stigma. The ille-gitimate child was once called *filius nullius*—nobody's child. Illegitimate children had, for example, no right to inherit from anybody, even from their mother. Not even their mothers were legally their parents. But the concept of *filius nullius* is long since gone. Today the illegitimate child is definitely somebody's child—the child of a real mother and, very often, a flesh-and-blood father too.

The late twentieth century was a period that stressed the concept of free choice, as we have said.[69] In such a period, it seemed paternalistic, authoritarian, and downright offensive to hide from people such important information as who they were, who gave birth to them, and where and why their mother (and father, perhaps) gave them up. If an adopted child tore away the veil of secrecy that hid the facts of their past, they had, in effect, the chance to choose between two identities, perhaps two religions, two ethnic groups, two races, two mothers, and occasionally two fathers as well.

This right to know was not cost-free. It could be very painful, both for the searcher and for the people searched for. And it was a right that conflicted with other possible rights—the rights of the birth mother, for example, or what she considered her right: the right to keep her secret hidden, the right to a kind of privacy. As we noted, in France, a woman has the right to give birth anonymously. Anonymous birth conflicts with the child's right to know; and a debate has taken place in France on this issue. What should have priority, the mother's choice (anonymity and privacy), or the child's choice? Recent French law has tried to reach some sort of compromise.[70]

In an interesting Dutch case, a young woman had been raised, and adopted by, foster parents. When she reached eighteen, she looked for and found her birth mother. She wanted very much to know who her biological father was. The mother refused to tell; she claimed she had been raped. The daughter asked the court to force her mother to give the name. The court refused. Yet in a later case a Dutch court was somewhat more willing to issue an order to divulge the name. Here too the mother claimed she had been raped, and gave this as a reason for keeping silent. But she had never reported the rape, in fact never mentioned it until late in the proceedings. The court thought she was lying.[71] In a German case before the Constitutional Court, a grown daughter brought a complaint against her mother. The daughter was illegitimate. Her mother had given her up; she had been raised by foster parents. She wanted to learn the name of her father, for personal reasons and perhaps for inheritance purposes. The mother resisted. During the time when she became pregnant, she said, she had had sexual relations with a number of men. Some of these men had since married and "lived in intact families." The mother's privacy rights (and the privacy rights of her lovers) collided with the daughter's (claimed) right to know the truth. The Constitutional Court did not really resolve the issue. Instead, it sent the case back down to the lower court, instructing it to consider a whole range of factors and to exercise a fairly broad discretion in reaching a decision.[72]

American law also reflects the clash between privacy and the adopted person's right to know. Some of the state statutes try for a balance of interests. Tennessee passed a law in 1996 granting to adopted children, when they became adults, access to their original birth certificates and other adoption records. The law also provided for a "contact veto." The birth parents could register this "veto," and if they did, the children would not be able to get in touch with the birth parents; it was a violation of the law to do so.[73] A birth mother calling herself Promise Doe and several other birth mothers, brought suit, claiming that the law was unconstitutional. It violated their right of privacy, they claimed. In 1997, a federal court denied their claim.[74] A birth, said the court, is "simultaneously an intimate occasion and a public event"; the government "has long kept records of when, where, and by whom babies are born." There is no "general right to nondisclosure of private information." Promise Doe and her fellow plaintiffs then tried the state court and the state constitution; but here too they lost.[75]

The Tennessee law tried to balance privacy and choice. Not everybody agrees with the law, the Tennessee court decision, and the attitude underlying these. An organization that calls itself "Bastard Nation: The Adoptee Rights Organization" is in strong opposition. It argues (on its Web site) that it would be wrong to "deprive one group of their rights in order to protect others from possibly having to face the consequences of their past choices."

In the next chapter, we will deal in more detail with other aspects of "privacy." With regard to adoption rights, however, in recent years choice has tended to trump privacy. The decay of sexual prudery has meant that society places less value on hiding a mother's guilty secret. Unmarried women giving birth are no longer social pariahs, and no longer need to keep their behavior quite so secret.

The Primacy of Choice

Choice is a pervasive concept in modern society. Of course, as mentioned earlier, freedom to choose cannot be absolute—if for no other reason than that my choice may encroach on your choice, my right may diminish your right; law and society may be forced to balance or elect one over the other. This was the case, for example, in the area of adoption rights.

Choice also, as pointed out earlier, is hemmed in by invisible barriers, unseen walls of culture and concept. Nonetheless, the domain of choice has widened in contemporary society. Areas of life that were once fixed at birth are now flexible, malleable. This is even—or especially— true of such matters as religion. The idea of an American Christian becoming a Muslim or a Buddhist would have been at one time absurd, or pathological. It no longer seems so absurd—or even unusual. The United States is, in general, a deeply religious country, compared to other countries of the Western world. From a relatively early date, waves of religious zeal have swept across the country—notably the first and second Great Awakenings. In our day, there is a kind of third Great Awakening.[76] But the zeal for religion is intensely personal; it is a search for a source of spirituality that fits the particular individual. The United States has been a fertile breeding ground for brand-new religions: Christian Science and the Latter-Day Saints (Mormons) are just two examples. This too is a symptom of the fluidity of religious ideas in America. There are hundreds of religions in the United States. None are "official." All (or almost all—"cults" are an exception) are considered worthy of respect. This means, then, that what is important is religion per se. Americans now seem more willing to vote for a Catholic, a Buddhist, or a Jew—but only if such a person appears to be serious about religion. To many Americans, all religions seem to have some sort of common base. The choice between them is not theological, it is personal. Hence, according to

Amanda Porterfield, "the barriers between traditions" have appeared to get lower, and "people crossed into other people's religious territories with remarkable ease"; obedience to "religion authority" has declined, and "respect for religious difference increased."[77] There is no such thing as a heretic any more. People marry across religions with great ease. Most people, to be sure, are not shopping around for a new religion. They stay with the one they were born into; but the option to shift is always there. Family tradition, in other words, does not inevitably control spiritual life; birth does not fix, once and for all, what faith one has, or the things one believes in.

Family may have less control over what the child is, becomes, believes, and does; but the family itself is normally not a matter of choice. You have a mother and father, grandparents, ancestors, brothers and sisters, cousins: this is ordinarily fixed and unchangeable, established once and for all the day your umbilical cord is cut; in fact, nine months before that. Nobody can blithely take on a new family—mother and father, relatives, uncles and aunts. The adopted child is an exception, one of the rare creatures for whom a choice might be possible. The rest of us, of course, cannot get ourselves reborn. But in a broader sense, in a highly mobile society a kind of choice *is* available. We can, as adults, decide how much family we want, how close we want to be with our families of origin. We can cling to our parents, our brothers and sisters, and so on; or we can move away, make ourselves scarce, confine our connection to a postcard or two and an occasional phone call. We can even reject our family entirely. All of this more or less as we see fit. The choice of estrangement—of shucking off the family—was almost impossible in a traditional society. It was also basically unthinkable.

The United States is more extreme in this regard than most Western countries. Adult children, even unmarried ones, do not usually live with their parents. In other countries, as we have seen, this is less common; but in every developed country, the ties of the extended family have gotten weaker. No doubt there is a difference between, say, Italy and Sweden; but the trends are everywhere the same. In the United States, it is not at all unusual for adult brothers and sisters to have little or nothing to do with each other; and it is very common for them to live thousands of miles apart. Millions of Americans also choose to live alone (or feel they have to). Millions choose to absorb themselves not in their family of origin, but only in the family they make for themselves: their spouses and children.

The idea of choice extends also to the decision to have a child. Adoption itself is, after all, all about choice. Fertile couples can choose to have children or not have children; to have one child, or two, or three, or however many they want. They can even choose to adopt. Adoption essentially levels the playing field between fertile and infertile couples—in theory at least. (The law and the supply of babies make adoption a lot harder than giving birth.) For fertile couples, contraception and abortion help make their choices realistic. It is hard to think of a technology that has had more influence on the modern world than contraception. Pills and condoms go a long way toward making parenthood voluntary. Along with adoption, in vitro fertilization, surrogacy, and the like, contraception moves childbearing from the realm of fate to the realm of choice. And more and more it has become *individual* choice, not a choice made jointly by two people. Joint decisions are still the usual case; a small but growing number of single women, however, decide to have a baby with or without a partner. Even for couples, either one, practically speaking, often has a veto right within the relationship. There can of course be trickery and pressure on one side or the other. Many women throughout history have had children forced on them through rape. There is no exact equivalent for men. No doubt some women (for example) secretly stop taking the pill and become pregnant against the wishes of their partners. But this is hardly the usual case.

Childbearing, then, has become a matter of choice, not a matter of fate. It is a matter of consent—normally. In Israel, a married couple, Danny and Ruti, wanted to have children. But Ruti, for medical reasons, was about to undergo a hysterectomy. This would normally mean an end to any hope of having babies. So, before the operation, Ruti went through a complex procedure to have eggs removed from her body. Danny's sperm then fertilized these eggs, which were frozen and held for possible implantation in a surrogate mother. Unfortunately, the marriage later broke up. Ruti still very much wanted a child and proposed using the fertilized eggs for this purpose. Danny refused to agree. Ruti brought suit to gain possession of the fertilized eggs, which were held by a hospital. Danny opposed this idea. In the end, after many stages of legal process, the Israeli Supreme Court held in favor of Ruti. It upheld her right to become a parent. Danny in this case had no right to prevent her—or to prevent himself from becoming a father, the father in fact of Ruti's child.[78] Without modern technology, the case could not have arisen. But the case is not about technology: it is about individual wants and desires and, above all, about choice—or, rather, it is about choices that came in conflict with each other. It is also about the role of courts in modern societies. In a traditional, hierarchical society, there are clean lines of authority, and clear answers to questions about who gets to decide. The more a society exalts choice, consent, volition and the more it reduces the vast molecules of society to individual atoms (legally speaking), the more it opens the door to collisions between volitions, to rights and choices that bump up against other rights and choices. Who then gets to decide? In instance after instance, in the world as it is today, the answer is: a judge.

Illegitimacy

Illegitimacy was at one time a powerful stigma. Bastard children were a living symbol of family dishonor and a social disgrace. They were a threat to a patriarchal order, and a threat to regularity in inheritance. They were the product of immoral, and illegal, sexual relations. The bastard was nobody's child, a miserable pariah stripped of the normal legal rights of legitimate children. The stigma remained strong in the nineteenth century, and even well into the twentieth.[79]

In the American South, during the days of slavery, the law did not recognize the right of slaves to marry. There were, of course, slave "marriages," that is, loving, long-term relationships; and some masters even encouraged these "marriages," which produced more slave children and tended to make slaves more productive and obedient.[80] But until the end of slavery, these relationships had no legal recognition whatsoever. Hence, technically, all children of slaves were illegitimate. This included the many children of slave women whose fathers were white slave owners, overseers, or other white family members. By law (and custom), all children of slave women, including these mixed-blood children, were slaves from birth. It would have been anomalous (and costly) to recognize these children as free because they had free fathers. As early as 1662, a law of Virginia made the point explicit: the children of slaves were also slaves: the "condition of the mother," not the father, was decisive.[81] To be sure, a few white fathers of slave children treated them with love, acknowledged them, cared for them, and set them free; sometimes these fathers even attempted to give them or leave them money and property. But slave owners usually ignored these children or, rather, treated them as they treated any other slaves. When slavery was abolished, the southern states validated slave marriages; the children of these marriages became legitimate.

In the later twentieth century the legal (and social) situation of the illegitimate child altered radically, as we mentioned. In an age of cohabitation, there is no place in the legal order for the concept of bastardy. In Western countries, the legal disabilities of the illegitimate child have essentially disappeared. These disabilities were peeled away one by one until, in contemporary society, illegitimacy, practically speaking, no longer exists. Under the English Family Law Reform Act of 1987, for example, a child whose parents are and remain unmarried (to each other) has essentially all the rights as any other child. (One exception is that the bastard son of a duke or an earl cannot inherit the title, an exception that makes little difference to the common person.)[82] The development in most countries followed a standard pattern. "Nobody's child" first gained rights to be the child of its own mother—inherit from her, for example. Then came rights to inherit from other relatives as well. The illegitimate child still has a somewhat more complicated legal situation than the child whose parents are married. But this is a fact problem, not a social problem. Often, nobody knows who the father is. Often, too, the putative father can choose to accept or disown the child.

The issue of legitimacy has constitutional significance in some countries. Article 53 of the Costa Rican Constitution provides that the "obligations owed by parents to their children born out of wedlock are the same as those owed to children of their marriage." In the United States, the Supreme Court has come to a similar constitutional conclusion. In *Levy v. Louisiana* (1968), Louise Levy was the unmarried mother of five children. She raised these children and supported them by working as a domestic. When she died, her children tried to bring a wrongful death action. But under Louisiana law, only legitimate children had the right to do so. The Supreme Court struck down the law. The Louisiana law, said the Court, was illegal discrimination; it violated the equal protection clause of the Fourteenth Amendment.[83]

Illegitimate children, of course, are innocent victims of circumstances; they have no say in the way they were born or conceived. But this innocence was not the underlying reason for the decision in *Levy*. In a companion case, the mother of an illegitimate child sued for damages after the death of the child. But she too, the Court ruled, could not be deprived of this right. Louisiana, in fact, was a laggard. State laws in general had removed the legal curse from illegitimacy. There are differences in detail, but the classical legal disabilities that dogged the life of the illegitimate child are gone.

The number of illegitimate births has risen sharply in the twentieth century. Here we have to distinguish between two very different situations. In one situation, quite common in Scandinavia, the parents live together, are committed to each other, share a life, but never bother to get married. Their lives are not very different from the lives of married people. To children in a stable, loving household, it can hardly make much difference whether Mother and Father have a marriage license and went through a ceremony or not. So the fact that in Iceland in the late 1990s over 60 percent of all children were born outside of marriage, and in Sweden over 50 percent, does not mean these children are the product of "broken homes."[84] It does mean that "marriage" (in the traditional sense) means less and less, socially and legally, in these countries. Nor can it matter much in Iceland, for example, whether a child is "legitimate" or not. If more than half of all children are "bastards," as they are in Iceland, it can hardly be much of a stigma.

Quite different is the case of children who, as the phrase goes, never had a father, or whose father was a bird of passage. A few of these are children of single women who wanted very much to have children, but either preferred to do without a husband, or simply had no obvious candidate available. These mothers are usually middle-class women. The biological father may be a medical student, donating sperm to a sperm bank. In addition, many poor women have babies from men who come and go or who drop out of the picture once the baby is born, or who, because of the woman's promiscuity, cannot be identified. Added to these are the very large number of children whose parents are divorced. Most of these children live with their mothers. Some have close ties with their fathers; some do not.

Families with one parent, especially families headed by a single mother, tend to be poor. Illegitimacy may not be a stigma; but these children do not need stigma to be very badly off. Their family is poor; their life chances are stunted and precarious. Correlations between poverty, crime, social disorganization, and single-parent families are stark and real. But the social problem is not illegitimacy; it is these children's severe social handicaps: no money, no opportunities, no networks, no access to quality education. With or without parents, poverty is bad for children.

What about the children of divorce? There is a raging controversy over the impact of divorce on children. They are legitimate, but they live in "broken homes." Does this scar them for life? Does it hurt their life chances? Are they likely to be badly adjusted, unhappy, neurotic? Some scholars think these children are at risk. Divorce, according to Judith Wallerstein and Sandra Blakeslee, robs children of something that is "fundamental to their development—the family structure." Their world tends to be, at least temporarily, "without supports." These are damaged children who tend to "grieve over the loss of the family"; this can work permanent injury.[85] Other scholars read the evidence quite differently. Children do not like divorce, yes, but most of them learn to cope and get on with their lives. Wherever the truth may lie, divorce is part of the lives of millions of children.

Child Custody

The changing nature of the family has also deeply marked the rules about child custody. At the beginning of the nineteenth century, in cases of child custody, preference was given to the father.[86] If a husband and wife separated, the children belonged as of right to the father, not to the mother. Indeed, not until 1839 did Parliament pass a law allowing a mother separated from her husband to petition a court for the right to have some access to her children.[87] The only exceptions to the general rule were the rare cases where the father was totally unfit—a criminal or a hopeless drunkard, for example.

In the course of the nineteenth century, custody doctrine shifted dramatically. The new rule ostensibly favored neither parent. The guiding principle was to be the "best interests of the child." In practice, women usually got custody, partly because men did not want it and partly because courts (and society in general) felt that children of "tender years" belonged with their mothers.[88] The shift in rules represented a shift in family life generally. The earlier law more or less reflected a kind of patriarchal family, with the father as the unquestioned head. His right trumped the mother's right. But as the years went by, this notion seemed more and more unsuitable. For one thing, it contradicted the Victorian image of motherhood. As a petition to the New York legislature put it in 1854, "There is no human love so generous, strong, and steadfast as that of the mother for her child."[89] Custody law thus shifted in such a way as to empower mothers—to recognize their special claims. But it also made the child the focus of legal attention. The child's interests, as opposed to the interests of the parents, had independent value and had to be recognized.

Most of the "patriarchal" decisions reported in cases in the early years—especially in England—came out of upper-class families. Fathers got custody in these cases, but nobody really expected fathers to take care of small children—to feed the babies or wipe their noses. Divorce was rare; legal separation was also exceptional. Men who were awarded custody of children had servants, or at the very least women relatives—a mother, a sister, or perhaps a new wife—to take over the job of actually raising the children. In the course of the nineteenth century, however, divorce became more common; it began to descend down the social scale. By the end of the century, working-class divorce was common in the United States (not yet in England). Divorce is the chief producer of custody disputes. In these cases, courts gave more and more recognition to the mother—the actual caregiver. Mothers were going to raise the children anyway; there were few fathers who could and would do so. It is not surprising, then, that the cases referred more and more frequently to mother love—how important it was, how precious; and that the doctrines of custody shifted in the direction of the mother. Children needed mothers more than they needed fathers.

The law in each country has its own peculiarities. But the broad lines of development are quite similar everywhere. Patriarchy as a legal doctrine has diminished all over the developed world. It has also become less of a social fact, though it is still quite powerful, and in some third world countries (Saudi Arabia, for example) it has hardly given way at all. Custody rules follow one general trend, at least in the wealthier countries. Some countries have been slower to change than others. In Taiwan before the 1990s there was a fairly strict rule giving preference to fathers. In 1994, the Grand Justices of Taiwan declared this rule unconstitutional; it was unlawful discrimination against women. The legislature then amended the law and adopted a new standard: the "best interests of the child." After this change, mothers began gaining custody in the overwhelming majority of cases.[90] In many countries, generous family allowances and day-care facilities make life a lot easier for single parents with custody of children. The United States is something of a laggard in this regard. Only recently was there any legal provision for maternity leave (or paternity leave, for that matter).[91]

In Taiwan, the new custody rule reflects social practice. Mothers are the primary caregivers (and always have been). This is true in all developed countries, including the United States and Canada. There are single fathers (or even not-single fathers) who raise and care for the kids; but they are very much in the minority. In theory, of course, fathers have the same rights as mothers. Mothers get custody not because the law says they should, but because fathers agree to this arrangement. Where fathers do contest and fight for their custody rights, they have a good chance to win, at least in the United States. There is also a great vogue for "joint custody" in the United States: that is, giving a divorced father and mother the same *legal* claim on the child. Here, as often, California was a pioneer: an amendment to the Civil Code in 1980 announced a "presumption" that "joint custody is in the best interests of a minor child," provided the parents agree to this arrangement.[92] By 1988, laws expressed such a preference in no fewer than thirty-six states;[93] and there is a similar preference in Finnish, Swedish, and German law.[94] Some states, however, have had second thoughts, and repealed the presumption.[95] And since a child cannot be in two places at once, joint custody in practice is not necessarily the same as joint custody in theory. Joint physical custody often means a lot of moving about—one day here, another day there. Most parents instead choose joint *legal* custody. One parent has the main burden—the child actually lives with that parent—but the other parent tries to play an important role in the child's life and has joint responsibility for important decisions (about schooling, for example). To be sure, in California the statute defines joint custody to mean "joint physical and joint legal custody,"[96] but the court can, if it wishes, distinguish between the two; and many couples do so in practice.

As we have seen, family law in the twentieth century has expanded the very definition of a family. The traditional "family" can no longer claim, in most Western countries, a monopoly of legitimacy. There are all sorts of new modalities. Many people are disturbed by the trends of the time. They object to the new modalities on moral or religious grounds; they usually argue that these new forms of family life are bad for society as well. Most people probably think children do best in traditional families: one man and one woman, married to each other and living together in a home. Millions of people think other arrangements are unacceptable, or bad for children.

But are the new, unorthodox families really so different from traditional families? I have already expressed some doubts. The key factors in family life are commitment, stability, and love. The law in some countries is receptive to "alternative" families, so long as they include some sort of commitment. "Domestic partners" can be a man and woman (married or unmarried), or two men, or two women. But they are supposed to be real partners, life partners, not two people who live together casually or temporarily. This is an issue with regard to marriage; but clearly, "best interests of the children" also means stability, commitment, and an atmosphere of nurturance and love.

Should same-sex couples be allowed to adopt children? This is a particularly controversial issue.[97] Some countries—for example, the Netherlands—explicitly forbid it.[98] In the United States, Florida bans the practice, and quite baldly: "No person . . . may adopt if that person is a homosexual."[99] But in other states, the issue is not so definitely foreclosed. In a state that allows the practice, a child can end up with two mothers and no father, or two fathers and no mother.[100] A similar question arises when a divorced woman with custody of children takes on a woman partner. The ex-husband sometimes swoops in and tries to get custody, on the grounds that his ex-wife's lifestyle is immoral, or bad for the children. The cases go both ways. The more recent ones show a good deal of tolerance.[101]

Traditionalists are horrified at the idea of same-sex marriage, and they do not want same-sex couples to adopt. These arrangements strike them as a sure sign of moral decay, not to be allowed by a civilized state. To legitimize such "families" would be revolutionary, and totally destructive—so they believe. But is this so? How "revolutionary" are these alternative families? In Israel, in the early years of Zionist immigration and socialist zeal, children were communally raised in some *kibbutzim* (agricultural settlements).[102] Children did not live with their parents; they lived with each other, under the care of child-care workers. Their parents basically had visiting rights. This was indeed a radical break with the traditional family: a real experiment in new ways to raise children. (The experiment has since been largely abandoned.) But what is so radical about two women who adopt or produce a child, so long as they live together in a long-term relationship? Two people (of whatever sex) raising children in a safe, comfortable home: in one sense, this is no innovation at all. Is it good for the children? Any warm, supportive environment is good for children. For the child, then, there is not much difference between orthodox and unorthodox families. For the *parents*, there may be big differences; for the children, no.

Traditionally, only legally married people had the right to have children—legitimate children, at any rate. Modern law and practice in some countries have given the right to others, too: to unmarried people and same-sex couples, through adoption, for example. These practices and laws expand the domain of choice. They give options to people who lacked these options before. Everywhere in the developed world, the trends are in the same direction—but not without struggle, backlash, and bitter opposition.

Biology Is Power

In the traditional family, children born to a married man and woman were legitimate. The husband was legally the child of the father.[103] Except in rare cases, the wife could not bastardize her own children by admitting she had lovers.

This was before the days of DNA testing. Paternity is often a matter of some doubt. Science has come to the rescue, and taken away some of the doubt. It is now possible, in many cases, to show that the husband is not the real father at all.[104] Still, asking who the biological father is may not be the right question. There are good reasons why a legal system might not want to let married women cast doubt on paternity. Two principles are in conflict here: biological and social parenthood—or, if you will, biological parenthood versus the welfare and interests of the child. The child may have an interest in finding or knowing his or her "real" father; but the child also has an interest in a stable home, and nothing, one imagines, could destabilize a home more than the mother's confession of adultery, or that her husband was raising another man's child, like a cuckoo in the family nest.

Arguably, social parenthood should trump biological parenthood. The father who gave his genes to the child has contributed far less than a man who raises and nurtures a child. But the pull of biology is powerful. In *People v. Sorensen*, a California case from 1968,[105] the defendant, Folmer Sorensen, was convicted of a crime—willful failure to provide for his child. Sorensen had been married; but medical evidence showed he was sterile. Somewhat reluctantly, he agreed in writing to let his wife have a child through artificial insemination. She gave birth to a baby boy. Several years later, Sorensen's wife left him. At this point, Sorensen got a divorce. She made no claim for support money—at the time. Later, though, she became sick and unable to work; she then asked Sorensen to contribute child support. Sorensen refused; and this was the basis for the criminal action. The California Supreme Court upheld his conviction. Sorensen was the legal father of the child. The child was Sorensen's legitimate son. The "anonymous donor of the sperm" was no more "responsible for the use made of his sperm than is the donor of blood or a kidney." The social father was the real father, the responsible father, even though the child owed nothing to him, biologically speaking. The Sorensen case represents the prevailing rule. If the mother is married, and if her husband has agreed to insemination, when a child is born, the child is legally his. He cannot back out or disclaim it.

As a general rule, a sperm donor is entirely anonymous. There have been a few cracks in the wall of anonymity, but not many and not very deep. No doubt many children born through this route have wondered or daydreamed about their unknown fathers. Some sperm donors have surely also imagined and wondered about their long-distance and indirect children. In at least one case, a sperm donor succeeded in getting a court to recognize him as a father. But this was an unusual case; the plaintiff had donated his sperm to a woman he knew, who lived with another woman and who wanted very much to have a baby. He agreed not to assert parental rights, but changed his mind once the baby was born.[106] He was not, of course, an anonymous donor.

The Illinois case of "Baby Richard" created something of a stir, in Illinois and elsewhere.[107] Otakar and Daniella, Czech immigrants, were living together; Daniella became pregnant. The couple split up. Daniella gave birth, but gave up the child, "Baby Richard," for adoption. Apparently she lied to Otakar, and told him the child had died at birth. Otakar was suspicious, investigated, found out the child was alive, and hired a lawyer to pursue the issue of custody. The adoptive parents resisted. By the time the case worked its way through the Illinois court system, the baby had spent years with his adoptive parents. The Illinois Supreme Court decided in favor of Otakar, the biological father. This set off a storm of protest and caused vigorous debate in Illinois (and elsewhere).

Why was this decision so unpopular? It wrenched a child from the arms of its "social" parents, the only parents it had ever known, and handed the child over to a stranger, a man who had never married the mother and whose claim was based on sheer biology—a random sperm cell in the night. Legally speaking, Otakar had a strong case. In this day and age, whether he and Daniella were married makes relatively little difference—at least to a father who acknowledges his child and asserts parental rights. Otakar had never given away his "natural" right to his "natural" son. Under state law, a parent only forfeits a child if he or she is evil or abusive, or consents to adoption. Otakar was in neither category. An Alabama court in 2001 came to a similar conclusion.[108] Here too a mother lied: she told an adoption agency she had no idea who the father was; and she told the father the child was born dead. The father was suspicious in this case too; he asked for a death certificate, checked state records, got in touch with funeral homes. After a long legal battle, he won custody of his child. This was, in some ways, a tougher case than Baby Richard's: this father, unlike Otakar, had behaved badly during the pregnancy. He was abusive to the mother, who had him once arrested for assault. But an abusive boyfriend is not necessarily an abusive father; in any event, the court felt that his behavior did not disqualify him and cost him his child. These two cases once more illustrate two principles stressed in these pages. First, "rights" and "choices" often collide, and expanding the zone of choice expands the collision zone as well. And second, the courts, for want of any alternative, emerge as institutions that resolve

Once the court eliminated the contract, it was left with a more conventional dispute over custody. There was a biological father, William Stern, and a biological mother, Mary Beth Whitehead; they had a child, but they were not living together; and they were at loggerheads over custody. This was (said the court) no different from a divorce case; and the sole consideration should be what was in the child's best interests. The court gave custody to William Stern; but Mary Beth Whitehead retained her rights as a mother, which included visitation rights. Mrs. Stern, the forgotten third party, had no right to adopt the child. Baby M. would never be legally hers.

The *Baby M.* case was something of a sensation—the media carried stories about it, and it was widely discussed in both legal and nonlegal circles. As a New Jersey decision, it was decisive only in New Jersey. Other states have faced the issue with varying results. In some states, the issue has never been resolved. In others, surrogacy is legal. In one California case in 1990, the surrogate mother, still pregnant, asked a court to declare the contract void and to grant her rights to her baby. The judge turned her down flat, gave custody to the genetic parents, and upheld the contract.[111] Other judges have been leery about surrogacy. Legislatures, too. It is the sort of practice that legislatures find easy to forbid and hard to legitimate. The opposition has a loud voice; and the supporters tend to be quiet, if not downright bashful. Some state laws have flat-out forbidden contracts of surrogacy. In other states the agreement is legal, but subject to conditions—in some, it is forbidden to pay the surrogate mother anything beyond her expenses.[112] Florida allows a "binding and enforceable gestational surrogacy contract." But such contracts are only legal if the "commissioning mother" is infertile or if pregnancy would hurt her or her fetus; and the "commissioning couple" may only agree to pay "reasonable living, legal, medical, psychological, and psychiatric expenses" of the surrogate mother, expenses that are "directly related to prenatal, intrapartal, and postpartal periods."[113]

Surrogacy is a going concern, however, despite the legal battles. The surrogate mother is usually the biological mother; in a few cases, she is merely a "gestational surrogate"—that is, the eggs belong to some other woman, and the surrogate is only renting out her womb. Either way, infertile couples who are desperate for a baby sometimes seize on the practice as a last resort. They may be blocked from the adoption market; or they may feel that half a loaf is better than none: the father at least can make a baby. An January 2003 ad in the *SF Weekly*, a free newspaper in San Francisco, offered $22,000 to young women willing to be surrogate mothers: "Be Someone's Miracle. . . . Help an infertile couple create a family."[114] A report in New Jersey in 1992 studied "broker/intermediaries" who arranged surrogate deals. They charged substantial fees. The report estimated that "as many as 1,200 children" had been "born through brokered arrangements," and probably another 1,000 had found surrogates without the help of brokers. A nontrivial number of surrogacy contracts—about 4.5 percent, apparently—had ended up as lawsuits or complaints; but these were mostly settled out of court.[115]

Surrogacy has been an issue outside the Untied States as well. In 1989, an estimated 1,000 babies were born to surrogate mothers in Germany; organizations were in place to make surrogacy deals, despite severe legal obstacles. In the Netherlands, surrogacy contracts are invalid; and the surrogate mother is the legal mother of the child. The only way to change the situation is to go to court and pursue regular adoption proceedings. Nevertheless, as in the United States, the practice continues, whatever the law may say. In France, for example, in 1982, a thirty-one-year-old woman bore a child for an anonymous couple; she was paid 50,000 francs. So long as the surrogate mother goes through with the deal, there is no lawsuit, whether or not surrogacy is "legal." Infertile couples are sometimes willing to take the risk. In a few countries, statutes explicitly legalize surrogacy, under certain conditions. One such country is Israel, by virtue of a 1996 law. By 2001 some thirty children had been born under this law in Israel. The battle over surrogacy continues, and will continue, for some time.[116]

What is especially interesting about surrogacy is that it has little or nothing to do with technology. As writers on surrogacy seem fond of pointing out, something like surrogacy is as old as the hills: Abraham's wife, Sarah, in the Old Testament, was barren; she told Abraham to take her servant, Hagar, and make a baby with her.[117] (Gestational surrogacy, of course, is a different story; it does require technological magic.) Artificial insemination, a crucial aspect of modern surrogacy (Abraham's technique was older and cruder), is also nothing new; breeders have been inseminating animals for about two centuries, and for humans the practice is more than fifty years old. All artificial insemination, after all, is a matter of surrogacy—as far as the father's role is concerned. But the idea of a woman surrogate would once have been utterly unthinkable. Selling an egg or a womb is more taboo than selling sperm. Male sperm donors are anonymous and impersonal. They never see the women they impregnate. But a surrogate mother feels the life inside of her, harbors it and nurtures it from seed to child, and goes through the pain and the ecstasy of childbirth.

The surrogate mother is almost always the genetic or biological mother.[118] Under the terms of the contract, she gives up her rights to be the social or psychological mother. This, critics say, amounts to baby-selling; and baby-selling is taboo, except for a few daring souls who defend it on the grounds that it makes everybody better off—baby, old mother, and new mother.[119] Those who oppose surrogacy contracts assert a powerful social definition of a mother. The mother carries the child inside her body; she bonds with the child, she may nurse the child at her breast. This connection is much more than a matter of genes and chromosomes (of which the man is an equal contributor). The connection is the romance and intimacy of pregnancy and childbirth, the mystery of life growing and maturing in the womb, the potential child taking food from the mother, attached to her, molding the very shape of her body.

Today, thanks to modern science, the notion of a biological mother has become a bit ambiguous. A child can have a womb mother and an egg mother. What happens if they both claim the child? One case already mentioned came out of a surrogacy contract. Most people perhaps feel the womb mother has a better claim, especially if she becomes the primary caregiver and the baby lives in her home. But could both mothers have rights? The egg mother's contribution is much like a father's: genetic material and little else. Under modern law, fathers have strong claims to custody, often formally equal to the rights of the mother (if they are married, for example). Yet a father's genetic contribution is pretty fleeting—one sexual instant and nothing more. When the sperm cell pierces the egg, the father's work is done. The "child" at that point is a single cell. The rest of the job is up to the mother. Yet this tiny sperm cell gives rise to powerful claims. It was, for example, the basis of Otakar's claim in the Baby Richard case. Usually in law (and life) this sperm cell is enough.

If we recognized both egg mother and womb mother as real mothers, a child might conceivably have three parents. The problem is that this bumps up against an important (implicit) social norm: two, and only two, is the optimal number of parents. Yet this principle, too, is eroding. In practice, many children have what amounts to three or four "parents," or even more. They have stepparents along with their biological parents. They may live with a mother and stepfather, who plays the role of a social and psychological father; at the same time, they visit and spend Sundays with their "real" father, and perhaps also the father's new wife, who may also act like some kind of mother. In many societies, other relatives— uncles, aunts, grandparents—have powerful, almost parental, claims. And hundreds of thousands of children in the United States are raised by grandparents.

The issue—in disputes between womb mothers and egg mothers, between foster parents and "real" parents, or between adoptive parents and birth parents—is the familiar one of "social parenting" versus "biological parenting." If we focus on the rights of the child, "social parenting" usually wins out. A powerful argument (and body of research) claims that a child is at risk if we pull him or her away from familiar, comfortable settings. According to this line of argument, Baby Richard should have stayed with his adoptive parents. The uproar over the Baby Richard decision shows the strength of the idea of social parenting; but biology has its claims, and in that case, they prevailed.

The Primacy of the Child

No phrase in family law is more pervasive than "best interests of the child." It is the governing principle in custody cases in the United States and many other countries. It is the principle that is supposed to rule all aspects of adoption law. By Section 3 of the United Nations Convention on the Rights of the Child, "In all actions concerning children, whether . . . public or private . . . , the best interests of the child shall be a primary consideration."[120] The principle seems obvious, even banal—and of course exceedingly vague. It does, however, reflect a historic shift of focus: from parental and family rights to the rights of individual children. To give rights to children, however, in practice means to give the state rights to intervene on their behalf. Very small children have no power to defend their "rights"; and since children in general are under the physical power of their parents, their "rights" must be lodged in proxies—governments, social agencies. Hence, the law not only decides disputes between parents, and between parents and children, it inserts its own interests and values, and sometimes imposes these on both parents and children.

At various points in this chapter, we have touched on this theme: in discussing, for example, the sad story of native children in Australia and the United States. Parents find themselves in battle against the state in other ways as well. Education, as we have mentioned, is one example. Education is now, in all Western societies, a state responsibility. Children go to school. Indeed, they *must* go to school until a certain age. The state decides what the children are going to learn, either centrally or through local school boards. The parents usually go along with these decisions—but not always. In the United States, religious parents fight to keep evolution out of the schools. Jehovah's Witnesses battled (successfully, in the end) against saluting the flag in public schools. The Amish of Wisconsin fought, also successfully, for the right to pull their children out of high school, before the secular world corrupted them. Secular parents have objected to religion in the schools—Bible reading, mandatory prayers, and so on. The Supreme Court of the United States has generally taken their side.[121] Devout parents have objected on precisely the opposite grounds: they feel schools are too hostile to religion. Parents of various stripes have complained about the books in school libraries, and about school texts, on the grounds that these are (depending on the parent) filthy or racist or prejudiced or perverted. In the United States, the educational system is radically decentralized. Local parents have a lot more say than parents do in (for example) England or France. Control is at issue: many parents want the power, individually or collectively, to decide what the schools should teach. The state has its own policies and concerns. In the long sweep of history, the parents seem to be losing.

But perhaps in a deeper sense the children, not the state, are the winners. This victory goes deeper than curriculum. What really saps the power of the family is not the school as such, but the general culture—the culture of self-realization and individualism; the culture of the media; the culture of the peer group. "Entertainment" is loud, insistent, and seductive—television very notably, and now the Internet. "Entertainment" has not only sapped the power of the family, it has also eroded the power of the state, though in a less flagrant way. These forces have brought about a change in the way society looks at children, how it handles children, indeed, how it even *defines* children. Education, for example, was once a matter of indoctrination and socialization. It treated children either as little adults or as shapeless pieces of clay, to be molded in the image of the (right sort of) grown-ups. Less emphasis—or no emphasis—was placed on "creativity," on "self-esteem," on developing the child's unique skills and personality.

By the end of the twentieth century, educational policy was strongly child-centered. It reflected the norm of expressive individualism. Education's implicit messages were messages of self-development. Getting ahead was an important goal; making a life for yourself was perhaps the most important value of all. Realizing your full potential. Becoming your own person. In the republic of choice, the child is supposed to have broad horizons, wide choices, great and open opportunities. The child is not the property of the parents, but a single unique being, a bud that will develop into one unparalleled rose. Education, and the rights and duties of children, reflect these dominant ideologies—more or less, depending on the society. Expressive individualism has some catching up to do in, say, Japan.

Whether making children "winners" and emphasizing individual growth is good or bad for society (and for the children themselves) is another question. There is no obvious answer. Social life and legal life are too complex to be summed up in a single formula. Children are precious, they have rights, they are society's hope for the future. But they are also (in the popular mind) incredibly fragile. They have to be protected—from bad or neglectful parents, to be sure; but also from evil influences. The draconian drug laws in the United States and in many other countries draw their passion and their fire from concern about children. Parents are terrified that their kids may fall victim to drug pushers, become addicts, and destroy their lives forever. Parents are also paralyzed by fear of sexual predators. They tell their children never to talk to strangers. And children must be protected from "harmful" and "immoral" influences. As sexual taboos have crumbled for adults, some parents feel an even stronger need to shield their children from indecency. The whole society seems obsessed with sex. The air is filled with dirty talk and dirty pictures. Especially in the United States, children are used as the excuse for forms of censorship that are legally intolerable for adults.[122] Grown-ups can read virtually any book they want and watch any movie they want. But many movies are taboo for children under seventeen; others demand "parental guidance." Television, which streams right into the home and which children can access by pushing a button, is hemmed in with more regulations than books are. Books freely use "dirty words" and graphic descriptions (or pictures) of sexual activity. Television has to be much more circumspect. Programs televised during "prime time"—hours when children are awake and might be watching—are subject to a code much more stringent than the code for books and movies. The problem is even greater—and more intractable—with regard to the Internet. Children can cruise the Web and gather information; but how can society protect their children from "filth" and protect what many people feel is the moral basis of civilization? A code of morality and the right to free expression are in battle here. But it is also a battle between the freedom of adults and the strong urge to shield children from a rough, salacious, and corrupting world.

There are, of course, millions of people who think society is far too permissive even with regard to grown-ups. This position seems, as of now, to be losing its battle, in the developed world. Adults can see, read, and do things that were once absolutely verboten. Some aspects of this right of adults to choose goes under the name of privacy—a word with many meanings. In its various forms and definitions, privacy has a direct bearing on marriage, sex, and procreation, hence on the family. It is to this subject that we now turn.

5

Privacy and the Republic of Choice

In prior chapters, we have examined the ways in which marriage and divorce law reflected deep changes in society, how families are socially defined and the way people in families relate to each other. Modern individualism, and the primacy of an ideology of choice, were of particular importance in this discussion. By "individualism" I have meant a decline in the power of categories that depend on status—gender, birth order, age, and position in society. More and more, law, like the broader society, focuses on the wishes, desires, and needs of individual people, freely chosen, within a broad band of possibilities. Each person is felt to have the right to select his or her own lifestyle, to craft his or her marriage and divorce, even to make basic decisions about family affiliation in general. How real these choices are is another question; but the *ideology* of choice is an important social fact. The domain of these choices in the American legal system overlaps a legal category that often goes by the name of the "zone of privacy." "Privacy" has two rather disparate legal meanings. There is a tort of "invasion of privacy," an action against someone who intrudes into spaces in our lives we have a right to keep hidden. And there is a constitutional right of "privacy," which refers to decisions about sex, contraception, abortion—life choices from which we can exclude the heavy hand of the state. In this chapter, I explore this mysterious and intriguing zone of privacy. The main focus is on the United States, but with some consideration of other countries.

As explained in the first chapter, privacy law and family law, in our times, have an intimate connection. The two branches of privacy law seem on the surface to have little to do with each other, or even appear to be, in some ways, contradictory. But both concern family life. The family, historically, was the domain of privacy in both of its legal senses. It was a private, safe world (for the middle class certainly) in which the state was not to intrude. It was also the locus—the only *legitimate* locus—for sex and for the breeding of children. Thus the story of privacy in the twentieth century is a story about family life; and it is also a story about the decline of families or, at any rate, their loss of power and control. In any event, choices about sex and marriage (the constitutional "zone of privacy") obviously involve and affect the family.

Invasion of Privacy

The tort of the invasion of privacy is older than the constitutional zone of privacy. The traditional common law, to be sure, had no such right of action. The modern tort is usually traced to a famous article by Samuel D. Warren and Louis D. Brandeis, "The Right of Privacy," published in the *Harvard Law Review* in 1890.[1] The two authors, respectable and wealthy men (Brandeis was later to become a Justice of the United States Supreme Court) were horrified at the nerve and impudence of the popular press. The newspapers of the day were "overstepping . . . the obvious bounds of decency." They were filled with "idle gossip"; they intruded "upon the domestic circle." The press even spread details of "sexual relations." To modern eyes and ears, even the most lurid of the newspapers of the 1890s seem fairly tame, or even prudish; but Warren and Brandeis lived in a different era, with different sensibilities; and they were appalled.

Technology was partly responsible for the situation that seemed, to these two writers, new and frightening. The "candid" camera—the Kodak—had just been invented. This marked a considerable leap forward in photography. Before the Kodak, cameras had trouble dealing with motion. If a photographer wanted to take your picture, you had to pose, you had to sit still, and, in short, you had to *want* to have your picture taken. But now "advances in photographic art" made it possible "to take pictures surreptitiously." Hence the crisis in privacy.

The crisis, or the problem, was not imaginary. In Germany, two men in Hamburg, of the type we would today call paparazzi, used a Kodak to take pictures of the old chancellor, Otto von Bismarck, as he lay on his deathbed. They were about to hawk these photographs for unbelievable sums when Bismarck's son went to court and put a stop to this crass behavior. In fact, the photographs were not published until 1998—a century later.[2]

It was precisely this sort of issue that Warren and Brandeis wanted to confront. They argued for a change in the law—for the creation of a new tort, for the recognition of a new right: a right to a quiet life, to anonymity. They wanted courts to protect this right against violators. But they couched their argument in classic terms. They never claimed total invention of the right. The common law, they insisted, already had within it principles that could remedy the situation. They tried to piece together scraps of precedent, bits of doctrine, to show that such a right would not really be a great leap forward, although of course practically speaking it was.

Clearly, the kind of "privacy" they were arguing for had an elite and traditional flavor. It aimed to shield respectable people from the prying eye of the camera. It condemned the hunger of the public, and the press, for sensation. The essay gave off more than a faint whiff of prudery. In many ways, Warren and Brandeis expressed quite old-fashioned and traditional values. They themselves were men of impeccable reputation. The right of privacy—the right to protect private life from the prying eyes of the press—would also protect members of the elite who were not quite so unsullied: the rich man, for example, who visited a brothel or who had some other skeleton in his closet.

The essay was also a reflection of what we might call the Victorian conception of privacy. The word "Victorian" today is almost a synonym for prudery. The Victorians strike us as fantastic prudes (though their prudery can be exaggerated). They never talked about sex—not openly. Victorian novels either ignore sex or at most drop a hint or two. The *Oxford English Dictionary*, the most scientific, elaborate dictionary in any language, on which work began in the late nineteenth century, left out two exceedingly common words, words known to every native speaker of English, because they were completely taboo. (The second edition, published in the late twentieth century, put these two words back in.) Literature and plays were censored. Pornography was a totally outlawed branch of literature.

This prudery was itself a form of privacy. It drew a curtain over a certain area of life. Sex was for husbands and wives, in the privacy of their home. Anywhere else it was taboo—like nudity. Prudery, in short, was a form of enforced privacy. Thus the tort of invasion of privacy began as a way to protect Victorian notions of prudery and privacy. It began with the sanctity of the family and of marriage. This depended on keeping sex, and even talk about sex, off the public agenda.

Warren and Brandeis constructed an elegant argument. But not many courts took up their challenge. Few of them recognized the right of privacy. In 1902, for example, the highest court of New York flatly rejected their idea. The plaintiff in the case was a young, pretty woman; a flour company and a box company used her picture, without her permission, on advertising posters. This was humiliating, she claimed—an invasion of her privacy. But the court refused to adopt the new tort into New York law.[3] At least with regard to commercial exploitation, the legislature of New York was of a different mind; it passed a law to provide at least limited protection of privacy. The act prohibited use of the "name, portrait or picture of a living person" for "advertising purposes" unless the owner of the name and the face gave permission.

The right to privacy made rather slow progress in other states as well. One of the relatively few cases that took up the notion came out of California in 1931.[4] The plaintiff was a woman who called herself Gabrielle Darley Melvin. She had led a dramatic life. At one point, she had been a prostitute. She had a lover (and pimp) named Leonard Tropp. He abandoned her; she followed him to Los Angeles and shot him dead. This resulted in a sensational 1918 trial for murder. The defense tried to paint Gabrielle as a pure, noble young girl who had been ruined and betrayed by Tropp; her lawyer also claimed that Gabrielle had killed him in self-defense. This was, to put it mildly, something of a stretch; but the jury apparently swallowed the story whole. They found Gabrielle not guilty, and she walked out of the courtroom a free woman. Years later, Hollywood made a movie, based more or less on her life, called *The Red Kimono*. It used her real name—the opening scene, in fact, shows a woman reading a newspaper account of the trial of Gabrielle Darley. Gabrielle sued the producers of the movie. She had given up her career of vice, she claimed, had married a respectable man, and settled down into bourgeois life. The movie had exposed her past, revealed her secrets to the world around her, and in so doing had invaded her privacy.

Once again, Gabrielle won her argument. The California appellate court agreed: the moviemakers had violated her rights and invaded her privacy. They had no justification, legal or moral, to parade before the world the secrets of a woman's past once she had taken her place in "respectable society."[5] The tone and the language of the case are strikingly reminiscent of the tone and language of Warren and Brandeis's article. And the ideology was the same: respectable people had a right to be shielded from the media, from the curiosity of the masses—regardless, apparently, of their past behavior.

In many ways, this case was exceptional. There were already signs that any claims to privacy for people in the public eye was diminishing. Since the 1930s, certainly, this kind of "privacy" has gone into serious decline in the United States. For celebrities, it is all but dead. People in the news—for whatever reason—have virtually no effective right of privacy. Almost anything about them is fair game for the media. The only question is who qualifies as a "public figure." Obviously, presidents, governors, senators, and others holding political office are public figures; but so are movie stars and basketball heroes, and famous industrialists and prominent lawyers. Probably also in the category of public figures are people who, for whatever cause, achieve fame or notoriety—criminals who commit sensational crimes, or the victims of sensational crimes, or notable victims in general. Almost anything you are or say or do, if it is important enough, or interesting enough, to get into the newspapers, can make you a public figure and thus rob you of some or all of your right of privacy. As one court put it, even people who "do not desire the limelight" have no right to prevent publicity "if the experiences that have befallen them are newsworthy, even if they would prefer that those experiences be kept private."[6]

In one well-known case, in 1940, the *New Yorker* published an article about William James Sidis. Sidis had been a child prodigy—a mathematical star who graduated from Harvard at the age of sixteen. Where is he now? asked the magazine. Basically, the answer was: poor Sidis was nowhere. He had flamed out at an early age. By 1940, Sidis was a kind of hermit, living alone in a shabby apartment, collecting streetcar transfers. He had a low-level job as a clerk. Sidis was (not surprisingly) mightily offended by the article; he sued the magazine for invasion of privacy. But he lost the case. The public, said the court, had a right to know what had become of this former child prodigy.[7] In a more recent case (1998), the plaintiff was arrested in South Carolina; the police charged him with a serious crime: dousing a woman with gasoline and setting fire to her mobile home. Later, they released the man, and he was never tried for the crime. A newspaper published a story about his travails. It reported, among other things, that a fellow inmate had raped the man in jail. The victim sued for invasion of privacy. The Supreme Court of South Carolina turned him down. It noted, "The commission of a violent crime between inmates of a county jail is a matter of public significance"; the public had a right, therefore, to learn the facts about this incident.[8]

Here again the case law reflects norms of the larger society. People like the idea of a right to privacy, even the kind that Warren and Brandeis were talking about—for themselves. But not for other people. It is characteristic of modern culture that the public thinks it has the right to know everything about everybody in public life. People in general also have a great curiosity, amounting almost to prurience, about other people's private lives. This is, of course, nothing new. Lurid crime news was a staple of the nineteenth-century press, particularly specialized newspapers, such as the *Police Gazette*. But mostly these papers reported news about crimes, and the vices of the low and depraved. The upper middle class enjoyed a certain amount of immunity from publicity.

The argument in the South Carolina case is not entirely unreasonable. Conditions in local jails, violence in local jails—these are matters that the public can be and should be interested in. If a newspaper sincerely wants to expose the horrors of life in local jails, this kind of muckraking should be encouraged, even if somebody finds the results of the exposé offensive. But why did the public have the right to know about the fate of poor Sidis, about his lonely life and his streetcar transfers? Perhaps because he was, or once had been, something of a minor celebrity. And ours is the age of the celebrity. A celebrity is not just a famous person; a celebrity is a famous and *familiar* person.[9] Celebrities are familiar because they are visible, because we know so much about them. We read about them in magazines and newspapers. But, even more significantly, we see them and hear them on television. We learn to recognize their faces; we hear their voices; we see how they walk; we come to recognize their every mole and tic.

There have always been famous people, public figures, in the past, but they were not "celebrities" in the modern sense. A century ago, how many people in England or Sweden or the United States actually saw the king, prime minister, or president in the flesh? Even their images were remote. Perhaps they could be seen on a coin or a postage stamp; but nothing more. The pope was a great, holy, and famous figure—who never left the Vatican. The Dalai Lama and the Emperor of Japan were godlike and distant figures, immured in their palaces. Today all of these men are celebrities, stars of the media. They travel about the world; vast crowds see them as they travel; but, more significantly, millions or billions more watch them on television. Every day on TV we learn all about them— their habits, the clothes they wear, their facial expression. The President of the United States is ubiquitous; the same is true of other heads of state and chiefs of government. All of her subjects see and hear Queen Elizabeth II in a way that Queen Elizabeth I, or even Queen Victoria, could not have imagined. Celebrities are the magical people we see on TV and read about in the gossip magazines or in the daily newspapers—we become acquainted with their activities, their quirks, their families and friends, even their cats and dogs. Because images of celebrities are constantly beamed into our homes, we have the illusion that we actually *know* these people. When Princess Diana died, millions of people were overwhelmed with grief; the whole United Kingdom fell into a paroxysm of mourning, and thousands of ordinary people bought tons of flowers and heaped them everywhere to honor her memory and express their grief. They were suffering because of the death of a woman they had never met—in the flesh. But she was near and close to them, she aroused deep feelings because she was so familiar—because they had read and seen and heard so much about her in magazines, news articles, and above all, on TV.

In our times, image and imagery are everything—and not just for movie stars. Political figures have become celebrities, along with rock stars, talk show hosts, soccer players, and miscellaneous television "personalities." Politicians rise and fall on the basis of their charm, their image, their "charisma." Ideology and policy seem almost secondary in the age of the media; the voters react to the person more than to the ideas. It follows from this that the private life of political leaders (and religious leaders, business leaders, cultural leaders) is no longer irrelevant. It is part of what makes them appealing—or repulsive. It is the basis on which we vote for or against. And this is the key, too, to a case like Sidis's. What had become of him was not irrelevant: his private life was in fact *the* crucial aspect of his being, once you concede that he was or had been a "public figure."

Obviously, poor Sidis was much less of a "public" figure than, say, the President of the United States. But the courts have expanded the definition of a public figure quite dramatically. Was Mike Virgil a celebrity? He was a prominent bodysurfer. *Sports Illustrated* ran a story about him. It talked about his surfing, to be sure, but it added a lot more details, particularly about his rather strange private life. Virgil "never learned how to read," apparently; and he did crazy things, like diving headfirst down a flight of steps, because he thought it was "groovy" and would impress the "chicks." Mike Virgil (whether he could read or not) became acutely aware of this story, which of course he resented. He sued the magazine, claiming it had invaded his privacy. An appeal court, writing in 1975, found the case troublesome: it was close to the borderline. Virgil had a point. There had to be limits to "morbid and sensational prying into private lives." Still, he *was* a well-known bodysurfer, and bodysurfing, after all, was a subject of "general public interest."[10]

Technically, there are two questions to be answered in a privacy case of the type that Mike Virgil brought. First, is this person a public figure? If the answer is yes, then almost anything goes. But second, even if he or she is not a genuine public figure, the media have not invaded a person's privacy if the story is newsworthy—that is, if the public has a legitimate interest in the person or the subject. If these conditions are met, the publication has a right to print its story. Both issues were involved in the case of Toni Ann Diaz, who sued the *Oakland Tribune* in the early 1980s.[11] Toni Ann Diaz was born Antonio Diaz, but had always suffered from a "gender identification problem." In 1975, she underwent "gender corrective surgery," and successfully. Antonio now became Toni. She kept her surgery secret, except for "immediate family and closest friends." She changed her high school records, her social security records, her driver's license, all to reflect her new gender. She enrolled in the College of Alameda, and in 1977 she was elected president of the student body. A reporter for the *Tribune* wrote a story in which he broke the news that the new president of the student body, Toni Diaz, was "no lady," but was "in fact a man whose real name is Antonio." The reporter added that this might be "no big deal, but I suspect his female classmates" in phys ed classes "may wish to make other showering arrangements."

When Diaz read this article, she became (she said) very depressed, suffered from "insomnia, nightmares, and memory lapses," and delayed enrolling in Mills College (a woman's school). She sued the *Tribune* on the grounds that the newspaper had "invaded her privacy by the unwarranted publicity of intimate facts." A jury awarded her fairly hefty damages. The appeal court reversed the case and sent it back for retrial, but on rather technical grounds (improper jury instructions). Presumably, the parties later settled out of court. The newspaper won a victory, of sorts; but there was also at least a moral victory for Diaz. She was simply not that much of a public figure, even though she was the "first female student body president of the College." In other words, she ranked much lower than a famous bodysurfer. Was her situation "newsworthy"? The court clearly did not like the rather smarmy article: it was "by no means an attempt to enlighten the public on a contemporary social issue." The jury was entitled to decide "whether the article was newsworthy or whether it extended beyond the bounds of decency." This left the ultimate decision somewhat up in the air. The definition of a public figure has expanded enormously (Toni Diaz fell short, but not by much), and so too of the definition of what is and what is not newsworthy; but there is still a gray area, an area of doubt. Almost anything goes—but not yet everything.

The courts may never resolve the problem, at least not to everybody's satisfaction. Freedom of the press is a precious thing and a basic liberty; but a person's right to some sort of privacy is arguably also precious. The public also has a hunger for "news." And the media have a hunger to make money by satisfying that hunger for "news." Invading people's privacy can be profitable. There is a market for tiny cameras, hidden camcorders, secret microphones, and other devilish paraphernalia; and there is certainly a market for the products of these devices. In one startling California case, *Shulman v. Group W Productions, Inc.* (1998),[12] Ruth Shulman was badly hurt in an auto accident, and trapped inside her car. A medical transport and rescue helicopter came to save her. A television cameraman came along as well. A film was made of people pulling Ruth out of the car and of her trip to the hospital by helicopter. The flight nurse, a woman named Carnahan, wore a tiny microphone, and it picked up her conversations with Ruth Shulman—including the moment when Ruth said, "I just want to die." All this was made part of a TV program and broadcast to the world.

The court was troubled by the case. No, Ruth was not a public figure.

But yes, her accident was newsworthy. The media had a right to report it. Yet under the circumstances, the court felt the media had gone too far. The secret microphone, the recording of conversations in the helicopter, a woman half-conscious, delirious, in pain—this was an invasive, intrusive act, taking place at a time and place where a person had no reason to think somebody would be listening, filming, recording. The right to tell the story did not include the right to intrude into Ruth Shulman's private agony.

Quite different was the case of John Neff, a boisterous fan of the Pittsburgh Steelers. In 1973, photographers took pictures of a group of fans, some of them somewhat drunk, as they jumped up and down, "waving banners and drinking beer . . . screaming and howling and imploring the photographers to take more pictures." One of these pictures, which *Sports Illustrated* published, showed Neff with his fly open. This photo was chosen from more than 7,000 pictures. Although the fly was "not open to the point of being revealing," the picture was "in utmost bad taste." The publishers, said the court, should have thought twice about publishing this picture; but courts were not authorized to set up "canons of good taste." The article—about the fans and their behavior—was "of legitimate public interest"; moreover, Neff was "catapulted into the news by his own actions." Despite some "misgivings," the court held that publication of the photograph was "protected by the Constitution."[13]

Courts in the United States see a problem, but not a solution; they find it hard to know where to draw the line between the public's right to know and the individual's right to privacy. There is apparently *some* line, some border, some zone of privacy or propriety that no newspaper or TV camera is allowed to cross. Where exactly it is located, nobody knows. Some newspapers (and television programs) would cross the line, if they could; in fact, they would prefer no line at all. Indeed, the boundaries keep moving. Material is tolerated—in the press, on TV— that would have been out of the question even one generation past. The talk shows on television explore subjects that would have been inconceivable before the 1980s. They wash dirty linen in public; people confess every aspect of their sex lives without apparent shame. We might also take note of the explosion of "reality" programs that appeared at the very end of the twentieth century. The first American example, perhaps, was a 1973 program called *An American Family*, which took a close, hard look at the Loud family. *The Real World*, a program in which a group of young people live together, under the beady eye of a camera, began its career in 1992. But the real outbreak of "reality" television came in 2000; as of early 2003, some 13 percent of prime time was devoted to this dubious genre.[14] The percentage was predicted to go even higher.

These shows may or may not be a passing fancy. The networks love these programs in part because they are cheap to make; real people do not command huge salaries, and production costs are low.[15] But this would count for nothing if the programs were unpopular, which they are not. The public has taken to them eagerly. Some of them have gained enormous audiences. People apparently love to see real people in situations of fear, horror, sexual exaltation, and other heightened emotions. They love to see and hear people letting it all hang out in public. The shamelessness that parades itself on television is truly extraordinary. But it is, after all, hardly typical. The public watches avidly as other people expose themselves; but in their own lives, most people want and need a zone of privacy, places that state and media cannot enter. Or, at the very least, they want to choose what parts of their lives to keep secret.

The boundaries between privacy and publicity are drawn differently in different countries. In some ways, American law is fairly extreme. Many European legal systems treat privacy with more respect than the United States. In those countries, private facts, even about public figures, cannot be quite so blatantly transmitted to the hungry public. Material about the private lives of famous people, especially political figures is only printable if this material has at least some relevance to the way they carry out official duties. In some countries, everything else is forbidden. In some instances, it is forbidden only if it is downright false.[16] The difference between the attitudes of American and German law came out in bold relief in a case decided by the German constitutional court in 1973.[17] The plaintiff wanted to stop a television program in which an actor playing the plaintiff, and using his real name, would appear. The plaintiff had been an accomplice in a sensational crime some years before—an attack on a munitions depot of the German armed forces. In the course of the attack, four soldiers were killed. The plaintiff took no part in the actual attack. He was a friend of the attackers, and his friendship had "a homosexual component." He was convicted, sentenced, and sent to prison; at the time of the dramatization he was due to be released, and he intended to return to his home town. Nobody claimed the program was inaccurate; still, the plaintiff claimed it violated his constitutional rights of "personality." It would interfere with his reintegration into society. He particularly objected to any mention of his sexual orientation. Under U.S. law he would no doubt be a "public figure" and have no chance of winning the case. But in Germany he did win. The court noted that the case was no longer current; stirring up the ashes in the "form of a documentary drama" would constitute a "severe incursion" into the plaintiff's personal rights; showing him as a criminal and a homosexual would only "strengthen the overwhelming disdain for these socially marginal people" and lead to negative assessments of the plaintiff.[18]

Are these European limits and boundaries effective? Perhaps we should ask, rather: Are they honored? This is a more troublesome question. The tabloid press of Europe seems as outrageous and intrusive as anything in the United States, whatever the cases and treatises say. The hunger for gossip, dirt, scandal, and sex seems every bit as great in Frankfurt or Paris or London as the hunger for these things in New York or Los Angeles. And the tabloid press pays very well for material to satisfy this hunger. Huge sums changed hands for such juicy items as topless photos of the Duchess of York, or exclusive rights to pictures of the wedding of racer Michael Schumacher in Germany. The money seems well spent. The topless duchess sold an extra 482,000 copies of the *Daily Mirror*.[19] A German mass-circulation rag, *Das Bild,* scored a stunning scoop in 1994 with a somewhat blurry photo taken with a telephoto lens showing the Prince of Wales on vacation, dressed only in his birthday suit. The page-one headline screamed: "Charles Naked!" Nothing in the photo suggested anything exceptional about Charles's physical equipment; but this historic scoop apparently sold a lot of newspapers. Buckingham Palace huffed and puffed; it called the "intrusion" an outrage and "completely unjustifiable"; but the palace apparently confined itself to a loud expression of annoyance, and nothing more.[20] In contrast, Michael Douglas and his bride, Catherine Zeta-Jones, in early 2003 brought a lawsuit against the cads who took and printed unauthorized and unflattering pictures of their wedding. They won a small amount; and the case, at this writing, is on appeal.[21]

The tort of "invasion of privacy" differed radically from the older actions of libel and slander. If I accuse somebody of being a horse thief, it is a good defense to his lawsuit if I can show that he was in fact a horse thief. But truth is not a defense to the tort of invasion of privacy. Sidis never claimed that the *New Yorker* was lying; he simply asserted that they had no right to tell the story. The American law of defamation has also been evolving, and in ways that seem strikingly parallel to developments in the law of privacy. In the famous 1964 case of *New York Times v. Sullivan*,[22] the U.S. Supreme Court examined for the first time the constitutional implications of the law of defamation. In the background was the civil rights movement in the South—the fierce struggle of southern blacks to end segregation and discrimination in all areas of life. A full-page advertisement in the *New York Times* ("Heed Their Rising Voices") asked for money to support the work of the civil rights movement. The ad was not completely accurate—at least not in every detail. It said, for example, that protesting students sang "My Country, 'Tis of Thee" at the Alabama State Capitol; actually, they sang "The Star-Spangled Banner." There were other statements, equally false, but equally trivial. Sullivan was a public official in Montgomery, Alabama. He claimed that the advertisement had libeled him; and he brought a lawsuit against the *New York Times* and four black clergymen. The case went to trial in Alabama before an all-white jury; the judge gave some very strong instructions, practically inviting the jury to punish the defendants; and the jury awarded each defendant to pay half a million dollars to Sullivan.

The Supreme Court unanimously overturned the award. Wrong statements, said Justice William Brennan, who wrote the main opinion, are "inevitable" in a free society; but a free society also needs "uninhibited, robust, and wide-open" debate on issues of the day. Public officials were not to collect damages for defamation against a newspaper or other medium of communication, even for wrong statements, unless the statements were made deliberately or with "reckless disregard" of whether the statement was true or false. Otherwise, freedom of the press might be impaired. To require a newspaper to "guarantee the truth" of all their "factual assertions" would be simply intolerable. Such a doctrine would stifle debate and discussion; it would inevitably lead to "self-censorship."

The *New York Times* case was dramatic, even revolutionary. It inserted the Court into an area it had basically never entered before. The Court was obviously aware of the social context—the threat to the civil rights movement. A decision against the *Times* would hand segregationists a mighty weapon to crush the civil rights movement, and to punish the northern press. The Court was also surely aware that the trial in Alabama was hardly a fair one. But the case turned out to have a wider meaning. It began a line of decisions that ran parallel to the privacy cases. Here too, the courts greatly expanded the concept of a "public figure." People in the limelight were not to complain about media coverage, even inaccurate coverage, so long as the mistakes were not "malicious" or "reckless." Public figures, in short, had no right to screen their private lives from the eyes and ears of the public. In *Curtis Publishing Co. v. Butts* (1967),[23] the "public figure" was a famous football coach. Early cases at least suggested that *New York Times v. Sullivan* might keep on growing, and that its doctrine could come to include anybody at all in the public eye, and for any reason—soccer players, movie stars, important businessmen, perhaps any person of any interest or significance, perhaps anybody whose name appeared in the paper or who was mentioned or shown on TV.

So far, at the level of the Supreme Court, this has not quite happened. In fact, the Court seemed at times to step back slightly. In *Gertz v. Robert Welch, Inc.* (1974),[24] the plaintiff, Elmer Gertz, was a lawyer. Gertz represented in court the family of a young man killed by a policeman. Welch was the publisher of *American Opinion,* an ultra-right-wing organ of the

John Birch Society. In print, Welch called Gertz a "Leninist," a stooge of the Communists; Gertz was part of a plot to discredit and frame the police. There were plenty of mistakes in Welch's piece. The Court held that Gertz was not a public figure; thus Welch was not free to defame him.[25] In a 1976 case, the plaintiff was Mary Firestone, third wife of an heir to a fortune based on rubber tires. She was a party in a sensational divorce case. There was testimony in the case of "extramarital adventures on both sides" that would, according to the judge, "make Dr. Freud's hair curl." But Mary Firestone was adjudged not to be a "public figure"; she had no role of "prominence in the affairs of society, other than perhaps Palm Beach society."[26] Nor was Ronald Hutchinson, in a 1979 case. Hutchinson, a scientist, had a research grant to study anger in monkeys; Senator William Proxmire ridiculed the research, sneeringly called it a study of why monkeys clench their jaws, denounced it in a speech in the Senate, and also in a press release and newsletter. Hutchinson, said the court, was not a public figure and had a right to sue.[27]

It is not clear, then, how far the doctrine extends. Decisions of the lower federal courts are hardly consistent. In *Braun v. Flynt* (1984),[28] the plaintiff, Jeannie Braun, worked for an amusement park in Texas. Her job included "working in a novelty act with 'Ralph, the Diving Pig.'" Ms. Braun would tread water, holding a bottle of milk with a nipple on it; Ralph would dive into the pool and drink from the bottle. *Chic*, a hard-core magazine full of "explicit photographs of female genitalia," published a picture of this marvelous exploit. Ms. Braun, who had been "raised in a private Catholic school," was horrified to see her photo in such a magazine; she was (she said) "very upset" and "felt like crawling in a hole and never coming out." She was a public performer, but not (according to the court) a "public figure." In another case, however, an eye clinic sued a television network, claiming it had been defamed. The program had accused the clinic of various ophthalmic misdeeds; but the clinic was declared a "public figure." Anita Wood, who had once had something of a singing career and had been (maybe) a girlfriend of Elvis Presley, was also held to be a public figure.[29]

In short, the boundaries of *New York Times v. Sullivan* remain indistinct. But that case, and the ones that followed, did give the media a privilege they had not had before. The line of cases increased their already enormous power. Unless they were actually "reckless," they had wide-ranging freedom to comment, report, and even misrepresent anybody who fit the vague category of "public figure." Thus the right of privacy, in the Warren and Brandeis sense, was steadily losing out in the "marketplace of ideas." The media can exercise the power that so horrified Warren and Brandeis. Gossip, prurient rumors, and scandals all leer from the pages of newspapers and magazines, and from TV channels as well.

The second aspect of privacy law is another story. The constitutional right that goes by this name has gained steadily in importance.[30] This "right," essentially, is the right to make fundamental life choices without state interference: the right to marry, use contraception, produce or not produce children. It is a right tightly bound up with issues of family life and sexual behavior. Moreover, it is related to "privacy" in a literal sense. Warren and Brandeis wanted to establish the right to be free of prying eyes. But to most people, "privacy" means the right to a bit of private space. To teenage children of the middle class, it means a room of one's own, slamming the door shut, and keeping parents out. For rebellious adolescents, it is a way of preserving the freedom to do what they want— listen to raucous music, perhaps even have sex in their room. Parents, of course, also want and need privacy. A government pamphlet on "child management," published in 1925, suggested that "whenever possible" children "should have a room separate from . . . parents." Otherwise, and especially under "the crowded living conditions . . . of . . . apartment life," children may be "forced to see rather revolting intimacies," which may "leave . . . scars."[31]

Freedom from "revolting intimacies" (or, conversely, the freedom to *have* "revolting intimacies") is impossible for poor people. It is strictly a middle-class privilege. Almost nobody had "privacy" in the Middle Ages; in the shacks and huts of peasants there was no such thing as personal space. When mother and father, children, chickens, and goats all shared a room, privacy in the bourgeois sense was nonexistent. This lack of privacy continued to be the case well into the modern era. In the colonial period in what is now the United States, there was "no escaping neighbors. . . . It was impossible to sustain privacy within households; the houses were too small, the rooms too cramped, the walls too thin."[32] In the early nineteenth century, in Leeds, England, "the average cottage was fifteen foot square"; and in London in the middle of the century, it was not "uncommon" for three or four families to share a "room of twelve foot square or less" in the "promiscuous intimacy of cattle."[33] Thus most people, throughout most of history, have had to have sex and make babies under conditions modern people would find immoral or intolerable. It was sex, by and large, without much nudity. Modern middle-class people dress and undress far more often than their ancestors. Nudity is on the whole rather modern (I ignore the ancient Greeks and Romans). Nudity needs modernity. It needs privacy. It needs modern bathrooms and showers. In other words, it requires a lot of spatial privacy. The so-called sexual revolution has thrived under conditions of modern privacy. It is hard to be sexually active unless you have your own room or apartment; if you are squeezed into a room with parents and brothers and sisters, having sex is more difficult. In college, it helps that dormitories are now co-ed, and that old rules about dating and visiting have gone by the boards.

Many factors, to be sure, lie behind the so-called sexual revolution. But notions of privacy surely played a role. Privacy, for one thing, helped to redefine what is thought of as "natural" in sexual behavior. There is an interesting passage in Alfred E. Kinsey's famous "report" on American sexual behavior. In the volume on the behavior of women (1953), Kinsey discusses nudity during intercourse. He waxes enthusiastic about making love while naked. After all, he writes, in the course of evolution, the "human species" evolved "out of unclothed mammalian stocks." Earlier generations, I imagine, would have objected strongly to arguments from animal evolution, and found totally irrelevant the fact that animals never wear clothes. Not Kinsey. To him, it seemed "reasonable" to "conclude that the avoidance of nudity during coitus is a perversion of what is, in a biologic sense, normal sexuality." Fortunately, he noted, this "perversion" was declining. A third of the women born before 1900 were "usually or always clothed" during sex; but a mere 8 percent of the women born in the 1920s avoided nudity.[34] As for men, 90 percent of the "upper level males" had sex in the nude, and "others would prefer it so, if circumstances allowed."[35]

Kinsey's book about the male (human) animal appeared in 1948; the book about women was published five years later. They set off a firestorm of comment and criticism. These were not the first sex surveys; but studies of sexual behavior had been rare and fairly timid.[36] Kinsey's surveys were bold; and he had a point of view. He believed very strongly that the laws against all kinds of sexual behavior—against everything but ordinary intercourse between married people—were absurd; moreover, most people in the United States, according to the laws on the books, were technically sex offenders. Kinsey's reports evoked horrified gasps and jeremiads; but the times did seem to be changing. And within a few years, the U.S. Supreme Court itself would confront a cluster of issues about sex, sexuality, and reproduction.

Contraception

The constitutional history of privacy begins, essentially, with a 1965 case, *Griswold v. Connecticut*.[37] Members of the Connecticut Planned Parenthood League challenged a Connecticut law, almost a century old, that basically made it a crime to sell or use contraceptives or to provide contraceptive information. A majority of the court agreed that this law was invalid, that it violated one of the constitutional rights of the people of Connecticut. But where in the text of the Constitution was this right to be found? The answer was far from obvious. The main opinion, by Justice William O. Douglas, all but admitted that nothing *literally* dictated the result in the case. Instead, Douglas talked vaguely and almost mystically about the spirit of the Bill of Rights, about "penumbras" and "emanations" from the words of the Constitution. These "emanations" implied a "zone of privacy" beyond the reach of the legislature. Other justices had their own pet theories of why the Connecticut statute was bad, though the Douglas opinion is the one most frequently quoted. Justice Arthur Goldberg, for example, zeroed in on the word "liberty," used in the Fourteenth Amendment; liberty, in his opinion, meant "those personal rights which are fundamental." Liberty was not "confined to the specific terms of the Bill of Rights." In any event, "liberty" embraced "the right of marital privacy." Other justices made still other arguments. That there was something fatally wrong with the Connecticut statute was the one thing most of them agreed on.

The Connecticut statute was therefore dead; but the significance of the case went far beyond this holding. After all, the Connecticut law was already practically a dead letter; and Connecticut was an extreme case to begin with. Birth control was popular—and controversial. The Catholic Church bitterly condemned birth control devices. But these devices were readily available. Enormous numbers of people used contraceptives, especially condoms, to limit the size of their families.[38] In Katherine Davis's survey of college women, published in 1929, 89.7 percent of the women surveyed felt that the use of contraceptives was justified. As one woman put it, "Unwanted children are very pathetic"; and another woman said that "a man and wife should not have more children than they can take care of."[39] A concerted movement, led by Margaret Sanger among others, had aimed to legalize birth control and to promote what its proponents considered rational family planning.[40] This movement had made enormous strides—although not enough to persuade the legislature of Connecticut. Still, Connecticut is one of the smallest of the states, and it was easy for most residents to get what they wanted by driving a short distance and crossing the line into New York. In most states, the laws had been liberalized. The law was hardly a barrier by the 1960s. Courts too had done their bit to undermine the strict laws that were once on the books. In a 1930 case, one condom company sued another condom maker for trademark violation.[41] The defendant countered that trademark protection was unavailable, if a business was illegal to begin with. The court disagreed. True, condoms could be used for illegal purposes (preventing babies). But they also had a perfectly proper use: prevention of disease. The plaintiff was entitled to protect his trademark with respect to the *legal* use of condoms.

The judges must have been perfectly aware that most people did not use condoms for medical reasons. The plaintiff sold about 20 million condoms a year—and they were hardly a monopoly. The defendant produced a witness who "testified that the article is infrequently prescribed by physicians, and is commonly sold by drug stores" without any prescription "to any customer who calls for it." This did not, however, sway the court.

The same attitude appeared in a case from 1933, *Davis v. U.S.*[42] Davis was "engaged in the business of handling druggists' rubber sundries" in Akron, Ohio. Defendants were tried and convicted of the crime of selling condoms, and shipping them in interstate commerce. This was a violation of the Comstock Act, which made it illegal to send across state lines any "article, or thing designed . . . or intended for preventing conception." The appeal court reversed the convictions. The trial court had committed error when it refused to let the defendant show evidence of "good faith and absence of unlawful intent." The defendant was entitled to argue that its sales were for medical purposes and disease prevention. Or, to put it another way, selling condoms was not per se a crime; at least not in the view of the federal court.

An attitude of impatience with the Comstock restrictions was even more evident in a case from 1936.[43] Here the full might of the U.S. government weighed in against a "package containing 120 vaginal pessaries more or less"; a woman gynecologist had imported these devices from Japan. She testified that she had ordered the devices to try them in her practice, to see if they were useful "for contraceptive purposes." She prescribes "the use of pessaries in cases where it would not be desirable for a patient to undertake a pregnancy." The Comstock Act, as we noted, absolutely banned the mailing or importing of articles "intended for preventing conception"; nothing in the statute even hinted at exceptions. The court admitted that in 1873, when Congress passed the law, it probably intended to "bar the use of such articles completely." But would Congress, if it knew the whole story, really want to outlaw "things which might intelligently be employed by conscientious and competent physicians" to save lives or promote the "well being of their patients?" Apparently not, or so the court thought. In any event, the government lost its case. Learned Hand wrote a rather odd concurring opinion. Left to himself, he said, he would have gone the other way. The meaning of the statute seemed perfectly plain. Of course, many people "have changed their minds about such matters" since the Comstock law was passed, but (in his opinion) the statute ought to stay alive (and presumably enforced) at least "until public feeling gets enough momentum" to bring about a change. Despite these sentiments, he was "content" to accept the opinion of the majority.[44]

Connecticut's statute, in short, had been a lonely one, and was getting lonelier; and so too of the attitudes behind it. Ordinary people used contraceptives; and almost anybody, even in Connecticut, could easily get hold of them. Hence the real significance of *Griswold* was its discovery, or invention, of a "right of privacy," or a "zone of privacy," arising from the Constitution's precious bodily "emanations." The case certainly provoked a good deal of criticism in legal circles. Quite a few scholars were worried (or outraged) by the boldness of the interpretive leap. It seemed obvious that this "zone of privacy" had no real grounding in the actual text. The reasoning was "curious, puzzling"; it was a "malformation of constitutional law"; it was "shot through with serious weaknesses," an "opinion whose concepts fall suddenly in a heap."[45]

True enough. Basically, the Court was reading expressive individualism into the text of the Constitution and into fundamental law. The American Constitution, one must recall, is (as Constitutions go) a rather ancient document. It is not easy to amend. Amendments, in fact, have been few and far between. But in another sense, the Supreme Court has been amending the Constitution ever since it went into effect, through the process of creative "interpretation" and the doctrine of the "living constitution." Modern declarations of human rights, and modern constitutions, have often been more explicit on the issue of "privacy," lifestyle, and related matters. The Universal Declaration of Human Rights, issued by the United Nations in 1948, asserts that people have the right to be free from "arbitrary interference with . . . privacy, family, home, or correspondence" (Art. 12).[46] The Spanish Constitution (Tit. I,

Art. 10) speaks of "the dignity of the person" and "the free development of the personality."[47] The South African Constitution states that everyone shall have "the right to respect for and protection of his or her dignity" and a right to "personal privacy."[48] Some American states, in part inspired by the cases that followed *Griswold,* have written privacy into their own constitutions. Alaska did so in 1972: the people's "right to privacy . . . shall not be infringed." Similar language appears in the Montana Constitution. In Florida (1980), every "natural person has the right to be let alone and free from governmental intrusion into the person's private life" (Const. Art. 1, sec. 23). California, too, added to its list of "inalienable rights" in the 1970s the right of "pursuing and obtaining safety, happiness, and privacy" (Const. Art. 1, sec. 1).[49]

At any rate, later Supreme Court cases picked up the concept of "privacy" in the *Griswold* case, expanded it, and extended its scope. The *Griswold* case had talked about the rights of married people; Connecticut's law intruded into the "intimate relation" of husband and wife. Did this mean that a state could, by law, limit the right to buy contraceptives to married people? The Supreme Court, in 1972, made it clear that the answer was no.[50] Massachusetts had precisely this kind of statute: it was against the law to distribute contraceptives to unmarried people. William Baird, after a lecture at Boston University, gave Emko Vaginal Foam to a woman, in front of a large crowd of people. He was arrested on the spot. This was not unexpected or unwanted; in fact, he told the police who were at the lecture to "do their duty"; as he said to the audience, "the only way we can change the law is to get the case into a court of law."[51] Baird was absolutely right. The Supreme Court struck down the statute. The "right of privacy," Justice Brennan said, is the right of the individual, "married or single, to be free from unwarranted governmental intrusion," on such matters as "whether to bear or beget a child."

That the concept of "privacy" could be extended in this way was hardly surprising. This was an age in which the social meaning of marriage was changing dramatically. It was an age more and more willing to accept substitutes for orthodox marriage. Attitudes toward sex were also more and more permissive. The Court took a further step in *Carey v.*

Population Services International (1977).[52] A New York statute made it a crime to sell or give contraceptives to minors under sixteen years of age; and no one but a licensed pharmacist could distribute contraceptives, to people of any age. The statute also made it a crime to advertise or display contraceptives. The Supreme Court struck down the statute. Minors had a right to make life choices, too. Indeed, the main opinion expressed doubts "whether limiting access to contraceptives will in fact substantially discourage early sexual behavior" and went on to say magisterially that the justices "take judicial notice . . . that . . . the incidence of sexual activity among minors is high." The ban on advertising was also obnoxious. The state may not "suppress" truthful information about "entirely lawful activity," and the Court brushed aside the argument that ads of contraceptive products "would be offensive and embarrassing" and that "permitting them would legitimize sexual activity of young people."

Abortion

The most dramatic extension of the privacy doctrine came in the famous case of *Roe v. Wade*, in 1973.[53] Here the issue was abortion. Many states had enacted restrictive abortion laws in the nineteenth century. Some of these laws had been liberalized in the course of the twentieth century; others had not. There had been at all times a strong demand for abortion, even after abortion was illegal. Women often managed to find someone willing to help them get rid of an unwanted fetus. Sometimes this ended in tragedy, but there were also skilled doctors, who had a flourishing underground practice.[54]

Roe v. Wade challenged two state abortion laws—one in Texas and one in Georgia, one quite restrictive (Texas) and one more liberal (Georgia). "Jane Roe" was the pseudonym of a woman named Norma McCorvey. In a sweeping seven-to-two decision, the Supreme Court struck down *all* existing laws on abortion. The "right of privacy," established in the *Griswold* case and its descendants, was broad enough to protect a woman's decision to put an end to her pregnancy. The main opinion—by Justice Harry Blackmun—located this expanded right of privacy in the due process clause of the Fourteenth Amendment. Blackmun's opinion did not give a woman or her doctor an absolute right to abortion up to the moment of birth. Blackmun divided pregnancy, legally speaking, into three trimesters. In the first trimester, the woman's right to an abortion was essentially unlimited. In the second trimester, states could regulate abortion in the interests of health. In the last trimester, the state had a greater interest in protecting the unborn child; states could, if they wished, severely restrict abortion, but not if the woman's life was at stake.

Very likely, Blackmun and the other justices in the majority saw the decision as a compromise. It did not give women total control over abortion. Nor, obviously, did it give the other side what it wanted. Many people considered abortion a sin and a crime—murder, in fact; the slaughter of innocent souls. They wanted a total ban on abortion. The decision was actually less of a compromise than Blackmun probably imagined. Women's groups were on the whole quite pleased. "Pro-life" forces were absolutely not. Millions of people loathed the decision. You cannot compromise with murder. Thus, from the very beginning, the decision stirred up a hornet's nest of controversy. Today, more than thirty years later, the controversy has by no means died down. It remains a fiery political issue, and a fiery legal issue as well. Religious conservatives are determined to get rid of *Roe,* by amending the Constitution if necessary. Congress has in fact nibbled away at the decision. The so-called Hyde Amendment ended federal funding of abortions for poor women, except to save the life of the mother. The Supreme Court upheld this restriction.[55] Conservative presidents promised to try to get the abortion decision overturned. They appointed Supreme Court justices who, they hoped, would vote *Roe v. Wade* out of existence. At one point, in 1992, this seemed likely. But in *Planned Parenthood of Southeastern Pennsylvania v. Casey*[56] a bare majority of the Court refused to do so.

Casey concerned a law passed in Pennsylvania, which contained many restrictions on abortion. A minor had to have parental consent, for example; and married women had to tell their husbands if they planned to get an abortion. Challenged in court, the statute gave the majority a chance to end the reign of *Roe v. Wade.* The Supreme Court in fact upheld most of the Pennsylvania law, but not the provision making married women tell their husbands of their plans. And a majority pointedly refused to overrule the earlier case. The new President, William Clinton, later appointed "pro-choice" justices to the Court so that the decision, for the time being, seemed to be secure. But the future of *Roe v. Wade* is still somewhat cloudy.

Abortion, family law, regulation of lifestyle, and sexual choices—these have been issues all over the developed world. Different countries resolve these issues in different ways; but they cannot avoid confronting them. Abortion is almost everywhere controversial. Some countries make it illegal under most or all circumstances. In most Latin American countries, abortion is either legally unavailable or severely restricted by law.[57] About a quarter of the world's population lives in countries that either ban abortion altogether or restrict it to a few rare situations (rape, incest, or saving the mother's life). According to a United Nations survey, as of 1999 only four countries banned abortion totally—that is, without even these few exceptions. Chile was one of the four; but even there abortion is in practice not quite so unattainable. In some countries, including Germany, Spain, and Poland, a constitutional court has confronted the issue. Neither in Germany nor Spain did the court go as far as the U.S. Supreme Court; and indeed, in one key German case, the court recognized that the unborn child itself had constitutional rights. Neither Germany nor Spain recognizes a "right" to abortion in the U.S. sense. The German constitution specifically protects the right to "free development of . . . personality"; but the Constitutional Court did not interpret this clause to create a Teutonic version of *Roe v. Wade.*[58] A Polish decision in 1997 invalidated an abortion law passed by Parliament on grounds that it infringed on the rights of the unborn child.[59] Poland then enacted a new abortion law, which allowed early abortion (up to twelve weeks), but only in cases of rape, incest, risk to the mother's health, or if the fetus is malformed.[60]

Most developed countries allow women to terminate pregnancy in the early stages, but most, like Poland, have hedged this right with certain restrictions (for example, mandatory counseling in France) or limited it to certain circumstances. Many otherwise narrow laws take a different tack if the woman was raped—that is, if her pregnancy was involuntary. Of course the texts of statutes rarely give a true picture of the law in action. Abortion is often easier in practice than in theory. For example, when a woman can get an abortion in the interests of mental or physical health, "mental health" is often a loophole of enormous proportions. It is, after all, quite easy to get depressed over an unwanted pregnancy, and a cooperative doctor can certify that your mental health requires getting rid of the fetus. Once upon a time there was migratory divorce; now there is migratory abortion. Pregnant Irish women can take a boat or plane to England. A number of countries permit abortion on demand, including China, Sweden, and the Czech Republic. Rates of abortion vary wildly. The law in force may be a factor, but if so it is hardly a determining factor. The abortion rate in Turkey, a country that permits abortion on demand, was minuscule in 1991; the rate in the United States was nine times as great, and in Romania sixty-six times as great.[61]

Gay and Transsexual Rights

For some time, *Roe v. Wade* seemed to be the high-water mark of the constitutional right of privacy in the United States. In 1986, in *Bowers v. Hardwick*,[62] the Supreme Court refused to take what many hoped would be the logical next step. The subject of the case was Georgia's sodomy law. Michael Hardwick, the defendant, was a bartender. Hardwick owed money on a fine for drinking in public. A policeman came to serve Hardwick with a warrant. Another resident of the apartment let the policeman in; he entered Hardwick's bedroom, and found him in the act of having sex with another man. The Georgia sodomy statute applied to "any sexual act involving the sex organs of one person and the mouth or anus of another." It was not restricted to homosexuals; even married couples, if they did the forbidden deeds, could be in violation of the statute. The penalty, theoretically, might be quite harsh: up to twenty years in prison. Needless to say, the law was sporadically enforced, if it was enforced at all; and it was never used against married couples. In fact, Georgia did not really want to prosecute Hardwick; Hardwick, however, insisted on challenging the law. A bare majority of the Supreme Court upheld the statute. Byron White, writing for the majority, argued that the privacy cases were about "family, marriage or procreation"; it was absurd to claim a constitutional right to homosexual behavior. Justice Blackmun disagreed; to say that the case was about a "fundamental right" to do sodomy was narrow and prejudicial. Rather, the case was about the "fundamental right" to be "let alone."

This was a five-to-four decision; and Justice Lewis Powell, the crucial fifth vote, later recanted: in October 1990 he told a law school audience that his vote was "probably" a mistake. Ironically, the Georgia Supreme Court in 1998 struck down this very statute.[63] The Georgia court blithely ignored *Bowers;* it appealed to its own constitution. The Georgia Supreme Court, and not the U.S. Supreme Court, was after all the supreme authority on that document.

The 1998 decision in Georgia—a state in the deep South—bears witness to a dramatic change in the climate of national opinion. As late as 1960, every state made "sodomy" a crime. By the end of the century, it had been wiped off the books in state after state, at least for consenting adults. The Supreme Court itself began to backtrack. It gave a clear signal to this effect in 1996. The case came out of Colorado. A number of cities and towns in Colorado—Boulder, Aspen, Denver—had adopted ordinances banning discrimination on the basis of sexual preference. Fundamentalist groups put a proposal on the ballot to amend the Colorado constitution and get rid of these ordinances. Under the proposal, no state or local government was to take any action to protect people on the basis of sexual preference. The proposal succeeded at the polls, under Colorado's referendum procedure. It was promptly challenged in federal court. Somewhat surprisingly, a majority of the Supreme Court agreed that the amendment violated the federal constitution. The Colorado provision, by singling out one category of people in this way, had violated the equal protection clause. The majority opinion did not even mention *Bowers v. Hardwick.*[64]

As of 2003, only thirteen states still made sodomy a crime—some southern states, together with Utah and Idaho. In four of these states, the crime was limited to homosexual acts. Texas had one such law. The Supreme Court agreed to hear a challenge to the Texas law; and in June 2003 the Court struck down the law, overruled *Bowers v. Hardwick,* and apparently consigned *all* existing sodomy laws to the ashcan of history. The right of privacy had won a smashing victory.[65]

Nonetheless, the whole issue of gay rights was and is intensely controversial—among members of the public, despite the holdings of the Supreme Court. The Colorado case illustrates the point. The Supreme Court weighed in on the side of gay rights (though not without a furious dissent by Justice Antonin Scalia). A voting majority of the people of Colorado had expressed opposition to gay rights ordinances. Yet what set off the "family values" campaign was the very fact that important cities in Colorado *did* guarantee gay rights. As noted, many states of the United States had years before wiped from their books the laws against sodomy. In most of the country, same-sex behavior had been no longer a crime. Openly gay men and women ran for office, sometimes won, and were occasionally appointed to government positions. Colorado is not the only state where communities have adopted antidiscrimination ordinances. In some places, these ordinances have been suggested, proposed, and then defeated; in some they have been abolished by popular vote, as in Colorado. But on the whole, public attitudes toward same-sex relations have relaxed dramatically.

According to the census, there are at least 1.5 million same-sex couples living in the United States. Nearly 200,000 of these couples are raising children. Many of these couples would like some sort of state recognition—some way of getting the legal and social advantages of marriage. Not all of the couples want to marry; but many do hunger for the recognition—the legitimacy—that marriage might bring.[66] But if anything horrifies conservatives more than gay rights ordinances, it is the specter of gay marriage. One small New England state—Vermont—in response to a court decision, set up a system of civil unions for gay and lesbian partners. This set off a panic in other parts of the country. Vermont seemed dangerous because the normal rule of comity, under a federal system, might force other states to recognize a "marriage" of this kind. That is, if it was valid in Vermont, it had to be valid in their state too. A frenzy of lawmaking followed; to ward off this plague state after state passed laws explicitly defining marriage as something between one man and one woman; nothing else would do. And Congress in 1996 passed a "Defense of Marriage" Act. Under this law, no state was required to "give effect to any public act, record, or judicial proceeding of any other state . . . respecting a relationship between persons of the same sex that is treated as a marriage." Wherever in the federal statute books the word "marriage" was used, it was to mean "only a legal union between one man and one woman as husband and wife."[67] In November 2003 a decision of the Massachusetts high court went even further than Vermont: it ordered the legislature to pass a law allowing gays and lesbians to marry.[68] This set off another panic attack, calls for a constitutional amendment, calls to do something, anything, to avert what was seen as a crisis. A woman who headed an organization called Concerned Women for America demanded instant action: "The time is now," she said; later, "when you see the American public disintegrating and you see our enemies overtaking us because we have no moral will," it will be too late.[69] In 2004, the mayor of San Francisco ordered city officials to issue licenses and marry same-sex couples. This only made the culture war more intense.

The "moral will" no doubt is connected with orthodox marriage in the mind of the woman just quoted. But unorthodoxy is sprouting everywhere in the United States, even in the flat fields of Kansas. The Kansas high court had to deal in 2002, for example, with a case concerning a transsexual. Marshall Gardiner, a rich old man of eighty-five, went through a wedding ceremony with J'Noel Ball, who was much younger. Gardiner died about a year later without making out a will. J'Noel claimed her statutory share of the estate as Gardiner's widow. But there was a problem: J'Noel was a transsexual. Born a male, J'Noel had even once been married to a woman, from whom he was divorced. Even before the divorce, J'Noel began a series of treatments and operations to change her sex from man to woman. She then married Marshall Gardiner. The Kansas Supreme Court turned down the "widow's" claim. The marriage was void. Only a biological woman—a woman from birth—could be a wife in Kansas. A "male-to-female post-operative transsexual" did not fit the "definition of a female."[70]

A lower court in Kansas had held otherwise; and cases in other states had been at least willing to give some legal recognition to transsexuals (people who change their identity through hormones and surgery). Under the law of Massachusetts, for example, if a person goes through "sex reassignment surgery" and has his or her name legally changed, that person has a right to have the birth certificate "amended to reflect the newly acquired sex and name."[71]

A transsexual was also involved in a case before the European Court of Human Rights in 1997. This time, it was a woman who had been "reassigned" as a man through the wonders of the operating table. This person, X, a British subject, had been living for many years in a relationship with Y, a woman. The woman had had artificial insemination and gave birth to a child. X wanted to be registered as the father of the child; this was refused. X then claimed that his rights had been violated and complained to the Court of Human Rights. X lost the case, partly on the grounds that countries of the Union had wide discretion on the law of family affairs.[72]

The whole idea of a transsexual in a way illustrates the power of the concept of choice in our society. To be sure, almost everybody is satisfied with his or her own sexual identity and cannot imagine changing it. But a few people feel that their birth gender was some kind of terrible mistake. Radical surgery, hormones—and the culture of choice—allow them to shift from man to woman, and from woman to man, at least in matters of behavior and sexual practices. But no surgery can change the nucleus of the cell, the genetic makeup; and this was, as we saw, decisive for the Kansas Supreme Court. In any event, sex-change surgery is an extreme measure. It is at the extreme edge, too, of the culture of individual choice—the edge of the idea of plastic identity.

Transsexuals first became news with the case of Christine (formerly George) Jorgensen, who became surgically a woman in Denmark in

1952. At the time the story caused something of a sensation. Another famous case involved Dr. Renée Richards, formerly a man, who won a lawsuit in 1977 allowing him to play tennis as a woman. Sex change is hardly routine even today; but it is no longer the stuff of headlines. And a number of European countries are now willing to go rather far in giving men and women who switch sexes all the rights and duties of their new identity.[73]

These cases, though unusual, illustrate a point. Despite intense controversy, backsliding, and legal firewalls against what some see as too much protection of private choices, the zone of legal options of lifestyle has increased enormously. People now claim and get rights to forms of behavior and ways of living that would have caused scandal, outrage, and disgrace in the past—that would have cost them their place in respectable society. In theory at least, some of this behavior might even have landed them in prison. In big cities in the United States, Scandinavia, and other parts of Western Europe (but not all), cohabitation has become almost normal. Same-sex behavior is perfectly legal and widely tolerated. Contraception and abortion are freely available. Censorship of literature, magazines, and movies is moribund or dead.

Privacy, in the sense of *Griswold* if not of *Roe v. Wade,* is firmly embedded in the law of the developed countries. The Universal Declaration of Human Rights (1948) announced, "No one shall be subjected to arbitrary inference with his privacy, family, home or correspondence"; and the European Convention on Human Rights (ECHR) (Article 8) also declared a right to "respect" for "private and family life." These are extremely vague provisions. Moreover, the ECHR has an escape clause wide enough to encompass almost anything. States can override Article 8 if the goal is "the prevention of disorder or crime" or "the protection of health or morals." But in fact, as interpreted by the courts, Article 8 has been quite expansive. Courts have seized on the word "private" and found great things hidden inside of it. The movement is in directions that run parallel to American developments—and then some. In *Dudgeon v. U.K.* (1981), for example, Jeffery Dudgeon, a shipping clerk in Belfast, Northern Ireland, brought a complaint before the European

Court of Human Rights. He invoked Article 8 against "the existence in Northern Ireland of laws which [made] . . . homosexual acts between consenting adult males criminal offences." These laws, the Court held, were indeed a violation of Article 8.[74]

Laws against same-sex relations have vanished or are vanishing, then, in Europe. Some countries have been open to the idea of allowing same-sex couples rights very much like marriage rights. Pioneers in this regard were the Scandinavian countries of Denmark, Norway, and Sweden. In Norway, for example, same-sex relations were decriminalized in 1972; discrimination on the basis of sexual preference was forbidden in 1981; and in 1993, Parliament enacted a "registered partnership" law. The legal status of registered partners is much the same as ordinary married couples—couples who registered, for example, needed to follow normal procedures for divorce if they wanted to dissolve these relationships.[75] In 1998, the Parliament of Catalonia passed a law on couples in stable unions ("uniones estables de pareja"); this law granted extensive rights to same-sex couples, including inheritance rights. There are analogous provisions in Aragon and Navarra.[76] In Germany, too, same-sex couples can now register as partners; if they do so, they have a legal relationship similar to the one in Norway—only a court can grant a "divorce."[77] Three states of the federal republic, including conservative Catholic Bavaria, challenged this law in court. They claimed the law violated constitutional guarantees protecting marriage and the family. But the Federal Constitutional Court, by a five-to-three margin, upheld the law. The court pointed out that, in 2000, there were at least 47,000 same-sex partners living in the federal republic and that more than half of them "expressed the wish to live in a legally binding partnership."[78] Giving rights to same-sex partners, said the court, did not contravene provisions protecting marriage. Indeed, the new law took marriage as a social model or ideal. The constitution protected the basic human need for intimate, reliable relationships; to give a legal basis to these relationships for same-sex couples in no way impaired the institution of marriage. These civil unions are a kind of halfway house. Actual marriage for same-sex couples is only a step away. Two provinces of Canada have actually taken this step, as of early 2004; and so has the state of Massachusetts.

Privacy and Its Discontents

Abortion is another privacy issue that remains steeped in controversy. Religious beliefs and legal technicalities bedevil the question of abortion. Underlying the tumult and the shouting are some basic facts of modern society. The technology of sex and reproduction affects abortion, and not only in the technical sense: it changes attitudes and expectations as well. It is not just that abortion is medically safe. Devices like the pill and even condoms spread a message: babies are a matter of free choice. Abortion is a less desirable, more drastic way of exercising this choice. But it is part of the same continuum.

In the United States, the abortion question is treated as an aspect of privacy; divorce, on the other hand, is dealt with under the heading of family law. But the two issues are organically connected. They both concern the master trend we have discussed throughout this book: the voyage of the family from status to contract, from rigidity to flexibility, from compulsion to choice. The trend is obvious; the voyage, however, has never been effortless and smooth. It is certain that on matters of lifestyle and "privacy," general attitudes have changed dramatically, especially in the last half of the twentieth century. That much seems clear, despite the hesitations, conflicts, struggles, and all the zigs and zags. What also seems clear is that changing conceptions of the individual—ideas about choice, freedom, and rights—underpin these developments. Doors are open in modern society that were tightly shut in the past. On issues of marriage, divorce, sexual preference, having children, not having children, family life or no family life, even questions of identity, the menu of choices has expanded.

Expanded: but within limits. Many choices are still forbidden. Incest is still taboo. Sexual freedom is essentially limited to consenting adults (or near-adults). Hardly anybody wants to change these rules. Moreover, there is a conservative core at the base of many changes in attitude and behavior. Commitment, marriage, stability: these are still ideals. Even J'Noel, the Kansas transsexual, wanted something like old-fashioned marriage. Rights for cohabiting couples are rights for couples who want to make a commitment. "Progressive" jurisdictions give rights to these couples—and even require something like a divorce when love begins to fade. Most same-sex couples in long-term relationships want some form of marriage; they want legitimacy. Some radicals (gays and straights) oppose gay marriage precisely because they oppose *all* marriage, which they denounce as a bourgeois and oppressive institution. But there is tremendous vitality still left in this bourgeois and oppressive institution.

It is a bit paradoxical that so many modern controversies—over sex life, abortion, and contraception—are defined legally as issues of privacy. "Privacy" in the sense of free choice of lifestyle seems miles away from "privacy" in the sense of secrecy, or "privacy" as a screen shutting off the world from a person's intimate life. For some people, "privacy" means the freedom to go naked, so to speak, perhaps even in public. The privacy that was so precious to Warren and Brandeis, the cloak of respectability, freedom from the prying eyes of the media, has lost some of its power and its luster, particularly for public figures.

Public figures, as we saw, are fair game for the media. Nothing about them is sacred. The tabloid press feeds off the sex life of presidents and prime ministers; these things are even fodder for the mainstream press. The tabloids smack their lips over every scandal: the young royals in England, the love affairs of princes, the sex lives of the rich and famous. Photographers with zoom lenses swarm like gnats around celebrities of stage, screen, and TV. The hunger for information goes far beyond sex and scandal. Does the President of France have a hearing aid? What kind of clothes does the Queen of England wear? Anything about the life, private or public, of a celebrity—the trivial and the ordinary as well as the sensational—is grist for the mill of television and the press.

In the past fifty years or so, the formative role of the media has become more important than ever. Vast economic, social, and technological changes since 1800 or so have utterly transformed family life, family structure, and family law; but nothing more so than the media. The media are a pervasive element in modern society. Their impact on culture in general, and on legal culture specifically, is incalculable. Television is particularly powerful and ubiquitous. For children, television has become, in James Steyer's phrase, the "other parent."[79] The family once had a monopoly on the job of training, teaching, and socializing young children. Schools take over and share the job at a certain point. But nowadays both family and schools have a mighty rival. Almost from the day a child is born, television in the home spreads its message. It imparts ideas, words, images. It shapes children's views of reality. According to a study cited in the *New York Times* in October 2003, almost 25 percent of the children in America under two years old have a TV in their room, and 59 percent of children between the ages of six months and two years watch television.[80]

In short, the typical middle-class child in Western countries absorbs an astonishing amount of imagery—television, DVDs, Web sites. And what do these children learn from the television they so avidly watch? Television imparts a definite ideology—an ideology of individualism, consumption, and desire. The child learns about a world of wanting, needing, buying, and using, a world of consumer products, a world of fads and fashions. As Kenneth Karst has pointed out, "babes in arms learn to recognize advertising logos and start to pronounce brand names soon after they say their first words."[81] Above all, children enter a world that revolves around the naked self. The child learns about heroes and superheroes. The child also gets to look inside the world of the rich and the famous—the world of celebrities. These are the people who dominate TV. They share it with cartoon characters. Humble, ordinary people are squeezed into the cracks and margins of the broadcast band. Television inflates and exalts the celebrity society. But it inflates at the same time the sense that people have a right to see, hear, and know *everything;* that nothing in the world of politics, sports, and public life can legitimately be kept private; that every detail, even the most intimate, is in the public domain. Because people see so much on television, they come to think that they could, and should, have unlimited access to the public sphere.

This may explain why there is so little support for privacy with regard to public figures while at the same time, there is so much support for privacy with regard to ordinary people. Ordinary people feel a right to choose, and a right to know, for themselves (though perhaps not for other people). We have mentioned the growing right of adopted children to learn the facts of their birth and the identity of their birth parents. They are animated by curiosity and a deep sense of this right to know, to choose, to have self-knowledge. Here, too, as we pointed out, there is a plain conflict of interests. Many birth parents (though not all) resent it when the veil of secrecy is violently wrenched away.

Television floods the house with sounds as well as images; it disrupts the intimate silences of the home. The Internet and the cell phone do the same. Millions of young people, in countries like Italy or Finland or Israel or the United States, are never "private" in the sense of solitude or being alone. They chatter all day on their cell phones; they would feel naked without a headset, a computer, a pager, a Palm pilot, or any other gadget that connects them to people, images, and sounds. Their lives revolve around technological communication. Businesspeople, too, can now be connected constantly and wherever they are to home, office, or the World Wide Web.

Choosing Privacy—or Not

In a way, then, many ordinary people choose to live life in a kind of fishbowl. Celebrity life is the extreme case of life in a fishbowl. Changes in the law and (more significantly) changes in the culture have weakened old restrictions on the media. The media no longer censor themselves; and nobody else censors them either. The older conception of privacy has become, as we saw, a victim of this development. The press, TV, and mass-market magazines are bold and invasive in a way that once would have seemed both wrong and downright illegal. Celebrity life has glamour; but the glamour comes at a price—the loss of privacy. Once your face is known and recognized, you become a kind of prisoner of fame. Yet life in the celebrity fishbowl is glamorous, enthralling, dazzling, infectious; it attracts the desire of millions of people.

Recently, the media have given ordinary people the chance to enter the world of glamour and publicity. Now perhaps everyone can become a celebrity—can have their fifteen minutes of fame. Hence privacy itself— the quiet, anonymous life—has itself become a matter of choice. Most people prefer to remain obscure and unknown; but a small, strident minority is willing to do anything, and make any sacrifice, in order to become a star. Reality TV gives a few people the chance to do so. These are the people who appear on *Big Brother* or *Survivor*. A few people have even flooded their homes with cameras and put themselves on the Internet. In the late 1990s Jennifer Ringley, a young woman in Washington, D.C., committed herself to a "life under Internet-ready cameras"; viewers could see her dressing, sleeping, eating, drinking orange juice.[82] She has had many imitators since then. In *Big Brother,* the camera stares at a group of ordinary people living together in a rented house. This program, or a variation on it, has been shown in at least seventeen countries. In the United Kingdom, when plans for the program were announced, some 5,000 people sent personal videos to the producers. It wasn't the modest prize money that attracted them, but the chance to become a star.[83]

There is a similar appeal to the so-called trash talk shows. These are programs where ordinary people talk about their lives and their problems. Of course, the truly ordinary problems of truly ordinary people are too boring for these programs. Hence they specialize in the lurid and sensational, especially sexual behavior that is (to put it mildly) out of the mainstream.[84] In August 1993 Sally Jessy Raphael, the host of one of these shows, set up a toll-free number to be used by women willing to call in and answer her question "Are you a mother who was raped by her son?"[85] A steady parade of men and women on these programs reveal the most intimate details of their lives. They talk about what it is like to be a transsexual, or an atheist, or a victim of abuse, or a dentist who sleeps with his patients, or a woman who has sex with her father-in-law, or a forty-five-year-old woman impregnated by a high school student, and so on. For some of the participants, the shows are cathartic. For some, the program has a political meaning. It gives them the chance to go before the public; it is the only forum where they can be heard, seen, and listened to. These participants "trade their privacy for the chance to place their items on the agenda."[86] For most participants, though, what attracts them is probably nothing more than the love of their tiny slice of fame.

Most people are not so willing to parade naked, so to speak, in front of the world. They value their quiet obscurity. They do not want to be on TV—at least not badly enough to do what it takes to get there. But if chance should give them an opening—if they live next door to a murderer, or are witnesses to a crime, or find themselves in some other way "in the news"—many of them will eagerly grasp the opportunity. The camera and the microphone seem to be almost addictive. In some ways, the hunger for fame seems almost epidemic in modern society. Ours is a society in which more and more people are isolated individuals, in which family ties have become more attenuated. The yearning to be "somebody" gnaws at the belly. And to be "somebody" means to be known outside of your narrow circle, which means to become news, to get your name in the papers, to go on TV. The fifteen minutes of fame seems to be worth the price.

The culture of privacy in modern society is complex, even internally contradictory. There may be no way to reconcile the two forks of the road. The demand for personal privacy is real enough. People want restrictions on dossiers, they want their medical records and their bank accounts kept private, they are afraid of identity cards, they are leery of surveillance, and so on. But these same people love invading the privacy of other people, especially famous people. They have no objection when the media invade the privacy of celebrities. A small number of people are even quite willing to give up their own privacy. Perhaps what people want is to choose how much privacy to consume and when and how they want to consume it—at least for themselves.

Privacy is also situational. The same people who, say, might feel an urge to go to a nudist beach would be horrified to discover a hidden camera in their bedroom or shower; they might even object to somebody taking pictures at the nudist beach. They hate the idea of surveillance; but by now they are used to it in some circumstances—TV monitors in stores and office buildings; metal detectors in airports, along with X-rays of their baggage and sometimes even pat-down searches of their bodies. They also value a kind of right I call the right to evanescence: the right to have things disappear. Much of what we write in the book of life we want to write with vanishing ink. It is a little like the fact that grown-ups often hate it when Mother trots out naked baby pictures. A person might be willing, even eager, to march in a parade, carry a banner, join a demonstration, make himself heard; but feels uncomfortable if someone with a video camera records the parade or the demonstration for posterity or takes notes. As a teacher, I stand in front of a small audience several times a week, sounding forth; but it makes me queasy when somebody in the class has a tape recorder. I want my jokes, my expressions, my halting utterances to go away as swiftly as they came.

People who jealously guard their own privacy are happy to peep into other people's windows, especially (but not exclusively) the windows of celebrities. The United States has become what one author calls a "voyeur nation."[87] Nor is the United States the only "voyeur nation." Some of what people want to watch is spectacle: ceremonies, funerals, coronations. These events are now available to millions, even billions, through TV. People like intimate glimpses of how the other half lives—or, to be more accurate, the other one percent, the people who are enormously wealthy. A program called *Lifestyles of the Rich and Famous* was once quite popular in the United States. The program went into celebrity homes, exploring the various rooms. You could see their kitchens, the sofas in their living rooms, the style of their bedrooms, the pictures on the wall. All over the Western world the new "reality" shows, as we said, are incredibly popular. The "reality" on these shows is not particularly real—that is, it is not real life; but it *is* real people, ordinary people, often doing stupid or crazy things or playing ridiculous games. Much of this "real life," of course, is staged; some is not. Thanks to TV and the Internet, "Lifestyles of the Ordinary but Unashamed" is a program everybody can watch—or even become part of.

Some of the fascination of celebrities—particularly those in show business—comes from the fragility of their relationships. They marry and divorce with great rapidity. Or, more and more, they connect and disconnect with great rapidity (whether they are married or not hardly matters). The gossip magazines breathlessly give us the ins and outs of all these relationships. To the disgust of people who believe in traditional family values, celebrities project a model of disconnections, including family disconnections. Or rather, they project a model of connections that are loose, fluid, and volatile. Sports heroes and rock stars wallow in promiscuity. Relationships seem passionate but shallow. At the same time, these celebrities are in a way part of the "family" of ordinary people; the public feels a sense of closeness, even intimacy, with them.

The technology of communication has opened up whole worlds of possibilities. It connects people across great distances. What the telephone and the telegraph began, e-mail and the Internet have expanded and completed. People can reach out and communicate almost instantaneously. Barriers of time and space seem no longer to exist. Young people, as we mentioned, talk all day long on their cell phones. They send messages to each other, and they get back answers; the businessperson reads e-mail on the airplane, and the hotel room has a fax machine and an Internet connection. Someday the whole world may be connected. But these are not traditional connections. They are just as much disconnections as connections. As connections, they are individual and voluntary. Some are fleeting and fluid. They come and go. The young woman on the sidewalk, talking to a friend on her cell phone, is connected to her friend, but in the contemporary world she is also more and more disconnected from family ties; she is no longer so dependent on them. The binds and hasps of an older, simpler society become weaker all the time.

One of the main themes of this book has been the rise of the individual and the dissolution of one version of the traditional family (though not of the family as such). Old ways of relating have been replaced by new forms of being alone, and new forms of being together. Marriage and divorce have become voluntary, individualistic. The child's role in the family has changed quite dramatically. For many people, relationships take on new and strange shapes. This is a world of cohabitation, in vitro fertilization, surrogacy, no-fault divorce, and many other legal and social institutions our great-grandparents never imagined, or never thought of as acceptable in polite society. Yet some new modes of togetherness are really variations on the theme of the classic family. The key to social life is still commitment. Perhaps it is a looser commitment, and perhaps more and more people choose *not* to commit; but commitment is still the glue that holds society together.

Any discussion of the world we live in has to contend with the power and the reality of the mass media (I have stressed this point). In many ways, technology and the media created the world as we know it today. Young people cannot imagine a world without television. Very young people cannot imagine a world without computers and the Internet. Television in particular powerfully competes with family life; it is a presence in the home, an invasion of privacy, although millions of people eagerly welcome this invader into their living rooms, family rooms, kitchens, and bedrooms. Television and the other media, and now the Internet, have helped to destroy the privacy of "public figures" and, to an extent, of everybody else. They have allowed some people to open up their souls and bodies to the whole watching world. Most of us reject this idea. We value our privacy. On the other hand, we have grown accustomed to some kinds of invasions of privacy, as I pointed out—cameras in banks, for example. When we buy goods on the Web, we know that somebody makes and keeps a record. Radar tracks us on the highway. Perhaps all this makes us uneasy. But what can we do?

Today there is a wider menu of choices of (legitimate) lifestyle than in the past. Somewhat oddly, this wide menu of choices also goes by the name of (rights of) privacy. And this kind of privacy has expanded in the twentieth century. "Traditional values" and the "traditional family" have lost their monopoly of respectability. "Family" is still meaningful; but we can define family in ways that would have startled our grandparents.

The media are important here, too, in widening the area of choice.

They enable individuals to reach out and find like-minded people. Whether your thing is antique silver or sadomasochism, you can find kindred spirits on the Web.[88] Yet the new technology is, ironically, a tremendous danger to privacy and choice as well. Information gathering and storing has become downright scary. Governments, the media, and big institutions have ways to intrude into people's lives, to find out their secrets, their medical histories, the bills they pay, their credit history, the books they read, the shows they watch, the Web sites they explore.[89] Wiretapping, to be sure, has been with us for a long time; but it is cumbersome and limited; it is hedged about with legal restrictions (whether these restrictions are effective is another question). Besides, until recently, nobody recorded telephone messages or conversations, and wiretaps were rare and perhaps confined to gangsters. What we said, did, and wrote was mostly gone with the wind. E-mail, however, is not so evanescent. It can come back to haunt us.

This is not all. Newer eavesdropping devices are positively Orwellian in their implications. There are devices that can hear a whisper on another continent, devices that can see through walls, devices that can invade and explore the body and soul of the citizen. Satellites can photograph a beetle crawling on the surface of the earth—or almost. Immense—infinite—amounts of data can be gathered, stored, and retrieved at low or no cost, and forever. Databases can be linked. The time may be coming when nothing is ever lost, when everything is or can be recorded. A power once thought to belong only to God would then belong to human governments—perhaps to big business too. The bloody tyrannies of the past, even such monsters as the Nazis, lacked the power to control every aspect of everybody's life. There are, practically speaking, no longer any limits—at least potentially. A new Hitler would be incredibly more powerful and even more dangerous. Joe and Jane Citizen, living placidly in a democratic society, expect privacy and anonymity in their daily lives or when talking on the phone, watching the news on television, shopping, walking down the street, or even when they surf the Web. But this privacy hangs by a thread. The technical power to destroy this anonymity and invade private lives is already here. Of course there are—at least theoretically—restraints. There are legal restraints, and there are political and social restraints. How well these work or will work is another question. The "war on terror," for example, has been a handy excuse for incursions into this sensitive and dangerous realm. Perhaps the most serious legal, political, and cultural struggle of the next generation will be the struggle over privacy—the struggle to contain and control technology and preserve our sacred, individual space.

Notes

1. Family Law in Context

1. H. F. Jolowicz, *Historical Introduction to the Study of Roman Law* (1954), p. 118.

2. Henry Sumner Maine, *Ancient Law* (1986 [1864]), p. 165.

3. Lawrence M. Friedman, *A History of American Law* (2nd ed., 1985), pp. 208–210.

4. Lawrence M. Friedman, *American Law in the Twentieth Century* (2002), pp. 10–11.

5. There were, to be sure, outbursts of intolerance: anti-Catholic riots, for example; and the Mormons, whose custom of polygamy outraged the rest of the country, were persecuted until they officially gave up the practice. See Sarah Barringer Gordon, *The Mormon Question: Polygamy and Constitutional Conflict in Nineteenth Century America* (2002).

6. Lawrence M. Friedman, "Is There a Modern Legal Culture?" *Ratio Juris* 7:117 (1994).

7. On this point, see Kenneth L. Karst, "Law, Cultural Conflict, and the Socialization of Children," *Cal. L. Rev.* 91:969, 1004 (2003).

8. Milton C. Regan, Jr., *Family Law and the Pursuit of Intimacy* (1993), p. 35.

9. Etsu Inagaki Sugimoto, *A Daughter of the Samurai* (1966).

10. Mary Ann Glendon, *The Transformation of Family Law: State, Law, and Family in the United States and Western Europe* (1989), p. 41. Under the Civil

Code of the Meiji in Japan, parental consent was needed for sons up to the age of thirty, and for daughters until twenty-five. But even this was offensive to conservatives, and the age limit was removed, making parental consent necessary as long as the parent was alive. See Fujiko Isono, "The Evolution of Modern Family Law in Japan," *Int'l J. of Law and the Family* 2:183, 193 (1988).

11. Ohio Rev. Code Ann. sec. 3101.01.

12. Milton C. Regan, Jr., *Family Law and the Pursuit of Intimacy* (1993), pp. 47–51.

13. See, in general, Lawrence M. Friedman, *The Legal System: A Social Science Perspective* (1975).

14. "Law" is here used in a broad sense—it is not simply the codes and doctrines, but the legal system, the legal order; the law as an actual living, functioning entity in society.

15. For the United States, see, for example, Lynn Mather, Craig A. McEwen, and Richard J. Maiman, *Divorce Lawyers at Work: Varieties of Professionalism in Practice* (2001).

16. See, for example, Kathryn Hendley, "Legal Development in Post-Soviet Russia," *Post-Soviet Affairs* 13:228 (1997).

17. See, for example, Roger Cotterrell, "Is There a Logic of Legal Transplants?" in David Nelken and Johannes Feest, eds., *Adapting Legal Cultures* (2001), p. 71.

18. Gordon S. Wood, *The Radicalism of the American Revolution* (1991), p. 44.

19. John Langbein, "The Twentieth-Century Revolution in Family Wealth Transmission," *Michigan L. Rev.* 86:622 (1988).

20. Lawrence M. Friedman, *The Republic of Choice: Law, Authority, and Culture* (1990).

2. Marriage and Divorce in the Nineteenth Century

1. There is a growing literature on the subject. See, in general, Michael Grossberg, *Governing the Hearth: Law and the Family in Nineteenth-Century America* (1985); noteworthy too are Nancy F. Cott, *Public Vows: A History of Marriage and the Nation* (2000); and Hendrik Hartog, *Man and Wife in America: A History* (2000).

2. See Grossberg, *Governing the Hearth,* pp. 69–75; Ariela R. Dubler, "Wifely Behavior: A Legal History of Acting Married," *Columbia L. Rev.* 100:957 (2000).

3. 1 Bl. Comm. *433: "Our law considers marriage in no other light than as

a civil contract." James Kent, *Commentaries on American Law* (1827), vol. 2, p. 71: "If a contract be made per verba de presenti . . . it amounts to a valid marriage . . . which the parties cannot dissolve"; Kent also uses the term "civil contract."

4. Epaphroditus Peck, *The Law of Persons or Domestic Relations* (1913), p. 4. There is, of course, the possibility of an antenuptial agreement.

5. See Wally Seccombe, *Weathering the Storm: Working-Class Families from the Industrial Revolution to the Fertility Decline* (1993), pp. 49–54; and R. B. Outhwaite, *Clandestine Marriage in England, 1500–1850* (1995).

6. See Stephen Parker, "The Marriage Act 1753: A Case Study in Family Law-Making," *Int'l J. of Law and the Family* 1:133 (1987). Lord Hardwicke's Act is 26 Geo. II, ch. 33.

7. 26 Geo. II, ch. 33, section 8. The law also did not apply to Scotland, "nor to any Marriages amongst the People called Quakers, or amongst the Persons professing the Jewish religion." Curiously enough, although Quakers and Jews were exempted, Catholics and Dissenters were not: they had to marry in an Anglican church, or not at all. The situation was at least partially remedied in 1836, when Parliament created a means of marrying civilly, or in a nonconforming church. Stephen Cretney, *Family Law in the Twentieth Century: A History* (2003), pp. 8–13.

8. For the minister's remarks, see Nancy F. Cott, *Public Vows: A History of Marriage and the Nation* (2000), p. 32.

9. Richard Godbeer, *Sexual Revolution in Early America* (2002), p. 127.

10. Mark M. Carroll, *Homesteads Ungovernable: Families, Sex, Race, and the Law in Frontier Texas, 1823–1860* (2001), p. 113.

11. Richard J. Hooker, ed., *The Carolina Backcountry on the Eve of the Revolution* (1953), p. 15.

12. A minor function was to save marriages—and the legitimacy of children—in cases where there was some technical flaw in the formal marriage ceremony. See, for example, Askew v. Dupree, 30 Ga. 173 (1860), discussed below, at pp. 23–24.

13. Fenton v. Reed, 4 Johns. 52 (N.Y., 1809).

14. Thomas v. James, 69 Okl. 285, 171 P. 855 (1918).

15. Robert Black, "Common Law Marriage," *U. of Cincinnati L. Rev.* 2:113, 133 (1928).

16. Clayton v. Wardell, 4 N.Y. 230 (1850).

17. Id., at 239.

18. Askew v. Dupree, 30 Ga. 173 (1860).

19. Meister v. Moore, 96 U.S. 76, 81 (1877).

20. See, in general, Karen Lystra, *Searching the Heart: Women, Men, and Romantic Love in Nineteenth-Century America* (1989).

21. Gall v. Gall, 114 N.Y. 109, 21 N.E. 106 (1889).

22. There was another issue in the case: Amelia had been married before she met Joseph Gall. This marriage was never legally dissolved. The first husband, however, John Jermann, had himself been married before Amelia—and this marriage too was never legally dissolved. Helena Jermann skipped out on her husband after two weeks of marriage. They signed a separation agreement, which John thought was equivalent to a divorce (it was not). Under New York law, Jermann had the right to remarry if his wife had been gone five years and he had no evidence that she was still alive. (Apparently she was). The jury decided this issue too in Amelia's favor—that is, that husband number one did *not* have the right to marry her; hence her marriage to Jermann was void. And if this marriage was void, then she was free to marry Joseph Gall.

23. Stephen Cretney, *Family Law in the Twentieth Century: A History* (2003), p. 161.

24. Lawrence Stone, *Road to Divorce: England, 1530–1987* (1990), pp. 371–372.

25. Gail Savage, "'The Magistrates are Men': Working-Class Marital Conflict and Appeals from the Magistrates' Court to the Divorce Court after 1895," in George Robb and Nancy Erber, eds., *Disorder in the Court: Trials and Sexual Conflict at the Turn of the Century* (1999), pp. 231, 233.

26. There is a large literature on the history of divorce in the United States. See, for example, Glenda Riley, *Divorce: An American Tradition* (1991); Nelson M. Blake, *The Road to Reno: A History of Divorce in the United States* (1962); and Norma Basch, *Framing American Divorce: From the Revolutionary Generation to the Victorians* (1999).

27. Lawrence M. Friedman, *A History of American Law* (2nd ed., 1985), p. 205.

28. Laws Md. 1847, ch. 130.

29. On the process, see Thomas E. Buckley, *The Great Catastrophe of My Life: Divorce in the Old Dominion* (2002).

30. Ibid., pp. 96–97.

31. Ibid., pp. 269, 271.

32. Mississippi, from 1803 on, gave courts of equity jurisdiction over divorce. Stats. Miss. Terr. 1816, p. 252. Desertion (for more than five years) and

adultery were the basic grounds for divorce. Yet in the laws of 1821, for example, a statute declared that "whereas" the Honorable Powhatan Ellis, acting as chancellor in Covington county, "did order, adjudge, and decree" that the bonds of matrimoney between John and Sally Coulter were dissolved, the legislature ("two thirds of both branches concuring [sic] therein") resolved that the "bonds of matrimony" between the Coulters were to be "dissolved and annuled." Laws Miss. 1821, ch. 57, p. 155. By Laws Miss. 1840, ch. 18, it was enacted that all decrees of divorce "shall be final and conclusive, as fully as though the same had been confined [sic] by act of the Legislature."

33. Conn. Stats. 1824, Tit. 23, p. 124. An editor's note (ibid.) explained that the statute was "not repugnant to the law of God, or the best interests of the community," even though some had thought that the "Saviour prohibited divorces . . . except for . . . adultery." The editor felt also that there was no country with "more conjugal purity and felicity than this."

34. N.H. Rev. Stats. 1851, ch. 148, p. 298.

35. See Ky. Rev. Stats. 1943, sec. 403.020(2)(f).

36. Allen Horstman, *Victorian Divorce* (1985), p. 79; see also Dorothy M. Stetson, *A Woman's Issue: The Politics of Family Law Reform in England* (1982), ch. 2; a distinction between male and female adultery was also to be found in the law of some Canadian provinces: D. C. McKie, B. Prentice, and P. Reed, *Divorce: Law and the Family in Canada* (1983), p. 38; on gender roles in the United States, see Naomi Cahn, "Faithless Wives and Lazy Husbands: Gender Norms in Nineteenth-Century Divorce Law," *U. of Ill. Law Review* 2002: 651.

37. Gen. Stats. Minn. 1913, sec. 8702, p. 1921.

38. Lawrence M. Friedman, *Crime and Punishment in American History* (1993), pp. 221–222. On the "unwritten law," see Hendrik Hartog, "Lawyering, Husbands' Rights, and 'the Unwritten Law' in Nineteenth-Century America," *Journal of American History* 84:67 (1997); Robert M. Ireland, "Frenzied and Fallen Females: Sexual Dishonor and the Unwritten Law in the Nineteenth-Century United States," *Journal of Women's History* 3:95 (1992).

39. On this trial, see Nat Brandt, *The Congressman Who Got Away with Murder* (1991).

40. Hartog, "Lawyering," p. 74.

41. On this trial, see Nancy F. Cott, *Public Vows: A History of Marriage and the Nation* (2000), pp. 107–108.

42. Cited in Richard H. Chused, *Private Acts in Public Places: A Social History of Divorce in the Formative Era of American Family Law* (1994), p. 44.

43. For example, in Florida, Laws Fla. 1874, p. 41. In some states (and Florida was one of them) only "open and notorious" adultery was a violation of the criminal code; occasional, secret acts of adultery were not criminalized.

44. U.S. Bureau of the Census, *Marriage and Divorce, 1867–1906*, Part 1, p. 14 (1909).

45. In countries with a Catholic majority, the resistance to divorce was naturally much more powerful. In revolutionary France, divorce was recognized; but the conservative reaction led to its abolition in 1814; not until 1876 did French law provide for divorce. See Dominique Lepetit, *L'Histoire de France du Divorce de 1789 à nos Jours* (n.d.), pp. 47–57.

46. Basch, *Framing American Divorce*, p. 87.

47. Joel Prentiss Bishop, *New Commentaries on Marriage, Divorce, and Separation* (vol. 1, 1891), p. 16.

48. Ibid., p. 21.

49. Ga. Stats. 1873, sec. 1715, p. 297.

50. Sheehan v. Sheehan, 77 N.J. Eq. 411, 77 A. 1063 (1910).

51. See Lawrence M. Friedman, "A Dead Language: Divorce Law and Practice before No-Fault," *Virginia L. Rev.* 86:1497 (2000).

52. See Lawrence M. Friedman and Robert V. Percival, "Who Sues for Divorce? From Fault through Fiction to Freedom," *J. Legal Studies* 5:61 (1976). In other legal systems, too, the wife was the plaintiff in a divorce case more frequently than the husband. See, for Germany, Dirk Blasius, *Ehescheidung in Deutschland, 1794–1945* (1987), pp. 159–160.

53. I am indebted to Albert Lopez, JSD candidate, Stanford Law School, for these data.

54. Basch, *Framing American Divorce*, p. 102; see also Friedman and Percival, "Who Sues for Divorce?"

55. Sam B. Warner, "San Francisco Divorce Suits," *Cal. L. Rev.* 9:175, 177 (1921); see also Joanna Grossman, "Separated Spouses," *Stanf. L. Rev.* 53:1613, 1633–1637 (2001).

56. Leon C. Marshall and Geoffrey May, *The Divorce Court: Ohio* (1933), vol. 2, p. 23.

57. Gilbert M. Ostrander, *Nevada: The Great Rotten Borough, 1859–1964* (1966), pp. 205–206.

58. Paul H. Jacobson, *American Marriage and Divorce* (1959), pp. 104–109.

59. The two Williams v. North Carolina cases are reported at 317 U.S. 287 (1942), and 325 U.S. 226 (1944); see Hendrik Hartog, *Man and Wife in America*, pp. 278–282.

60. On the situation in the early twentieth century, see the discussion of the validity of migratory divorces in Peck, *Law of Persons*, pp. 190–196.

61. The case was Rosenstiel v. Rosenstiel, 26 N.Y. 2d 64, 262 N.Y. Supp. 2d 86, 209 N.E. 2d 709 (1965); see William E. Nelson, *The Legalist Reformation: Law, Politics, and Ideology in New York, 1920–1980* (2001), pp. 230–231.

62. Steven Mintz and Susan Kellogg, *Domestic Revolutions: A Social History of American Family Life* (1988), p. 108.

63. J. P. Lichtenberger, *Divorce: A Social Interpretation* (1931), pp. 345–347.

64. See, in general, A. James Hammerton, *Cruelty and Companionship: Conflict in Nineteenth-Century Married Life* (1992).

65. Friedman, *A History of American Law*, 2nd ed., pp. 208–211; Norma Basch, *In the Eyes of the Law: Women, Marriage, and Property in Nineteenth-Century New York* (1982). The disabilities of coverture were not as total as the law suggested; there were ways to defuse coverture or to detour around it, but these were cumbersome and expensive.

66. On this point, see William L. O'Neill, *Divorce in the Progressive Era* (1967).

67. William J. Goode, *After Divorce* (1956), pp. 136–137.

68. Elaine Tyler May, *Great Expectations: Marriage and Divorce in Post-Victorian America* (1980).

69. Robert L. Griswold, *Family and Divorce in California, 1850–1890: Victorian Illusions and Everyday Reality* (1982), p. 25.

70. Roderick Phillips, *Untying the Knot: A Short History of Divorce* (1991), p. 239.

3. Marriage and Divorce in the Modern World

1. For an overview, see John B. Crawley, "Is the Honeymoon Over for Common-Law Marriage: A Consideration of the Continued Viability of the Common-Law Marriage Doctrine," *Cumberland Law Review* 29:399 (1999).

2. Fla. Stats. Ann. sec. 741.211; Idaho Code, sec. 32–201, in force January 1, 1996: "Consent alone will not constitute marriage; it must be followed by the issuance of a license and a solemnization as authorized and provided by law."

3. Mary E. Richmond and Fred S. Hall, *Marriage and the State* (1929), pp. 293–294.

4. Thomas Clifford Billig and James Phillip Lynch, "Common-Law Marriage in Minnesota: A Problem in Social Security," *Minn. L. Rev.* 22:177 (1937).

5. Morton Keller, *Regulating a New Society: Public Policy and Social Change in America, 1900–1933* (1994), p. 19.

6. Otto E. Koegel, "Common Law Marriage and Its Development in the United States," in *Eugenics in Race and State*, vol. 2 (Scientific Papers of the Second International Congress of Eugenics, New York, 1921) (1923), pp. 252, 260.

7. Otto E. Koegel, *Common Law Marriage and Its Development in the United States* (1922), p. 120.

8. Conn. Rev. Stats. 1821, Title 22, sec. 14, p. 152. On abortion in general, see James C. Mohr, *Abortion in America: The Origins and Evolution of National Policy* (1978); on England, see Jeffrey Weeks, *Sex, Politics, and Society: The Regulation of Sexuality since 1800* (2nd ed., 1989), pp. 70–72.

9. Lawrence M. Friedman, *Crime and Punishment in American History* (1993), p. 229; Michael Grossberg, *Governing the Hearth: Law and the Family in Nineteenth-Century America* (1985), pp. 165–195.

10. On the United States, see Leslie J. Reagan, *When Abortion Was a Crime* (1997); on England, see Angus McLaren, "Abortion in England, 1890–1914," *Victorian Studies* 20:379 (1977).

11. Friedman, *Crime and Punishment*, p. 230.

12. Quoted in Reva Siegel, "Reasoning from the Body: A Historical Perspective on Abortion Regulation and Questions of Equal Protection," *Stanford Law Review* 44:261, 298 (1992).

13. On this, see Gaines M. Foster, *Moral Reconstruction: Christian Lobbyists and the Federal Legislation of Morality, 1865–1920* (2002), p. 50; see also James A. Morone, *Hellfire Nation: The Politics of Sin in American History* (2002), pp. 248–256.

14. Comstock and Cook are quoted in Nicola Beisel, *Imperiled Innocents: Anthony Comstock and Family Reproduction in Victorian America* (1997), p. 41.

15. Morone, *Hellfire Nation*, pp. 255–256.

16. Weeks, *Sex, Politics, and Society*, p. 125.

17. Quoted in Steven Mintz and Susan Kellogg, *Domestic Revolutions: A Social History of American Family Life* (1988), p. 108.

18. On the eugenics movement see Mark H. Haller, *Eugenics: Hereditarian Attitudes in American Thought* (1963); see also the discussion in Charles E. Rosenberg, "The Bitter Fruit: Heredity, Disease, and Social Thought in Nineteenth-Century America," *Perspectives in American History* 8:189 (1974). On the eugenics movement in England, see Weeks, *Sex, Politics, and Society*,

pp. 128–138; and Richard Allen Soloway, *Birth Control and the Population Question in England, 1877–1930* (1982).

19. Isabel Rennie, *The Search for Criminal Man: A Conceptual History of the Dangerous Offender* (1978), p. 79. Dugdale's book was *"The Jukes": A Study in Crime, Pauperism, Disease, and Heredity* (1877); "Juke" was not the actual name of the family.

20. See Scott Christianson, "Bad Seed or Bad Science?" *New York Times*, Feb. 8, 2003, p. B9.

21. Friedman, *Crime and Punishment*, p. 335, 336; Henry Herbert Goddard, *The Kallikak Family: A Study in the Heredity of Feeble-Mindedness* (1913), p. 108.

22. Laws Cal. 1909, ch. 720, p. 1093; Laws Ind. 1907, ch. 15, p. 377.

23. Harry H. Laughlin, "The Present Status of Eugenical Sterilization in the United States," in *Eugenics in Race and State*, vol. 2 (Scientific Papers of the Second International Congress of Eugenics, 1921) (1923), pp. 286, 290; on the sterilization movement in general, see Philip R. Reilly, *The Surgical Solution: A History of Involuntary Sterilization in the United States* (1991).

24. On the indeterminate sentence, see Friedman, *Crime and Punishment*, pp. 159–161.

25. Thomas Speed Mosby, "Eugenics," *Case and Comment* 21:22, 24 (1914). I am indebted to Catherine Crump for this reference.

26. 274 U.S. 200 (1927).

27. Ironically, the number of generations of imbeciles in this case was probably, in fact, a big fat zero. Neither woman was actually feeble-minded. And Carrie's child, who died young, was described by her teachers as "bright." Ben A. Franklin, "Teen-Ager's Sterilization an Issue Decades Later," *New York Times*, Mar. 7, 1980, p. A16.

28. On this point, see Michael Grossberg, "Guarding the Altar: Physiological Restrictions and the Rise of State Intervention in Matrimony," *American Journal of Legal History* 26:197, 217–224 (1982).

29. For Connecticut, see Laws Conn. 1895, ch. 325, p. 667. For Indiana, see, in general, Edward W. Spencer, "Some Phases of Marriage Law and Legislation from a Sanitary and Eugenic Standpoint," *Yale L. Journal* 25:58 (1915). For Washington state, see Laws Wash. 1909. ch. 174, p. 633; for Wisconsin, Laws Wisc. 1913, ch. 738. The Wisconsin case is Peterson v. Widule, 157 Wis. 641, 147 N.W. 966 (1914). Interestingly, eugenic restrictions on marriage never made much headway in the South, despite considerable agitation in this direction; see Edward J. Larson, *Sex, Race, and Science: Eugenics in the Deep South* (1995), pp. 99–100.

30. Peterson v. Widule, 157 Wis., at 647–648; 147 N.W. at 968.

31. Chester G. Vernier, *American Family Laws,* vol. 1 (1931), pp. 199–202.

32. Richmond and Hall, *Marriage and the State,* pp. 370–371.

33. Vernier, *American Family Laws,* vol. 1, pp. 191–195.

34. Gould v. Gould, 78 Conn. 242, 61 A. 604 (1905).

35. Richmond and Hall, *Marriage and the State,* p. 60.

36. Fred S. Hall, *Medical Certification for Marriage* (1925), pp. 44, 46–47. The subtitle of Hall's book is "an account of the administration of the Wisconsin Marriage Law as it relates to the venereal diseases."

37. Larson, *Sex, Race, and Science,* pp. 22–23.

38. There is a sizable literature on this subject. See, for example, Peter Wallenstein, *Tell the Court I Love My Wife: Race, Marriage, and Law—an American History* (2002).

39. Interracial sex during slavery had been, of course, positively epidemic—slaveowners slept freely with slave women and produced thousands of mixed-race slaves. There were also instances of stable unions between whites and blacks. See Martha E. Hodes, *White Women, Black Men: Illicit Sex in the Nineteenth-Century South* (1997).

40. Ark. Stats. 1928, sec. 6084, p. 1449.

41. Pace v. Alabama, 106 U.S. 583 (1882).

42. Wallenstein, *Tell the Court,* p. 139.

43. See Ore. Rev. Stats. 1920, sec. 2163, p. 1256. A marriage was also void if a white married someone with more than one-half Indian blood. Chinese were also ineligible to become naturalized citizens, and were forbidden from entering the country as immigrants, after the late 19th century. See, in general, Lucy E. Salyer, *Laws Harsh as Tigers: Chinese Immigrants and the Shaping of Modern Immigration Law* (1995).

44. For California, see Cal. Civ. Code, sec. 60; for Mississippi, Miss. Code 1942, sec. 459. For a breakdown of the state laws as of around 1930, see Vernier, *American Family Laws,* vol. 1, pp. 204–209.

45. Koegel, "Common Law Marriage," p. 261.

46. Edward W. Spencer, "Some Phases of Marriage Law and Legislation from a Sanitary and Eugenic Standpoint," *Yale L. Journal* 25:58, 69 (1915).

47. *New York Times,* Jan. 8, 1914, p. 1.

48. Wis. Laws 1917, ch. 218, sec. 21. This law provides that marriages are "void" if they do not comply with another statute, which stated that a marriage could be "validly contracted . . . only after a license has been issued."

49. Perez v. Sharp, 32 Cal. 2d 711, 198 P. 2d 17 (1948).

50. McLaughlin v. Florida, 379 U.S. 184 (1964). The Court in this case specifically overruled an earlier decision in Pace v. Alabama, n. 41, supra.

51. 388 U.S. 1 (1967).

52. Quoted in Rachel F. Moran, *Interracial Intimacy: The Regulation of Race and Romance* (2001), p. 97. On the *Loving* case generally, ibid., pp. 95–99.

53. *Report of the Hartford Vice Commission, Hartford, Conn.* (1913), p. 83.

54. On the "red-light abatement" movement, see Friedman, *Crime and Punishment*, pp. 328–332; and Thomas C. Mackey, *Red Lights Out: A Legal History of Prostitution, Disorderly Houses, and Vice Districts, 1870–1917* (1987).

55. For Colorado, see Colo. Rev. Stats. 1953, ch. 90-1-6 (5); for Connecticut, Gen. Stats. Conn. 1949, Tit. 59, ch. 365, sec. 7302, p. 2661; Ind. Rev. Stats. 1965, sec. 44-213. See also Laws Ill. 1949, p. 1081, requiring "serological tests" for syphilis.

56. Okla. Rev. Stats., Tit. 43, sec. 31; Ann. Laws Mass. ch. 207, sec. 28a.

57. "Marriage Laws of the Fifty States, District of Columbia, and Puerto Rico," http://www.law.cornell.edu/topics/Table_Marriage.htm (visited Feb. 3, 2003); see, for example, Cal. Fam. Code, sec. 4300.

58. West Ann. Ind. Code sec. 31-11-4-4.

59. Ariz. Rev. Stats. sec. 25-121.

60. The statutes in question are: D. C. Code Ann. sec. 46-403; Cal. Family Code, sec. 352 (this also forbids a license for those "under the influence of an intoxicating liquor or narcotic drug"); Me. Rev. Stat. Ann. tit.91-a, sec. 701(3); Tenn. Code Ann. sec. 36-3-109; Miss. Code Ann. sec. 93-1-5(f). I am indebted for these references to Catherine Crump.

61. This is so except for the sterilization of the retarded, under certain circumstances, usually with parental consent. See, for example, Cal Probate Code sec. 1950–1969.

62. 316 U.S. 535 (1942).

63. Virginia: *Washington Post*, May 3, 2002, p. B1; South Carolina: *Greenville News*, Jan. 9, 2003, p. 2B; North Carolina: *Durham Herald-Sun*, Jan. 4, 2003, p. C8; Oregon: *The Oregonian*, Dec. 3, 2002, p. A1; California: *San Francisco Chronicle*, Mar. 12, 2003, p. A20.

64. Kelly v. Renfro, 9 Ala. 330 (1846).

65. Ginger S. Frost, "'I Shall Not Sit Down and Crie': Women, Class, and Breach of Promise of Marriage Plaintiffs in England, 1850–1900," *Gender and History* 6:224 (1994).

66. Joel Prentiss Bishop, *New Commentaries on Marriage, Divorce, and Separation* (1891), vol. 1, p. 100.

67. Karen Lystra, *Searching the Heart* (1989), p. 117.

68. This statement of course has to be qualified: not having sex, or refusing to have sex, could be grounds for an annulment of a marriage in some states; and physical inability to have sex was grounds for annulment more generally.

69. Koegel, *Common Law Marriage*, p. 128.

70. Bishop, *New Commentaries*, vol. 1, p 147, sec. 354.

71. See Ginger S. Frost, *Promises Broken: Courtship, Class, and Gender in Victorian England* (1995), pp. 1–10.

72. Charles J. MacColla, *Breach of Promise: Its History and Social Considerations* (1879), p. 38.

73. For a careful study of the English cases, see Frost, *Promises Broken*.

74. See Nathan P. Feinsinger, "Legislative Attack on 'Heart Balm,'" *Michigan L. Rev.* 33:979 (1935).

75. Laws Pa. 1935, no. 189, p. 450; Laws Mass. 1938, ch. 350, p. 326; Laws Cal. 1939, ch. 128, p. 1245; Laws Ill. 1947, p. 1181.

76. Susie L. Steinbach, "Promises, Promises: Not Marrying in England, 1780–1920" (Ph.D. diss., Yale University, 1996), p. 306.

77. The Law Commission, *Breach of Promise of Marriage* (1969), p. 6.

78. Frost, *Promises Broken*, p. 174.

79. Such a cause of action was allowed in Massachusetts, in De Cicco v. Barker, 339 Mass. 457, 159 N. E. 534 (1959), even though there was nothing in the statute that specifically authorized it. The plaintiff got back the six-carat diamond ring he had given to the woman he thought he was going to marry.

80. Tuttle v. Swanson, 9 R. F. L. 59, 1972 Carswell BC 40.

81. Thibault v. Lalumiere, 318 Mass. 72, 60 N.E. 2d 349 (1945).

82. Paul E. Fuller, "An Early Venture of Kentucky Women in Politics: The Breckenridge Congressional Campaign of 1894," *Filson Club History Quarterly* 224 (1989).

83. David M. Buss, Todd K. Shackleford, and Lee A. Kirkpatrick, "A Half Century of Mate Preferences: The Cultural Evolution of Values," *J. Marriage and the Family* 63:491, 501 (2001). "Good cook and housekeeper" had a similar evolution: it was sixth in men's list of valued traits in 1967, but fourteenth in 1996. Ibid. In the early 1970s, 56.4 percent of American women surveyed thought that premarital sex was "always or almost always wrong," while in the late 1990s, only 40 percent thought so; 46 percent of the men thought it was "always or almost always wrong" in the 1970s, but just under 30 percent in the late 1990s. Arland Thornton and Linda Young-DeMarco, "Four Decades of

Trends in Attitudes toward Family Issues in the United States: The 1960s through the 1990s," *J. Marriage and the Family* 63:1009, 1022 (2001).

84. 73 Md. App. 367, 533 A. 2d 1358 (1987).

85. Quinn v. Walsh, 49 Mass. App. Ct. 696, 732 N. E. 2d 330 (2000).

86. Maxine B. Virtue, *Family Cases in Court* (1956), pp. 90–91.

87. The case is Sheehan v. Sheehan, 77 N. J. Eq. 411, 77 A. 1063 (Ct. of Chancery of N. J., 1910).

88. Virtue, *Family Cases,* pp. 118, 140.

89. The study is reported in a note, "Collusive and Consensual Divorce and the New York Anomaly," *Col. L. Rev.* 36: 1121, 1131 (1936); see Lawrence M. Friedman, "A Dead Language: Divorce Law and Practice before No-Fault," *Va. L. Rev.* 86:1497, 1512–1513 (2000).

90. Colin S. Gibson, *Dissolving Wedlock* (1994), p. 96–97.

91. On the Queen's Proctor, see Wendie Ellen Schneider, "Secrets and Lies: The Queen's Proctor and Judicial Investigation of Party-Controlled Narratives," *Law and Social Inquiry* 27:449 (2002). The situation in Canada in the first part of the twentieth century was also complex. There was probably plenty of collusion, but the courts were less willing to close their eyes to it. As in England, the "king's proctor" was an official who acted on behalf of the state in divorce cases, snooping about to see if there was conniving or colluding. In Nova Scotia, this official was called a "watching counsel." These busybodies appear to have been at least somewhat effective. See James G. Snell, *In the Shadow of the Law: Divorce in Canada, 1900–1939* (1991), pp. 104–106.

92. I am indebted to Albert Lopez for the figures on San Mateo County. For Alameda County, see Joanna Grossman and Chris Guthrie, "The Road Less Taken: Annulment at the Turn of the Century," *Am. J. of Legal History* 40: 307 (1996).

93. *Thompson's Laws of New York* (1939), Part 2, N.Y. Civil Practice Act, sec. 1137, 1139, 1141.

94. Bishop, *New Commentaries,* vol. 1, p. 193.

95. Paul H. Jacobson, *American Marriage and Divorce* (1959), p. 113.

96. See William E. Nelson, *The Legalist Reformation: Law, Politics, and Ideology in New York, 1920–1980* (2001), pp. 51–54, 231–236.

97. Pawloski v. Pawloski, 65 N.Y. S. 2d 413 (Sup. Ct., Cayuga County, 1946).

98. Truiano v. Truiano, 121 Misc. Rep. 635, 201 N.Y.S. 573 (Sup. Ct., Special Term, Warren County, 1923). In fairness to Florence, it has to be said that under a federal statute at the time of the marriage, she would have lost her citizenship (and taken on her husband's citizenship). This would have cost her her

job. After the couple separated, the law was changed, in 1922, under the Married Women's Citizenship Act, 42 Stat. 1021 (act of Sept. 12, 1922). This was in effect at the time of the Truiano annulment case; but this fact, said the court, "cannot relieve defendant of the fraud, or cause denial to the plaintiff of the relief which she asks," since she would not have married James had she known of his blemish.

99. Ryan v. Ryan, 156 Misc. 251, 281 N.Y.S. 709 (Sup. Ct., Spec. Term, N.Y. County, 1935).

100. Jen Ross, "Separate Ways: Divorce to Become Legal," *Washington Post,* Mar. 30, 2004, p. C1. Malta apparently still does not allow absolute divorce.

101. Cited in Virtue, *Family Cases,* pp. 145–146.

102. Michael Asimow, "Divorce in the Movies: From the Hays Code to *Kramer vs. Kramer,*" *Legal Studies Forum* 24:221 (2000).

103. Act of March 3, 1933, ch. 62, sec. 1.

104. J. Herbie DiFonzo, *Beneath the Fault Line: The Popular and Legal Culture of Divorce in Twentieth-Century America* (1997), pp. 78–79.

105. Friedman, "A Dead Language," p. 1497.

106. Vt. Laws 1933, ch. 140, sec. 3117; Gen'l Stats. Kansas 1935, sec. 60–1501 (11).

107. 39 Cal. 2d 858, 250 P. 2d 598 (1952).

108. Herbert Jacob, *Silent Revolution: The Transformation of Divorce Law in the United States* (1988).

109. Cal. Civ. Code, sec. 4506.

110. See DiFonzo, *Beneath the Fault Line,* pp. 112–137.

111. Herma Hill Kay, "A Family Court: The California Proposal," *Cal. L. Rev.* 56:1205, 1230 (1968).

112. Rhode Island Rev. Stats., sec. 15-5-3.1.

113. Jacob, *Silent Revolution,* p. 102.

114. Utah Code Ann. (1998), sec. 30-3-1; Tenn. Code sec. 36-4-101. Ohio Rev. Code (2000), sec. 3105.01.

115. Gordon Ireland and Jesus de Galindez, *Divorce in the Americas* (1947).

116. I am indebted to Eliane B. Junqueiro for this information about Brazil. See also Eliane B. Junqueiro, "Brazil: The Road of Conflict Bound for Total Justice," in Lawrence M. Friedman and Rogelio Perez-Perdomo, eds., *Legal Culture in the Age of Globalization: Latin America and Latin Europe* (2003), pp. 64, 74–75.

117. Mary Ann Glendon, *Abortion and Divorce in Western Law: American Failures, European Challenges* (1987), pp. 71–76.

118. For Switzerland, see Andrea Büchler, "Family Law in Switzerland: Re-

cent Reforms and Future Issues—an Overview," *European J. of Law Reform* 3:275, 279 (2001); for Austria, see Monika Hinteregger, "The Austrian Matrimonial Law—a Patchwork Pattern of History," *European J. of Law Reform* 3:199, 212 (2001).

119. Stephen Cretney, *Family Law in the Twentieth Century: A History* (2003), p. 391.

120. Robert Bellah et al., *Habits of the Heart: Individualism and Commitment in American Life* (1985), pp. 82, 334, 336; see Lawrence M. Friedman, *The Republic of Choice: Law, Authority, and Culture* (1990), for the role of expressive individualism in modern law.

121. Glendon, *Abortion and Divorce in Western Law*, p. 108.

122. Barbara Dafoe Whitehead, *The Divorce Culture* (1997), p. 54.

123. Catholic laity also apparently do not agree with the church's stand on contraception. The proof of this is to be found in the low birthrates in otherwise devout countries. It hardly seems likely that good Polish and Irish and Italian Catholics are simply not having sex, or that some massive epidemic of infertility has overwhelmed these countries.

124. Jutta Limbach and Margret Rottleuthner-Lutter, "Ehestabilität in Spannungsfeld von Schuld- oder Zerrüttungsprinzip," *Kritische Vierteljahresschrift für Gesetzgebung und Rechtswissenschaft* 1988, no. 3: 266.

125. Some observers, however, see the beginnings of a "resurgence" in alimony payments, partly because of "a renewed focus on the job sacrifices women often make throughout a marriage and the value of their traditional role as family caretakers." Kyle Johnson, "In Resurgence of Alimony, New View of Women," *Christian Science Monitor,* Nov. 30, 1999.

126. For a discussion, see Jacob, Silent Revolution, pp. 159–164.

127. See, for example, Allen M. Parkman, *No-Fault Divorce: What Went Wrong?* (1992).

128. La. Rev. Stat. Ann. sec. 272 (West 2000).

129. There is, of course, no guarantee that couples who are married in a covenant marriage, and who lack formal grounds for divorce, will not resort to the kinds of collusion that were common before the no-fault revolution.

130. Ariz. Rev. Stats. sec. 25-901. People already married can convert their marriage into a covenant marriage (sec. 25-902). The Arkansas version is Ark. Code sec. 9-11-801 through 9.11-811 (adopted in 2001).

131. Ariz. Rev. Stats. sec. 25-903.

132. Laura Sanchez et al., "The Implementation of Covenant Marriage in Louisiana," *Va. J. of Social Policy and the Law* 9:192 (2001).

133. Mark Eastburg, "Marriage Strengthening Strategies for Communities: The Greater Grand Rapids Community Marriage Policy Experience," *Va J. of Social Policy and the Law* 9:224 (2001).

134. Norval Glenn, "Is the Current Concern about American Marriage Warranted?" *Va. J. of Social Policy and the Law* 9:5 (2001).

135. Aaron C. Ahuvia and Mara B. Adelman, "Formal Intermediaries in the Marriage Market: A Typology and Review," *J. Marriage and the Family* 54:452 (1992).

136. *Palo Alto Daily,* Oct. 16, 2002, p. 38.

137. Theresa Montini and Beverly Ovrebo, "Personal Relationship Ads: An Informal Balancing Act," *Sociological Perspectives* 33:327, 332 (1990).

138. These ads are from *Welt am Sonntag,* Sunday, Nov. 2, 2003, p. 42.

139. *New York Times,* Dec. 29, 2002, Sunday Styles Section, p. 9.

140. Jennifer Egan, "Love in the Time of No Time," *New York Times,* Nov. 23, 2003, p. 66.

141. The ads in "alternative" journals are more explicit on this point; this is also true of many of the people who pursue on-line dating (ibid.).

142. *Palo Alto Daily,* Oct. 16, 2002, p. 38. This writer also gave his height and weight: 6'4" and 210 pounds.

143. For example, Cal. Penal Code, 1872, sec. 266a.

144. Mark M. Carroll gives another reason for these laws in nineteenth-century Texas: the aim of the law was not to punish extramarital sex, or lapses of "public decorum," but rather to discourage desertion. "Living in adultery necessarily entailed desertion." Mark M. Carroll, *Homestead Ungovernable: Families, Sex, Race, and the Law in Frontier Texas, 1823–1860* (2001), p. 151.

145. Report, *Vice Commission of Philadelphia* (1913), pp. 9, 10.

146. In Northern Nigeria, sharia courts have ordered women to be stoned to death for having sex outside of marriage. See *New York Times,* Aug. 20, 2002, p. 1. A woman's adultery is also an extremely serious matter in such countries as Saudi Arabia.

147. Julia A. Ericksen, *Kiss and Tell: Surveying Sex in the Twentieth Century* (1995), p. 122.

148. 42 U.S. Code sec. 710: "abstinence education" is defined as a program that has "as its exclusive purpose" teaching the "social, psychological, and health gains to be realized by abstaining from sexual activity," and teaching also that all school-age children are expected to be chaste and that "a mutually faithful monogamous" marriage is the "expected standard of human sexual activity."

149. Lorraine Ali and Julie Scelfo, "Choosing Virginity," *Newsweek*, December 9, 2002, pp. 61, 66.

150. J. P. Lichtenberg, *Divorce: A Social Interpretation* (1931), p. 339.

151. See "Report on Kinsey," *New York Times*, Dec. 11, 1949, p. E9.

152. Ericksen, *Kiss and Tell*, p. 85.

153. Martin Burgi, "Schützt das Grundgesetz die Ehe von der Konkurrenz Anderer Lebensgemeinschaften?" *Der Staat* (2000), pp. 487–488.

154. Claude Martin and Irene Théry, "The Pacs and Marriage and Cohabitation in France," *Int'l J. of Law, Policy and the Family* 15: 135, 136 (2001).

155. Velina Todorova, "Family Law in Bulgaria: Legal Norms and Social Norms," ibid., 148, 166.

156. Encarna Roca Trias, "Familia, Familias y Derecho de la Familia," *Annuario de Derecho Civil* 43:1055, 1062 (1990).

157. Constanza Tobio, "Marriage, Cohabitation, and the Residential Independence of Young People in Spain," *Int'l J. of Law, Policy, and the Family* 15:68, pp. 78–79.

158. Marvin v. Marvin, 18 Cal. 3d 660, 557 P. 2d 106, 134 Cal. R. 815 (1976).

159. Carroll v. Lee, 148 Ariz. 10, 712 P. 2d 923 (1986); Boland v. Catalano, 202 Conn. 333, 521 A. 2d 142 (1987). Connecticut as a state did not recognize common law marriage, but even though (said the court) "cohabitation alone does not create any contractual relationship or, unlike marriage, impose other legal duties," that does not militate against "contractual enforcement of [an] . . . implied agreement to share."

160. Hewitt v. Hewitt, 77 Ill. 2d 49, 394 N.E. 2d 1209 (Ill., 1979).

161. Laws Minn. 1980, ch. 553.

162. Harry Willekens, "Long Term Developments in Family Law in Western Europe: An Explanation," in John Eekelaar and Thandabantu Nhlapo, eds., *The Changing Family: International Perspectives on the Family and Family Law* (1998), pp. 47, 56.

163. The case is Miron v. Trudel, [1995] 2 SCR 418. One justice dissented.

164. Nicholas Bala, "Court Decisions on Same-Sex and Unmarried Partners, Spousal Rights, and Children," *The International Survey of Family Law* (2001 ed.), 43, 48–50.

165. San Francisco is an example. See San Francisco, Cal., Administrative Code, ch. 62, sec. 62.3, "Establishing a Domestic Partnership"; and San Francisco, Cal., Charter, Appendix A, A8.500-2, "Domestic Partner Benefits."

166. See *New York Times*, Nov. 30, 2002, Section A, page 1.

167. For a discussion, see Wolfram Mueller-Freienfels, "Cohabitation and

Marriage Law—a Comparative Study," *Int'l J. of Law and the Family* 1:259, 263–267 (1987).

168. Stephen Parker, *Informal Marriage, Cohabitation, and the Law, 1750–1989* (1990), p. 113.

169. Ibid., pp. 113–114.

170. Lawrence M. Friedman, *American Law in the Twentieth Century* (2002), p. 232.

4. Who Are Our Children?

1. In an unusual case, Wisconsin v. Yoder, 406 U.S. 205 (1972), the Supreme Court engrafted a kind of exception on the mandatory attendance laws. The issue was the refusal of a very conservative and traditional religious group, the Amish, to send their children to high school. In high school, said the Amish, the children would learn values incompatible with the religious values of the Amish, which included a withdrawal from secular society. Making its children go to (secular) high school, they argued, would damage the community as a whole. The Supreme Court allowed the Amish to exempt themselves from Wisconsin's attendance law. Justice William O. Douglas, who dissented, pointed out that the majority decision paid no attention to the rights and interests of the children themselves.

2. The Supreme Court has emphasized this in a number of cases—for example, in Troxel v. Granville, 530 U.S. 57 (2000). The case concerned the rights of grandparents to visit their grandchildren. This right has statutory recognition everywhere (see, for example, Cal. Family Code, sec. 3103, 3104). The Troxel case arose under the statute of Washington state: Did that statute go too far by allowing courts to override the wishes of a parent in granting visitation rights to grandparents? The Court said yes, under the provisions of that particular statute.

3. 16 and 17 Geo. V., Ch. 29. There were a number of interesting provisions in the law. The applicant had to be twenty-five years old; generally speaking, no adoption was allowed if the applicant was "less than twenty-one years older than the infant." If the sole applicant was a male "and the infant . . . is a female," no adoption was allowed except under "special circumstances." There were also complex provisions with regard to inheritance. See also George K. Behlmer, "What's Love Got to Do with It? 'Adoption' in Victorian and Edwardian England," in E. Wayne Carp, ed., *Adoption in America: Historical Perspectives* (2002), p. 82; Stephen Cretney, *Family Law in the Twentieth Century: A History* (2003), pp. 598–606.

4. Jean Carbonnier, *Droit Civil 2/La Famille: L'Enfant, Le Couple* (20th ed., 1999), pp. 339, 352; Peter Tuor et al., *Das Schweizerische Zivilgesetzbuch* (11th ed., 1994), p. 299; Claudia Fonseca, "The Politics of Adoption: Child Rights in the Brazilian Setting," *Law and Policy* 24:199, 207 (2002).

5. Laura J. Schwartz, "Models for Parenthood in Adoption Law: The French Conception," *Vanderbilt J. of Transnational Law*, 28:1069 (1995). A distinction between types of adoption was found also in Chilean law—full adoption, of children under eighteen, was irreversible and basically the same as adoption in other countries; there was also simple adoption, which was temporary. Claudia Reyes Duenas, "Legal and Social Aspects of the Adoption of Chilean Children," in Eliezer D. Jaffe, ed., *Intercountry Adoptions: Laws and Perspectives of "Sending" Countries* (1995).

6. See Helena M. Wall, *Fierce Communion: Family and Community in Early America* (1990), p. 99.

7. See Jamil Zainaldin, "The Emergence of a Modern American Family Law: Child Custody, Adoption and the Courts, 1796–1851," *Northwestern U. Law Review* 73:1038 (1979); Chris Guthrie and Joanna L. Grossman, "Adoption in the Progressive Era: Preserving, Creating, and Re-Creating Families," *Am. J. Legal History* 43: 235 (1989).

8. Julie Berebitsky, *Like Our Very Own: Adoption and the Changing Culture of Motherhood, 1851–1950* (2000), p. 20.

9. For Kentucky: Laws Ky. (Private and Local) 1844–45, ch. 117, pp. 133–134 (adopted Jan. 29, 1845). For Mississippi: Laws Miss. 1846, ch. 60, p. 231. The Mississippi statute also stated that "all illegitimate children shall inherit the property of their mothers." Ibid., sec. 4. For Texas: Laws Texas 1850, ch. 39, p. 36 (approved Jan. 16, 1850). Under the Texas law, if the person adopting the child has, or later has, a child "begotten in lawful wedlock," the adopted child or children "shall in no case inherit more than the one-fourth of the estate of the party adopting him or her, which can be disposed of by will."

10. Laws Mo. 1857, p. 59 (act of Feb. 23, 1857). The act was quite narrow: the adopted child was to have the same rights as a blood child against his adoptive parents, including inheritance rights, but the statute did not affect "other parties"; its thrust was "wholly confined to persons executing the deed of adoption."

11. Laws Mo. 1917, p. 193.

12. Mary Ann Mason, *From Father's Property to Children's Rights: The History of Child Custody in the United States* (1994), p. 75.

13. Epaphroditus Peck, *The Law of Persons; or, Domestic Relations* (1913), p. 250. In Illinois, an adopted child could not take "property from the linear or collateral kindred" of the adoptive parents "by right of representation." Ill. Rev.

Stat. 1921, ch. 4, sec. 5, pp. 142–143. This means, for example, that if the adoptive father died and then his sister died without children or a will, the adopted child could not take a share in the estate as the surviving child of the sister's closest relative, her brother.

14. Laws Texas 1931, ch. 177, sec. 9, p. 302.

15. Cal. Probate Code, section 6451. There is an exception: if, say, a child's father dies and the mother remarries and her new husband adopts the child, the adopted child can still inherit from his or her "natural" father.

16. For one overview, see Fred L. Kuhlmann, "Intestate Succession by and from the Adopted Child," *Washington University Law Quarterly* 28:221 (1943).

17. Chester G. Vernier, *American Family Laws,* vol. 4, *Parent and Child* (1936), p. 410.

18. Fonseca, "The Politics of Adoption," pp. 201–205; Claudia Fonseca, "Inequality Near and Far: Adoption as Seen from the Brazilian Favelas," *Law and Society Review* 36:397 (2002).

19. See Marilyn Irvin Holt, *The Orphan Trains: Placing Out in America* (1992); Miriam Z. Langsam, *Children West: A History of the Placing-Out System of the New York Children's Aid Society, 1853–1890* (1964).

20. See Rickie Solinger, *Beggars and Choosers: How the Politics of Choice Shapes Adoption, Abortion, and Welfare in the United States* (2001).

21. See, in general, David Wallace Adams, *Education for Extinction: American Indians and the Boarding School Experience, 1875–1928* (1995).

22. Cited in Cynthia G. Hawkins-León, "The Indian Child Welfare Act and the African American Tribe: Facing the Adoption Crisis," *Brandeis J. of Family Law* 36: 201, 202 (1997).

23. The Indian Child Welfare Act of 1978 was passed to prevent the "breakup of Indian families." 92 Stat. 3069 (act of Nov. 8, 1978).

24. Rajiv Chandrasekaran, "Australia's 'Stolen Generation' Seeks Payback: Aborigines Want Apology for Kidnappings," *Washington Post,* July 6, 2000.

25. In 1986, out of a total of 104,000 domestic adoptions, 50.9 percent were "related adoptions" and 49.1 percent were "unrelated adoptions." To this last figure must be added the 10,000 or so international adoptions, for a total of some 61,000 "unrelated adoptions" (compared to 53,000 "related adoptions"). Kathy S. Stolley, "Statistics on Adoption in the United States," *The Future of Children* 3: 26, 29 (Spring 1993) (special volume on adoption).

26. E. Wayne Carp and Anna Leon-Guerrero, "When in Doubt, Count: World War II as a Watershed in the History of Adoption," in Carp, ed., *Adoption in America,* pp. 181, 190–193.

27. Katherine O'Donovan, " 'Real' Mothers for Abandoned Children," *Law and Society Review* 36:347, 360–365 (2002). In Germany, some cities have "baby flaps" *(Babyklappen)*—safe places "in which a woman who has given birth can leave an infant, with the knowledge that the baby will be taken care of" (ibid., 365–368), a practice strikingly reminiscent of some medieval customs.

28. Barbara Melosh, *Strangers and Kin: The American Way of Adoption* (2002), p. 4.

29. Leslie Kaufman, "Cash Incentives for Adoptions Seen as Risk to Some Children," *New York Times,* Oct. 29, 2003, p. 1. This newspaper account was stimulated by a scandal—a New Jersey family that had adopted many children was accused of starving four of them.

30. Quoted in Helen L. Witmer, *Independent Adoptions: A Follow-Up Study* (1963), p. 38.

31. Melosh, *Strangers and Kin,* p. 18. The baby-farm problem was an old one; for an account of the issue in England, see Ruth Ellen Homrighaus, "Wolves in Women's Clothing: Baby-Farming and the *British Medical Journal,* 1860–1872," *J. Family History* 26:350 (2001). How bad the baby farms actually were is not easy to tell.

32. E. Wayne Carp, *Family Matters: Secrecy and Disclosure in the History of Adoption* (1998), pp. 33–34.

33. Elizabeth Bartholet, "International Adoption: Propriety, Prospects, and Pragmatics," *Journal of the American Academy of Matrimonial Lawyers* 13:181, 184 (1996).

34. Madelyn Freundlich, *The Impact of Adoption on Members of the Triad* (2001), pp. 107–111.

35. Barbara Yngvesson, "Placing the 'Gift Child' in Transnational Adoption," *Law and Society Review* 36:227, 233 (2002).

36. Laws Tex. 1931, ch. 177, sec. 8, p. 302.

37. The cases are discussed in Rita J. Simon and Howard Altstein, *Adoption, Race, and Identity: From Infancy to Young Adulthood* (2nd ed., 2002), pp. 39–55.

38. See, for example, In re Custody of Temos, 450 A. 2d 111 (Pa. Super., 1982). This was a complex case. The mother had custody after a divorce. She developed a relationship with a black man. The father then sought custody. He won in the trial court. Race, however, was only one of several factors in the decision. The appeal court reversed, and was extremely sharp and outspoken on the race point, asserting that race was never to be considered a factor in custody cases.

39. Palmore v. Sidoti, 466 U.S. 429 (1984).

40. Berebitsky, *Like Our Very Own,* p. 169.

41. Simon and Altstein, *Adoption, Race, and Identity,* p. 87.

42. See, in general, Sandra Patton, *Birth Marks: Transracial Adoption in Contemporary America* (2000).

43. Simon and Altstein, *Adoption, Race, and Identity,* pp. 218–219.

44. See Mary Lyndon Shanley, *Making Babies, Making Families* (2001), pp. 35–36.

45. This law was P.L. 103-382, sec. 551, of 1994; see Rachel F. Moran, *Interracial Intimacy: The Regulation of Race and Romance* (2001), p. 133. The 1994 law was repealed in 1996, P.L. 104-188.

46. 25 U.S.C. sec. 1901–1923. Originally, 92 Stat. 3069, act of Nov. 8, 1978.

47. Similarly, Neb. Rev. Stats. sec. 43-1504, echoing the federal statute; see also Okla. Rev. Stats. Title 10, sec. 40.

48. Mississippi Band of Choctaw Indians v. Holyfield, 490 U.S. 30 (1989).

49. Moran, *Interracial Intimacy,* p. 150.

50. See the discussion in Sandra Patton-Imani, "Redefining the Ethics of Adoption, Race, Gender, and Class," *Law and Society Review* 36:813 (2002).

51. In some cases, however, courts did recognize the rights of children who thought they were adopted and were raised in a family as adopted children, but then discovered that the adoptive parents had not gone through the statutory process. In such cases, some courts recognized a kind of common-law (or "equitable") adoption for inheritance purposes. See, for example, Thomas v. Malone, 142 Mo. App. 293, 126 S. W. 522 (1910).

52. Laws Minn. 1917, ch. 222, p. 335.

53. On this point, see, in general, Carp, *Family Matters.*

54. Melosh, *Strangers and Kin,* p. 36.

55. Laws Ill. 1967, p. 2273.

56. Carp, *Family Matters,* p. 67.

57. Berebitsky, *Like Our Very Own,* pp. 138–142.

58. Vernier, *American Family Laws,* vol. 4, p. 453. In two states—Ohio and Wisconsin—the adopting parents could annul the adoption if the child developed these defects before reaching the age of fourteen (ibid.). In Delaware, the court had broad powers to annul an adoption, if it was fair and proper and in the best interests of the child, at any time; and the child, if over twenty-one, could personally bring such a petition (ibid., p. 455). For the California law, see Laws Cal. 1937, ch. 366, sec. 2, pp. 786–787.

59. Lawrence M. Friedman, *American Law in the Twentieth Century* (2002), p. 445.

60. Barbara Yngvesson, "Negotiating Motherhood: Identity and Difference in 'Open' Adoptions," *Law and Society Review* 31:31, 71–72 (1997).

61. The agencies, for example, were often unwilling to allow unmarried women to adopt children; on this, see Berebitsky, *Like Our Very Own*, ch. 4.

62. Quoted in Judith S. Modell, *A Sealed and Secret Kinship: The Culture of Policies and Practices in American Adoption* (2002), p. 77. For a discussion of the reputation of foster care, see ibid., pp. 75–97.

63. The reasons for this development are complex and not entirely clear. See Carp, *Family Matters,* ch. 4.

64. Barbara Melosh, "Adoption Stories: Autobiographical Narrative and the Politics of Identity," in Carp, *Adoption in America,* pp. 218, 226.

65. Carp, *Family Matters,* pp. 142–143.

66. Colorado Rev. Stats. section 19-5-305 (1) (supp. 2003).

67. 23 Ohio St. 3d 69, 491 N.E.2d 1101 (1986). The cases in general are discussed in Pat McDonald-Nunemaker, "Wrongful Adoption: The Development of a Better Remedy in Tort," *J. American Academy of Matrimonial Lawyers* 12:391 (1994).

68. The search movement is described in Carp, *Family Matters,* ch. 5 and 6.

69. I developed this theme in *The Republic of Choice: Law, Authority, and Culture* (1990).

70. O'Donovan, "'Real' Mothers," pp. 362–364.

71. Caroline Forder, "An Undutchable Family Law: Partnership, Parenthood, Social Parenthood, Names, and Some Article 8 ECHR Case Law," *International Survey of Family Law* (1997) 259, 305–306.

72. Nr. 624 BverfG, 1997, in *Zeitschrift für die Gesamte Familienrecht* 44: 869 (1997).

73. Tenn. Code Ann. 36-1-127(c), 128.

74. Doe v. Sundquist, 106 F. 3d 702 (6th Circuit, 1997).

75. Doe v. Sundquist, 2 S.W. 3d 919 (Tenn., 1999). In an interesting case out of Florida, G.P. v. Florida, 842 So. 2d 1059 (D. Ct. of App., Fla, 4th District, 2003), four women objected to a provision in Florida's law on private adoptions. Each of the women had executed formal consent for adoption of their babies. Each claimed they did not know who the father was. The statute required the women, in effect, to give a list of the men they had sex with, and who therefore possibly could have been the father. The appeal court called this a gross invasion of the women's privacy. It was an interference with their right "not to disclose the intimate personal information that is required when the father is unknown." The statute was in this regard unconstitutional.

76. See, in general, Amanda Porterfield, *The Transformation of American Religion: The Story of a Late Twentieth-Century Awakening* (2001).

77. Ibid., p. 230.

78. The case is discussed in Dalia Dorner, "Human Reproduction: Reflections on the *Nachmani* case," *Texas International Law Journal* 35:1 (2000). The case was decided in 1996. The author of this article, Dalia Dorner, was an Associate Justice of the Supreme Court of Israel and took part in the decision (she voted with the majority). Danny at the time of the case had remarried and had children with his new wife.

79. On the nineteenth-century treatment of illegitimate children, see Michael Grossberg, *Governing the Hearth: Law and the Family in Nineteenth-Century America* (1985), pp. 196–233.

80. Marvin L. Michael Kay and Lorin Lee Cary, *Slavery in North Carolina, 1748–1775* (1995), p. 8.

81. Mason, *From Father's Property*, p. 43.

82. Stephen Cretney, *Family Law in the Twentieth Century: A History* (2003), p. 564.

83. Levy v. Louisiana, 391 U.S. 68 (1968).

84. For the figures, see Kathleen Kiernan, "The Rise of Cohabitation and Childbearing outside Marriage in Western Europe," *Int'l J. of Law, Policy and the Family* 15:1, 13 (2001). The Nordic figures are exceptional for Europe. Extramarital births were under 10 percent in Italy, Switzerland, and Greece.

85. Judith S. Wallerstein and Sandra Blakeslee, *Second Chances: Men, Women, and Children a Decade after Divorce* (1989), pp. 12–13.

86. See, in general, Mason, *From Father's Property;* Michael Grossberg, *Governing the Hearth: Law and the Family in Nineteenth-Century America* (1985), ch. 7.

87. Dorothy M. Stetson, *A Woman's Issue: The Politics of Family Law Reform in England* (1982), p. 32.

88. Mason, *From Father's Property*, p. 61.

89. Quoted in Michael Grossberg, *Governing the Hearth*, pp. 244–245.

90. Hung-En Liu, "Mother or Father: Who Received Custody? The Best Interests of the Child Standard and Judges' Custody Decisions in Taiwan," *Int'l J. of Law, Policy, and the Family* 15:185 (2001).

91. The federal law is the Family and Medical Leave Act of 1993, 29 U.S.C. sec. 2601. There are also state laws: for example, Cal. Govt. Code sec. 12945.2, which requires employers to "grant a request by any employee with more than

12 months of service . . . to take up to a total of 12 workweeks in any 12-month period for family care and medical leave." This specifically includes "[l]eave for reason of the birth of a child of the employee."

92. Cal. Civ. Code, sec. 4600.5(a). See Patricia Anne Golembiewski, "California's Presumption Favoring Joint Custody: California Civil Code Sections 4600 and 4600.5," *Cal. Western L. Rev.* 17:286 (1981); Cal. Family Code, sec. 3080: "There is a presumption . . . that joint custody is in the best interest of a minor child . . . where the parents have agreed to joint custody."

93. Mason, *From Father's Property*, p. 130.

94. Kirsti Kurki-Suonio, "Joint Custody as an Interpretation of the Best Interests of the Child in Critical and Comparative Perspective," *International J. of Law, Policy and the Family* 14:183, 188 (2000).

95. For example, Cal. Civil Code, sec. 4600(d).

96. Cal. Family Code, sec. 3002.

97. See Felicia Meyers, "Gay Custody and Adoption: An Unequal Application of the Law," *Whittier Law Review* 14:839 (1993). The state of New Hampshire explicitly prohibited any "homosexual" from adopting a child; but it recently amended its adoption statute and eliminated this phrase. N.H. Rev. Stats section 170-B:4, as amended in 1999.

98. Isabelle Lammerant, *L'Adoption et les Droits de L'Homme en Droit Comparé* (2001), p. 177.

99. Fla. Rev. Stats. sec. 63.042 (3). In Lofton v. Kearney, 157 Fed. Supp. 2d 1373 (S.D. Fla., 2001), a federal district court upheld the statute.

100. See Shanley, *Making Babies, Making Families*, ch. 5.

101. Contrast, for examples, Doe v. Doe, 284 S.E. 2d 759 (Va., 1981), and M. J. P. v. J. G. P., 640 P. 2d 966 (Okla., 1982). In *Doe,* a divorced woman had custody of her son; she entered into a relationship with a woman. Her former husband had by then remarried; he and his new wife tried to get the child—indeed, the new wife wanted to adopt the boy. The Virginia court refused. Despite her "unorthodox life-style," the court ruled, the mother was "a fit parent," devoted to her son. In the Oklahoma case, however, the father got custody of a little boy when the (divorced) mother "established . . . [a] homosexual relationship, and went so far as to invite forty friends to a 'Gay-la Wedding' in a church." See Kenneth L. Karst, "Law, Cultural Conflict, and the Socialization of Children," *Cal. L. Rev.* 91:969 (2003). Karst cites an Alabama case as recent as 2002—Ex Parte H. H., 830 So. 2d 21 (Ala. 2002)—in which a custody decision went against a lesbian mother (ibid., 974n).

102. See Melford E. Spiro, *Children of the Kibbutz* (1965).

103. The Latin maxim is often quoted: "pater ... est, quem nuptiae demonstrant." See Jean Carbonnier, *Droit Civil: 2/La Famille* (20th ed., 1999), p. 223.

104. On this point, see, for example, Anders Eriksson and Åke Saldeen, "Parenthood and Science: Establishing and Contesting Parentage," in John Eekelaar and Petar Šarčević, *Parenthood in Modern Society: Legal and Social Issues for the Twenty-First Century* (1993), p. 75.

105. People v. Sorensen, 66 Cal. Rptr. 7, 437 P. 2d 495 (1968).

106. Thomas S. v. Robin Y., 599 N.Y.S. 2d 377 (1993).

107. See In re Petition of Kirchner, 164 Ill. 2d 468, 649 N.E. 2d 324 (1995).

108. Ex Parte C.V., 810 So. 2d 700 (Ala., 2001).

109. There is a considerable literature on surrogacy and the law. See, for example, Martha A. Field, *Surrogate Motherhood: The Legal and Human Issues* (1990).

110. In the Matter of Baby M, 109 N.J. 396, 537 A. 2d 1227 (1988).

111. Discussed in Shanley, *Making Babies, Making Families*, pp. 111–112.

112. On this point, see also R. R. v. M. H., 426 Mass. 501, 689 N.E. 2d 790 (1998).

113. Fla. Stat. Ann. 1997, sec. 742.15.

114. *SF Weekly*, Dec. 31, 2002–Jan. 7, 2003, Vol. 21, no. 48, p. 112. The ad also offers $5,000 for "egg donation." Egg donors must be between the ages of twenty-one and thirty; surrogates must have "at least one child."

115. New Jersey Commission on Legal and Ethical Problems in the Delivery of Health Care, *After Baby M: The Legal, Ethical, and Social Dimensions of Surrogacy* (1992), p. 39.

116. For Germany, see Silvia Dietrich, *Mutterschaft für Dritte* (1989), pp. 15–19; for the Netherlands, Trees A. M. te Braake, "Regulation of Assisted Reproductive Technology in the Netherlands," *Texas International Law Journal* 65:93, 111 (2000); for France, Dietrich, *Mutterschaft*, p. 202; for Israel, Rhona Schuz, "Surrogacy in Israel: An Analysis of the Law in Practice," in Rachel Cook, Shelley Day Sclater, with Felicity Kaganas, eds., *Surrogate Motherhood: International Perspectives* (2003), pp. 35, 53.

117. Joan Heifetz Hollinger, "From Coitus to Commerce: Legal and Social Consequences of Noncoital Reproduction," *University of Mich. J. of Law Reform* 18:865, 866 (1985).

118. This is not necessarily the case. It is possible for a couple to hire a surrogate mother to be the "womb mother," with the couple supplying both eggs and sperm. Hence a couple could "acquire the option of producing a child who

is genetically linked to *both* parents without the necessity of undergoing pregnancy or childbirth." Field, *Surrogate Motherhood,* p. 43. This situation, however, must be very rare, if it occurs at all.

119. See Elisabeth M. Landes and Richard A. Posner, "The Economics of the Baby Shortage," *Journal of Legal Studies* 7:323 (1978).

120. The Convention was adopted in 1989 by the General Assembly. See Dominick McGoldrick, "The United Nations Convention on the Rights of the Child," *Int'l J. of Law and the Family* 5:132 (1991).

121. The Jehovah's Witnesses case is West Virginia Board of Education v. Barnette, 319 U.S. 624 (1943); the Wisconsin Amish case is Wisconsin v. Yoder, 406 U.S. 205 (1972). See Engel v. Vitale, 370 U.S. 421 (1962), on prayer in the public schools (not allowed); and Abington School District v. Schempp, 374 U.S. 203 (1963), on Bible reading in the schools (also not allowed).

122. On this point, see in general Marjorie Heins, *Not in Front of the Children: "Indecency," Censorship, and the Innocence of Youth* (2001).

5. Privacy and the Republic of Choice

1. Samuel D. Warren and Louis D. Brandeis, "The Right of Privacy," *Harvard L. Rev.* 4:193 (1890).

2. Fedor Seifert, "Postmortaler Schutz des Persönlichkeitrechts und Schadensersatz—Zugleich ein Streifzug durch die Geschichte des allgemeinen Persönlichkeitsrechts," *Neue Juristische Wochenschrift* 52:1889 (1999).

3. Roberson v. Rochester Folding Box Co., 171 N.Y. 538, 64 N.E. 442 (N.Y. 1902).

4. Melvin v. Reid, 121 Cal. App. 285, 297 Pac. 91 (1931).

5. In part, the court relied on the California constitution, which mentions (Art. 1, sec. 1) the right to the pursuit of happiness. Somehow, the court found a right of privacy imbedded in this phrase—a rather creative piece of interpretation. It is also interesting to note that the case very likely rested on a lie—Gabrielle's lie. She claimed she had become a respectable woman; but this was probably pure fiction. In fact, she was apparently still a prostitute, and she continued for years in that business, ending up as a madam in an Arizona town. Moreover, her various husbands and lovers had a habit of turning up dead. See Leo W. Banks, "Murderous Madam," *Tucson Weekly* (June 5, 2000). The lawsuit, therefore, may have been the product of gall and greed. Ironically, the movie in question, *The Red Kimono,* takes Gabrielle's point of view and shows her in a very favorable light. At the end of the movie, she finds love, happiness, and redemption.

6. Haynes v. Alfred A. Knopf, Inc., 8 F. 3d 1222 (C.A. 7, 1993).

7. Sidis v. F-R Publishing Co., 113 Fed. 2d 806 (C.A. 2, 1940).

8. Doe v. Berkeley Publishers, 496 S.E. 2d 636 (S. Car. 1998).

9. On this theme see Lawrence M. Friedman, *The Horizontal Society* (1999), pp. 27–43.

10. Virgil v. Time, Inc., 527 Fed. 2d 1122 (C.A. 9, 1975).

11. Diaz v. Oakland Tribune, Inc., 139 Cal. App. 3d 118, 188 Cal. Rptr. 762 (1983).

12. 18 Cal. 4th 200, 955 P. 2d 469, 74 Cal. Rptr. 2d 843 (1998).

13. Neff v. Time, Inc., 406 F. Supp. 858 (D.C. W.D. Pa, 1976).

14. Emily Nelson, "Reality Bites TV Comedy," *Wall Street Journal,* Feb. 24, 2003, p. B1; Bill Carter, "TV Networks Plan Flood of Reality for Summer," *New York Times,* Feb. 24, 2003, p. C1.

15. David Lieberman, "Will Reality Bite TV Networks?" *USA Today,* March 4, 2003, B1.

16. See Tilman Hoppe, "Gewinnorientierte Persönlichkeitsverletzung in der europäischen Regenbogenpresse," *Zeitschrift für Europäisches Privatrecht* (2000), p. 29.

17. *Entscheidungen des Bundesverfassungsgericht* 35, no. 16, p. 202 (1973); see Ingo von Münch and Philip Kunig, eds., *Grundgesetz-Kommentar,* vol. 1, p. 148 (2000). On the cultural differences between the U.S. and Europe, see James Q. Whitman, "The Two Western Cultures of Privacy: Dignity versus Liberty," *Yale L. Journal* 113:101 (2004).

18. *Entscheidungen des Bundesverfassungsgericht* 35, at 230.

19. Hoppe, "Gewinnorientierte," pp. 31–32.

20. This incident is recounted in "German Paper Prints Nude Charles Photo," *Rocky Mountain News* (Denver), Sept. 8, 1994, p. 70A; see also "Prince May Act over Nude Photos in German Paper," *The Herald* (Glasgow), Sept. 8, 1994, p. 4.

21. Sarah Lyall, "London Journal: The Wedding Pictures: Two Stars in Court Drama," *New York Times,* Feb. 11, 2003, p. A4. On the status of the case in early 2004, see *The Express,* Jan. 24, 2004, p. 7; *Entertainment Law Reporter* 25, no. 8, January 2004.

22. 376 U.S. 254 (1964).

23. 388 U.S. 130 (1967).

24. 418 U.S. 323 (1974).

25. But the Court also held that in a case of this sort, the plaintiff could recover only for "actual injury"; there was to be no *per se* rule—that is, automatic recovery without showing evidence of loss or damage.

26. Time, Inc. v. Firestone, 424 U.S. 448 (1976). This was a libel action; and

there was a serious question (to my mind at least) whether the article in the magazine was actually false.

27. Hutchinson v. Proxmire, 443 U.S. 111 (1979). A serious issue in the case was whether Proxmire's philistine ranting was privileged because he was a U.S. senator.

28. 726 F. 2d 245 (C.A. 5, 1984).

29. Desnick v. American Broadcasting Companies, Inc., 233 F. 3d 514 (C.A. 7, 2000) (the eye clinic); Brewster v. Memphis Publishing Co., 626 F. 2d 1238 (C.A. 5, 1980) (the Anita Wood case).

30. See Howard Ball, *The Supreme Court in the Intimate Lives of Americans* (2002).

31. D. A. Thom, *Child Management* (Children's Bureau, U.S. Department of Labor, Bureau Publication No. 143, revised, Oct. 1925), p. 20.

32. Helena M. Wall, *Fierce Communion: Family and Community in Early America* (1990), p. 12.

33. Jeffrey Weeks, *Sex, Politics, and Society: The Regulation of Sexuality since 1800* (2nd ed., 1989), p. 66.

34. Alfred C. Kinsey et al., *Sexual Behavior in the Human Female* (1953), p. 365. The percentage of women who were having sex in the nude was apparently increasing, "much to the consternation of the manufacturers of night clothing" (ibid., p. 366).

35. Alfred C. Kinsey et al., *Sexual Behavior in the Human Male* (1948), p. 581. Kinsey remarks that "there can be no question of the fact that intercourse without clothing is biologically normal." Also, "more males prefer to have intercourse in the light, and more females prefer it in the dark." Ibid.

36. See, in general, Julia A. Ericksen, *Kiss and Tell: Surveying Sex in the Twentieth Century* (1999).

37. 381 U.S. 479 (1965). On the background of this case and the legal history of the constitutional right of privacy, see David J. Garrow, *Liberty and Sexuality: The Right to Privacy and the Making of Roe v. Wade* (1994).

38. See Andrea Tone, *Devices and Desires: A History of Contraception in America* (2001).

39. Katherine Bement Davis, *Factors in the Sex Life of Twenty-Two Hundred Women* (1929), pp. 372–373.

40. See David M. Kennedy, *Birth Control in America: The Career of Margaret Sanger* (1970).

41. Youngs Rubber Co. v. C. I. Lee & Co., 45 F. 2d 103 (C.A. 2, 1930). This case and others are discussed in Joshua Gamson, "Rubber Wars: Struggles over

the Condom in the United States," *Journal of the History of Sexuality* 1:262 (1990).

42. Davis v. U.S., 62 F. 2d 473 (C.A. 6, 1933).

43. United States v. One Package, 86 F. 2d 737 (C.A. 2, 1936).

44. The majority opinion also mentioned that the original draft of the Comstock law had contained the words "except on a prescription of a physician . . . given in good faith," but that these words were not in the final text. The reason why the words dropped out "seems never to have been discussed on the floor of Congress" (ibid., at 740). The court seemed to be suggesting that Congress was not very clear on the meaning of its own law, which is perhaps true, but a rather weak argument. It is hard to resist the conclusion that the court simply did not like the law.

45. Garrow, *Liberty and Sexuality,* pp. 263–264.

46. The declaration also asserts, "Marriage shall be entered into only with the free and full consent of the intending spouses" and that men and women "of full age" have the "right to marry and to found a family" and have "equal rights as to marriage" (Article 16).

47. This latter phrase also appears in Art. 27, with regard to education.

48. South African Constitution, Ch. 3, secs. 10, 13.

49. For these developments, see Ken Gormley and Rhonda G. Hartman, "Privacy and the States," *Temple Law Rev.* 65:1279 (1992).

50. Eisenstadt v. Baird, 405 U.S. 438 (1972).

51. Quoted in Garrow, *Liberty and Sexuality,* pp. 320–321.

52. 431 U.S. 678 (1977).

53. 410 U.S. 113 (1973).

54. See Leslie J. Reagan, *When Abortion Was a Crime: Women, Medicine, and the Law in the United States, 1867–1973* (1997); and Rickie Solinger, *Beggars and Choosers: How the Politics of Choice Shapes Adoption, Abortion, and Welfare in the United States* (2001), ch. 2.

55. See Maher v. Roe, 432 U.S. 464 (1977).

56. 505 U.S. 833 (1992).

57. Claudia Lima Marques, "Assisted Reproductive Technology (ART) in South America and the Effect on Adoption," *Texas International Law Journal* 35:65, 68–71 (2000).

58. See Mary Ann Glendon, *Abortion and Divorce in Western Law* (1987), pp. 33–39.

59. See Ryszard Cholewinski, "The Protection of Human Rights in the New Polish Constitution," *Fordham International L. J.* 22:236, 261–262 (1998).

60. *Agence France Presse,* March 7, 2004.

61. Rita J. Simon, *Abortion: Statutes, Policies, and Public Attitudes the World Over* (1998), pp. 51–52.

62. 478 U.S. 186 (1986).

63. Powell v. State, 270 Ga. 327, 510 S.E. 2d 18 (1998).

64. Romer v. Evans, 517 U.S. 620 (1996).

65. Lawrence v. Texas, 539 U.S. 558 (2003). Liberty, according to Justice Anthony Kennedy, who wrote the main opinion, "presumes an autonomy of self that includes freedom of . . . intimate conduct."

66. See Kathleen E. Hull, "The Cultural Power of Law and the Cultural Enactment of Legality: The Case of Same-Sex Marriage," *Law and Social Inquiry* 28:629 (2003).

67. Michael S. Wald, "Same-Sex Couple Marriage: A Family Policy Perspective," *Va. J. of Social Policy and the Law* 9:291, 292 (2001); the law was PL 104-199, of Sept. 21, 1996. Many states have their own versions forbidding gay marriage, for example Miss. Code sec. 93-1-1(2).

68. Goodridge v. Department of Public Health, 404 Mass. 309, 798 N.E. 2d 941 (2003). See *New York Times,* Nov. 19, 2003, p. 1.

69. *New York Times,* Nov. 20, 2003, p A29.

70. In the Matter of the Estate of Marshall G. Gardiner, 42 P. 3d 120 (Kansas, 2002). The court claimed, as courts usually do, that it was merely interpreting the relevant statute (on marriage). One oddity of the case is that it implies that if J'Noel were to go through a marriage ceremony with a woman, this marriage, though apparently lesbian in nature, would be valid in Kansas.

71. Mass. Stats. Tit. VII, ch. 46, sec. 13(e).

72. ECHR judgment of April 22, 1997, Series A, no. 753, as discussed in Lorna Woods, "Decisions on the European Convention on Human Rights during 1997," in *British Year Book of International Law 1997* (vol. 68, 1998), pp. 371, 404–405.

73. See Thomas M. Franck, *The Empowered Self: Law and Society in the Age of Individualism* (1999), pp. 162–177.

74. ECHR Dudgeon case, decision of Jan. 30, 1981, Series A, no. 45. The court recognized that although some people might be "shocked, offended or disturbed by . . . private homosexual acts, this cannot on its own warrant the application of penal sanctions when it is consenting adults alone who are involved." Ibid., at 23.

75. See Marianne Roth, "The Norwegian Act on Registered Partnership for Homosexual Couples," *U. of Louisville J. of Family Law* 35:467 (1997).

76. Constanza Tobio, "Marriage, Cohabitation and the Residential Independence of Young People in Spain," *International J. of Law, Policy and the Family* 15:68, 75 (2001); Encarna Roca, "Same-Sex Partnerships in Spain: Family, Marriage, or Contract?" *European J. of Law Reform* 3:365 (2001).

77. On the property rights created under this law, see Gregor Rieger, "Das Vermögensrecht der eingetragener Lebenspartnerschaft," *Z. für das Gesamte Familienrecht* 48:1497 (2001); for the earlier law, see Jörg Wegner, "Die Ehe für Gleichgeschlechtliche Lebensgemeinschaften," *Zeitschrift für Rechtssoziologie* 16:170 (1995).

78. BverfG, l BVvF1/01, July 17, 2002.

79. James P. Steyer, *The Other Parent: The Inside Story of Media's Effect on Our Children* (2002).

80. Tamar Lewin, "A Growing Number of Video Viewers Watch from Crib," *New York Times*, Oct. 29, 2003, p. 1.

81. Kenneth L. Karst, "Law, Cultural Conflict, and the Socialization of Children," *Cal. L. Rev.* 91:969, 1004 (2003). Karst goes on to say that in "consumer products lies self-presentation, a performance that passes for self-realization." Ibid.

82. Libby Copeland, "Guy Breaks up Cam-Girls but Internet Shows Go On," *Orlando Sentinel*, Sept. 2, 2000, p. E10.

83. Germaine Greer, "Watch with Brother," *The Observer*, June 24, 2001, Observer Review Pages, p. 1.

84. See Gini Graham Scott, *Can We Talk? The Power and Influence of Talk Shows* (1996); and Joshua Gamson, *Freaks Talk Back: Tabloid Talk Shows and Sexual Nonconformity* (1998).

85. Patricia Joyner Priest, *Public Intimacies: Talk Show Participants and Tell-All TV* (1995), p. 13.

86. Ibid., p. 190.

87. Clay Calvert, *Voyeur Nation: Media, Privacy, and Peering in Modern Culture* (2000).

88. On this point, see Lawrence M. Friedman, *The Horizontal Society* (1999), pp. 26–27.

89. See Iñigo de la Maza Gazmuri, "Privacidad y Comercio Electronico," in his edited book *Derecho y Tecnologías de la Información* (2002), p. 265.

Index

illegitimacy, 22–24, 34, 126–130;
adoption and, 99, 120; slavery and,
126–127
immigration, 47–48
indeterminate sentencing laws, 50
India, 7
Indian Child Welfare Act, 110–111
individual: advertising aimed at, 5–6;
choice and, 1–2, 14–16, 65, 77
individualism, 146; expressive, 77–78,
120, 143, 167
inheritance, 14; adoption and, 101–
102, 209nn9,10,13, 210n15; illegitimacy and, 127
Internet, 182, 186, 187, 188
invasion of privacy, 146, 147–164
Ireland, Gordon, 75–76
Islamic societies, 7
Israel, 125–126, 139

Jacob, Herbert, 72–73
Japan, 6–7, 13, 191n10
Jehovah's Witnesses, 142
Jorgensen, Christine (George),
176–177
"Jukes" (Dugdale), 49

Karst, Kenneth, 181
Kay, Herma Hill, 74
Key, Philip Barton, 30–31
Kinsey, Alfred E., 163–164
Kinsey reports, 86–87, 163–164,
219nn34,35
Kodak camera, 147–148
Koegel, Otto E., 46, 55
Korean War, 107

Latin America, 107, 171
law, 12–13, 192n14; living, 35, 38, 61,
74; official, 34, 38. *See also* family
law
legal system, as part of society, 11–12

legislative divorce, 28–29
Levy v. Louisiana, 128
liberty, and Fourteenth Amendment,
165. See also *Griswold v. Connecticut*
Lichtenberg, J. P., 86
Lifestyles of the Rich and Famous, 185
living law, 35, 38, 61, 74
Lohman, Ann ("Madame Restell"),
47, 48
longevity, and inheritance, 14
Lord Hardwicke's Marriage Act (1753),
18
Louisiana, 30, 80
Louisiana Civil Code of 1825, 30
love, romantic: and sexuality, 61–62
Loving, Mildred Jeter, 56–57
Loving, Richard, 56–57
Loving v. Virginia, 56–57
Lystra, Karen, 61–62

Maine, Henry, 2
majority values, and religious tolerance, 3–4
marriage, 73–74; annulment of, 69–70;
arranged, 6–7; bigamy, 21–23, 37;
bond, 19–20; breach of promise,
60–67, 202nn68,79; bureaucracy
and, 45–46; changing social definitions of, 39–41; choice and, 25,
56–60; as civil contract, 17–18,
25–27, 45, 61, 192n3; Community
Marriage Policy, 81; companionate, 40–41; covenant, 80–81,
205nn129,130; coverture, 41,
197n65; gay, 1, 11, 95, 174–180;
illegitimate children and, 22–24; as
individual choice, 7–8, 25, 56–60,
65, 77; informal, 18–19; licenses,
58–59, 201n60; medical certificate
requirements, 52–54, 57–58; miscegenation, 54–55, 56–57, 200nn39,43;
modern conception of, 77–78, 83;